litterae textuales

A SERIES ON MANUSCRIPTS AND THEIR TEXTS

EDITED BY

J.P. GUMBERT
M.J.M. DE HAAN
A. GRUYS

THE QUEDLINBURG ITALA

THE

QUEDLINBURG ITALA

The Oldest Illustrated Biblical Manuscript

Inabelle Levin

E.J. Brill – Leiden – 1985

Cover design Gerrit Noordzij

ISBN 90 04 07093 1

This book is dedicated
to the memory of my mother
RUTH C. LEVIN (1914-1984)
and of my sister
ELAINE C. BARD (1937-1970)
whose love of learning, so generously
shared with others, lives on.

Contents

Acknowledgements

This book began as a report presented in Hugo Buchthal's graduate seminar on the Vatican Vergil and Late Antique manuscript illumination which he taught at the Institute of Fine Arts during the Spring of 1967. Under his guidance my seminar report developed into a doctoral dissertation accepted at New York University in 1971. This phase of my work was supported by a Fulbright-Hays Fellowship to Rome (1968-1969) and a dissertation fellowship from the Institute of Fine Arts (1969-1970). I spent several subsequent summers expanding my research. Early drafts of this book were written during my year of residence as a Visiting Fellow at Dumbarton Oak's Center for Byzantine Studies in Washington, D.C. (1976-1977).

I am especially grateful to the Baltimore Hebrew College Publication Fund and to its principal benefactor, Mr. Gerald Goldberg, for supporting the publication of this book. Generous financial contributions were also made by my parents, Jacob and Ruth C. Levin, and by friends and family.

I would also like to thank Virginia Brown, Victor Elbern and Anne Marie Weyl-Carr for their valuable advice and assistance when I was preparing this monograph for publication. During various stages of my work I benefitted from consultations with Levon Avdoyan, Bernhard Bischoff, Larissa Bonfante-Warren, Frank E. Brown, James Nelson Carder, Evanghelos Chrysos, Caecilia Davis-Weyer, Bonifatius Fischer, Kenneth G. Holum, Herbert Kessler, Ernst Kitzinger, Gerhard Koeppel, Richard Krautheimer and Jean Owens Schaeffer.

Valuable technical assistance and an atmosphere which was always friendly and hospitable to research were provided by the directors and librarians of the Deutsche Staatsbibliothek and Staatsbibliothek Preussischer Kulturbesitz in Berlin; the Biblioteca Apostolica Vaticana in Vatican City; the Deutsche Archäologische Institut, American Academy, and Biblioteca Hertziana in Rome; Dumbarton Oaks Center for Byzantine Studies in Washington, D.C.; Pierpont Morgan Library, New York Public Library, the Metropolitan Museum of Art and Institute of Fine Arts in New York; Frick Fine Arts Library of the University of Pittsburgh; Freiberger Library of Case Western Reserve University, and the Cleveland Museum of Art in Cleveland.

I would also like to thank Mary Wheeler, Donna M. Stein, Carmella Ullman Chiswick and my family for encouraging me to embark on this project.

Washington D.C., 1981.

Introduction

The Quedlinburg Itala, a Latin manuscript of Samuel and Kings, was written and illustrated in Rome during the first part of the fifth century. As the oldest extant illustrated Biblical manuscript it has long served as a reference point for scholars interested in the formation of narrative biblical cycles. Its large and exceedingly beautiful script, generous spacing and margins, the large format of its fine white parchment folios and its full-color miniatures establish the deluxe character of this manuscript. Only five folios of the original codex have been found; they contain six pages of text and fourteen miniatures grouped within frames to fill the other four pages. Folios 1 to 4 are preserved in Berlin, Deutsche Staatsbibliothek, ms. theol. lat. fol. 485, and f. 5 is kept in the Quedlinburg Cathedral Treasury. The pictures were badly damaged when the manuscript was used as scrap material by a seventeenth-century bookbinder who pasted them on cardboard book backings. When the folios were removed, paint impressions remained on the cardboard; those impressions are now kept in Berlin, Staatsbibliothek Preussischer Kulturbesitz, ms. theol. lat. fol. 485 (Abklatsch). Despite the fragmentary condition of the Quedlinburg Itala, we can, nonetheless, learn a great deal about this manuscript and its relation to Late Antique and Early Christian art.

THE IMPORTANCE OF THE MANUSCRIPT

The manuscript contains so many rarely preserved features that it has considerable art historical importance for furthering our understanding of a period from which so little survives. Its miniatures contain one of the earliest narrative cycles of Old Testament Kings. Detailed instructions to the artists, discovered under the pictures on ff. 1, 2 and 4 and brief sketches and instructions on f. 3 were originally meant to have been hidden by the paint. Their presence suggests that these precepts were intended to guide the artists in devising a new cycle of illustrations. When this rare set of instructions is thoroughly analyzed it tells us a good deal about workshop practices and the methods used to compose a narrative cycle.

Along with the famous Vatican Vergil, our manuscript shares the distinction of preserving the oldest surviving painted miniatures. Both codices were produced during a period when the change from roll to codex stimulated the development of new designs for decorating and illustrating manuscripts.[1] Few pictorial cycles survive from the Late Antique and Early Christian period in any medium, and most extant works have been heavily restored; therefore, the Quedlinburg Itala provides important information about contemporary styles and painting techniques. The antique appearance of the miniatures reflects their artists' interest in Roman landscape, narrative and imperial imagery. Analysis of these characteristics serves, in turn, to shed further light on the role of these traditions in the work of contemporary artists. Furthermore the illustrations affect our understanding of Medieval illumination because several Carolingian and Ottonian manuscripts incorporate similar iconographic and formal motifs.

This rare example of an Old Latin, pre-Vulgate text of Samuel and Kings deserves further study. Ancient Latin manuscripts can seldom be assigned to specific centers, however, art historical evidence indicates that the Quedlinburg Itala was written and illustrated in Rome. It contains three scripts of considerable paleographical interest. The text was written in uncial; the instructions preserve an unusual example of Roman cursive rarely found in a manuscript; and the labels mix early half-uncial letter forms with mature uncials.

1. Weitzmann, 'Book Illustration'.

2. G. A. von Mülverstedt, 'Das Itala-Fragment', *Zeitschrift des Harz-Vereins für Geschichte und Altertumskunde*, 7 (1876): 251-63; W. Schum, 'Das Quedlinburger Fragment einer illustrierten Itala', *Theologische Studien und Kritiken*, 49 (1876): 121-34; A. Düning, 'Ein neues Fragment des Quedlinburger Itala-Codex', *Quedlinburger Gymnasialprogramm* (1888): 1-24; V. Schultze, *Die Quedlinburger Itala-Miniaturen der königlichen Bibliothek in Berlin, Fragmente der ältesten christlichen Buchmalerei* (Munich, 1898); and the same in *Grundriss der christlichen Archäologie* (Munich, 1919).

PREVIOUS RESEARCH

The discovery of the leaves between 1865 and 1888 generated the publication of brief studies by von Mülverstedt, Schum, Düning and Schultze.[2] On the whole, they limited themselves to discussing the history of the manuscript, and briefly describing the contents of the leaves. Von Mülverstedt's identification of the text with the so-called 'Itala', reputed to be Augustine's favorite Latin translation of the Septuagint, is no longer accepted, but the codex retains this name.[3] Early efforts to decipher the instructions met with little success, and the fourth-fifth century date usually assigned to the leaves was based on limited paleographical analysis.

The first thorough study of the text, paleography and art historical issues was published by Hermann Degering and Albert Boeckler in 1932.[4] Their volume of illustrations set new standards for accurate facsimile reproductions. Although these illustrations are remarkably reliable, they must be used with the following precautions. The colors are almost perfect, but slightly muted and muddied. The printer did not reproduce all of the remaining fine gold lines originally spun over almost every solid form. The pale beige color used to paint the ground is so similar to the bare parchment that it is difficult to distinguish between them without examining the manuscript. This differentiation is critical to determining the original representation of space in each miniature.

Although several of Degering's major theories are challenged and disproven, it is important to remember that he made a considerable contribution to our understanding of this manuscript. He reconstructed much of its history and recognized that it could not be identified with Augustine's 'Itala', but was simply one of several pre-Vulgate translations of the Septuagint Kings.[5] In his very valuable transcription of the text, instructions and labels, he corrected the errors of earlier scholars and produced far more accurate readings.[6] He analyzed scribal practices and letter forms with great precision. His attribution of the entire text and instructions on ff. 1, 2 and 4 to one scribe still seems reasonable.[7] With painstaking care he reconstructed the layout of the manuscript and the original number of text folios.[8] He had remarkable insight into the principles used in the physical and thematic relationship of the illustrations to the text.[9]

The art historical study by Albert Boeckler remains as solid a contribution to scholarship today as it was when he first wrote his monograph almost fifty years ago. There are, however, many important issues which he did not consider. His meticulous description of each miniature and paint impression is, on the whole, quite accurate, and his reconstruction of missing parts on the basis of comparisons with Roman pictorial conventions was methodologically sound and usually yielded reliable results.[10] Boeckler presents us with a sensitive and perceptive description of the style.[11] Moreover, through numerous detailed comparisons he documented the kinship of the Quedlinburg Itala miniatures with the Vatican Vergil illustrations and the S. Maria Maggiore nave mosaics. This led him to propose that both manuscripts were made in the same workshop.[12] He also recognized that these three cycles shared a common repertory of models derived from Roman pictorial traditions developed during the first and second centuries.[13]

Since 1932 several scholars, in the course of their research on Late Antique and Early Christian manuscripts and mosaics, have made observations which contribute to a further understanding of the Quedlinburg Itala. In his monograph on the Vatican Vergil, J. de Wit noted that both manuscripts reflect a strong predilection for imperial imagery.[14] He proposed that their artists referred to a similar repertory of motifs in developing new cycles to illustrate their respective manuscripts.[15] Having concluded that the Vatican Vergil was probably produced in the 420's, he placed the Itala close to 400 A.D.[16] Since that time, his dates for both manuscripts have been generally accepted.[17] Now his dating of the Quedlinburg Itala must be challenged.

Our understanding of narrative illustration in Ancient and Byzantine manuscripts has been greatly expanded by the scholarship of Kurt Weitzmann.[18] He has described the impact of imperial art, especially of its epic style, on the Itala and other manuscripts of the period.[19] By synthesizing the fragmentary information found in Late Antique manuscripts and their Medieval copies, he has been able to formulate an historical perspective of illumination in this period which enables us to

3. See von Mülverstedt, pp. 251-63; however, modern scholars consider that it is impossible to identify the text to which Augustine was referring in this passage in *De Doctrina Christiana*, 2.15. See, for example, the comments of J. N. Birdsall, 'The New Testament Text', vol. 2, *Cambridge History of the Bible* (Cambridge, 1969), p. 372.

4. H. Degering and A. Boeckler, *Die Quedlinburger Italafragmente*, 2 vols. (Berlin, 1932), henceforth cited as Degering or Boeckler.

5. Degering, pp. 8-16, 21-29.

6. Degering, pp. 29-64.

7. Degering, pp. 86-89.

8. Degering, pp. 87ff., 110-118.

9. Degering, pp. 110-119.

10. Boeckler, pp. 121-54.

11. Boeckler, pp. 165ff.

12. Boeckler, pp. 165ff., esp. p. 169. For the shelf mark and studies of the Vatican Vergil see the Bibliography of Works of Art Most Often Cited, at the end of this book.

13. Boeckler, pp. 150-82.

14. J. de Wit, *Die Miniaturen des Vergilius Vaticanus* (Amsterdam, 1959), pp. 146ff., 159f.; henceforth referred to as de Wit.

15. de Wit, pp. 205-10.

16. de Wit, pp. 165ff.

17. Both manuscripts are generally considered to be products of the early fifth century. See, for example, Weitzmann, 'Book Illustration', p. 114, on p. 104, he places the Itala at the end of the fourth century; and Kitzinger, *Byzantine Art in the Making*, pp. 67ff., figs. 118, 120, 122.

18. In particular see Weitzmann, *Roll and Codex*; and a collection of many of his important articles in *Studies in Classical and Byzantine Manuscript Illumination*, ed. H. L. Kessler (Chicago, 1971).

19. See Weitzmann, 'Book Illustration', pp. 96-125.

achieve new insights into workshop practices. Weitzmann rejected Boeckler's theory that the Quedlinburg Itala contains an original cycle. He proposed, instead, that the instructions were only meant to guide the artist in transferring an established prototype to a new format.[20] This controversial issue is carefully examined in chapter four.

In his recent publication of the fifth-century mosaics at S. Maria Maggiore, Beat Brenk added to Boeckler's already lengthy list several more precise comparisons of formal motifs used in the mosaics and the Vergil and Itala miniatures.[21] He theorized that modelbooks developed to aid artists producing triumphal paintings and reliefs would have been the likely intermediaries between these three cycles.[22] This attractive theory must remain an open issue because concrete evidence of such technical guides has not survived.

THE PURPOSE OF THIS STUDY

A number of issues raised by these scholars need reexamination and will be the subject of further investigation in this book. The manuscript's date, the significance of the instructions and the origin of the pictorial cycle have been hotly debated and will be reconsidered. My reappraisal of the miniatures has enabled me to offer new insights into their style and iconography and their relationship to Roman pictorial traditions. Woven throughout this monograph are numerous new observations about a variety of workshop practices and the contributions of the scribe and artists to developing this cycle of illustrations. Advances in our knowledge of Late Antique art gained since 1932 will enable me to clarify the art historical position of the Quedlinburg Itala and to examine issues which Boeckler was not able to consider.

The scope of my paleographical study is limited to issues which are important to my art historical inquiry; therefore I am primarily concerned with the date and provenance of the three scripts. The paleography of these fragments and the text still await full publication by specialists.[23]

Degering's attribution of the text to the famous scribe, Furius Dionysius Filocalus (active ca. 350-380), must be rejected. His historical analysis of the paleography is too narrowly considered and disagrees with other evidence which suggests a fifth-century date for the scripts. Moreover, he was incorrect in assuming that Jerome's translation of Kings established a late fourth-century terminus for the production of such Old Latin texts.[24]

Although E.A. Lowe and Bernhard Bischoff proposed an early fifth-century date for the manuscript, neither of them presented paleographic evidence to support his suggestion.[25] Because a wide margin of error ought to be allowed when dating script of this period, paleographic and art historical evidence should be weighed together in reaching a conclusion.

Discussions of the date of our manuscript inevitably consider the close stylistic kinship of its miniatures with the Vatican Vergil illustrations and the S. Maria Maggiore nave mosaics. Boeckler's decision to place the Quedlinburg Itala early in the third quarter of the fourth century was based on his belief that the mosaics were made under the patronage of Pope Liberius (352-366) and on his desire to conform with Degering's conclusions.[26]

The reattribution of the mosaics to the pontificate of Sixtus III (432-440) necessitated a reexamination of the Quedlinburg Itala's date. Nonetheless, Byvanck and Bianchi Bandinelli continued to assign the manuscript to the 350's. Their conclusions were based on particularly distorted stylistic analyses and incorrect studies of the antiquarian details.[27] We must seriously question whether they were entitled to separate the manuscripts and mosaics by eighty years. Nordenfalk placed the Quedlinburg Itala at the beginning of the fifth century, as did de Wit and Brenk in their respective monographs on the Vatican Vergil and S. Maria Maggiore.[28] A later date will be proposed.

Up till now, the assortment of dates proposed for this manuscript have not been based on a critical study of all its internal evidence. My conclusions will examine a wide range of relevant material: stylistic comparisons, antiquarian details, official insignia, iconography, pictorial topoi, artistic milieu and paleography.

Heretofore, scholars have always assumed that the illustrations were the work of one artist, but careful stylistic analysis indicates that at least two and possibly three painters illustrated the extant miniatures.

Three early Roman modes formed the character of the Itala's cycle: imperial imagery, especially its triumphal aspects; epic narative; and illusionistic landscape painting. We will investigate the source of these influences and how their use affected the style and iconography of this cycle.

20. Cf. Weitzmann's comments in *Roll and Codex*, pp. 100, 248; and in 'Book Illustration', pp. 104-105.

21. Brenk, *Mosaiken*, pp. 126ff., 146ff., 167ff., 175-80.

22. See his conclusions, Brenk, *Mosaiken*, pp. 178-80.

23. Guido Schoenberger's graduate seminar on paleography taught me the rudimentary techniques; Prof. Virginia Brown gave me valuable advice throughout every stage of my work. I have relied heavily on the publications of E.A. Lowe and benefitted from the generosity of Bernhard Bischoff and Bonifatius Fischer, who answered several questions about the script and text by letter.

24. Degering, pp. 93-94, 109-110.

25. Lowe in *CLA*, 8: no. 1069 placed the manuscript in the fourth/fifth century, but in the late 1960's he told V. Brown that the script could have been written during the first half of the fifth century. See Bischoff's remarks in 'Scriptoria', pp. 485-86.

26. Boeckler, pp. 182ff.

27. See Byvanck, 'Antike Buchmalerei: I', pp. 241-51; and Bianchi Bandinelli, *Miniatures of the Iliad*, p. 141.

28. See Nordenfalk, *Painting*, p. 93; de Wit, pp. 156-57; and Brenk, *Mosaiken*, pp. 178-79.

While exploring the artistic and cultural milieu which influenced the character of the Quedlinburg Itala, I have, for the first time, compared the miniatures to other art of their generation beyond the standard comparisons with the Vatican Vergil and the S. Maria Maggiore mosaics.

An inquiry into the origin of the Quedlinburg Itala's pictorial cycle involves determining whether it is related to other representations of Old Testament Kings and investigating the relationship of the miniatures to the text and instructions. This is the first time that the iconography of the miniatures will be compared with other Kings' illustrations.

Further investigation into the extent to which the artists either followed the scribe's written instructions or deviated from them explains the role of scribe and artists in formulating the pictorial cycle. Since Boeckler proposed that the instructions guided the artist in the invention of a new series of illustrations there has been considerable controversy over whether the cycle is original or simply copies pre-existing illustrations. Until now no one has tested either theory by examining all of the available evidence.

AN EXPLANATION

The extensive damage to the folios has made it impossible for the reader to obtain an accurate assessment of the material without detailed descriptions or the opportunity to spend long hours examining the original leaves and paint impressions divided between East and West Berlin. Therefore the first two chapters of this book present a thorough description of the scripts and miniatures and a transcription of the instructions and labels.

In chapter two, where my descriptions often agree with Boeckler's, I have decided not to distract the reader with frequent footnotes. Consequently the numerous new observations which I have contributed have become thoroughly intermeshed with Boeckler's work. I have limited the footnotes to our points of disagreement and to the contributions of other scholars. The reader should understand that I consider the first two chapters a tribute to the precise and perceptive contributions of Degering and Boeckler. Unfortunately only a few hundred copies of their monograph were published, therefore their work remains inaccessible to many scholars.

PROLOGUE

Discovery and History of the Quedlinburg Itala

The first discovery of the surviving leaves occurred in 1865 when Georg A. von Mülverstedt, Director of Archives in Magdeburg, found ff. 3 and 4 in the city's Preussische Staatsarchiv pasted as end papers in the bookcovers of the Quedlinburg parish financial accounts of 1617 to 1618; he identified the text with the help of Eduard Jacobs and Friedrich Wiggert.[1] In 1869 Gustav Brecht, Mayor of Quedlinburg, found in the city archives the first two folios glued inside the covers of the Quedlinburg police edicts, and in 1888 Adalbert Düning, Archivist of St. Servatius parish church in Quedlinburg, discovered the fifth page, which was being used as a cover for the church's Registry of Communicants of January 1619 to 1626.[2] From the same cover Hermann Degering removed two small fragments from the top of a sixth page, but all that remained on them was the title *Regnorum Lib.*[3]

The four illustrated pages were detached from the covers and sent with the impressions to Berlin, Preussische Staatsbibliothek, where they were catalogued as ms. theol. lat. 485, but the fifth page and fragments of the sixth page remained in the treasury of S. Servatius. Both Düning and Degering made a thorough search of government and church archives in Magdeburg and Quedlinburg and vicinity, but were unable to find other fragments. After World War II the four illustrated folios were returned to the Deutsche Staatsbibliothek in East Berlin, and f. 5 was replaced in S. Servatius' treasury in Quedlinburg,[4] however, the paint impressions on the book covers were sent to the Staatsbibliothek Preussischer Kulturbesitz in West Berlin.

The dismemberment of the Quedlinburg Itala can be traced to Asmus Reitel, a seventeenth-century Quedlinburg bookbinder who used the manuscript as scrap material, covered the pictures with paste and glued them inside the three bookcovers in which they were found. He most likely used the other folios in a similar manner, but all traces of them have been lost. Reitel wrote his name on the binding of the financial accounts from which ff. 3 and 4 were detached. After careful examination of the three books, Degering decided from the nature of their dated contents and the evidence of whether the pages were bound before or after they were written, that the manuscript had been used as binding material in 1618. Attempts by Degering to retrace the history of this manuscript prior to 1618 seem to be based on conjecture rather than fact.[5]

The Quedlinburg Itala was still being read in the late sixteenth century according to the evidence of Latin and German mottos written on the lower edge of f. 3r. There are also fifteenth-century entries added on the first two pictures of f. 1.[6]

1. See von Mülverstedt, pp. 251-63.
2. Von Mülverstedt, *loc. cit.*, also described the pages found by Brecht. Cf. Düning, pp. 1ff.; his inaccurate date of 1614-1621 was corrected by Degering, pp. 6-9.
3. They were described by Degering, pp. 8ff.
4. The present location of the folios and fragment was confirmed in a letter written to me on May 5, 1978 by Dr. Hans-Erich Teitge, Abteilungsdirektor, Berlin, Deutsche Staatsbibliothek, Handschriftenabteilung.
5. Degering, pp. 8-16, has reconstructed the history of this manuscript.
6. The contents and script style of these later entries were studied by Degering, pp. 15-16, 82-83, pl. 16, figs. 31-36. In a letter written to me on July 29, 1982, Prof. J. P. Gumbert corrected Degering's dates of these entries.

CHAPTER ONE

The Text and Scripts

The Old Latin text of Samuel and Kings is written in large regular uncial on fine white parchment: 5 leaves plus 1 fragment.[1] All leaves have been trimmed and the largest preserved dimensions are 312 mm. (f. 3) × 277 mm. (f. 4). Written in *scriptura continua* in two columns of twenty-six lines; rulings and single bounding lines are drawn with a sharp stylus on the flesh side. The black ink of the script has faded, and the first three lines of ff. 1v, 2v, and 4v are written in red following the illustrations on the recto. Major sections of text begin with the first word (*Et* in every case) projecting into the margin, with the first letter written somewhat larger. Each illustration is associated with verses that are emphasized in this manner. Running titles at the top of each page, 'Regnorum' on the verso and 'Lib I-II-III-(IV)' on the facing recto, designate the text as the four books of Kings according to the Septuagint system.

CONTENTS AND CONDITION OF THE FOLIOS

f. 1v: 1 Samuel 9: 1-8. 305 × 205 mm.; part of the left column was cut away. The imprint of two pictures on the right margin occurred when f. 2r was pasted on top and remained after it was pulled away.

f. 2v: 1 Samuel 15: 10-17. 311 × 252 mm. Binding threads and needle holes remain on the left edge of the recto. It is uncertain whether this very narrow 17 mm. inner margin retains its original width or possibly results from a later trimming and rebinding of the codex. The outer margin is missing, but 47 mm. remain on the top and bottom margins. The 1618 bookbinding damaged the left column.

f. 3r: 2 Samuel 2: 29-3: 5; using only 22 lines. 312 × 202 mm. Half of the right column was cut away, but a 5 mm. upper margin and a 58 mm. lower margin remain. Late sixteenth-century Latin and German mottos and a drawing are on the lower margin.

f. 4v: 1 Kings 5: 2-9; the last two letters 'lo' are completed at the beginning of f. 5r with 'cum' to form the word 'locum'. 298 × 277 mm.: the 40 mm. left margin is the widest remaining outer margin. The red picture frame of f. 3v left an impression when it was pasted on the right margin. The right column was damaged by the book spine in 1618; cf. dates '1617-1618'.

f. 5r: 1 Kings 5: 9-6: 1 continues the text from f. 4v. f. 5v: 1 Kings 6: 1-7. 308 × 238 mm.; cut in two parts at lower margin. A seventeenth-century title is written on the lower left margin.

f. 6: two small fragments contain the title *Regnorum Lib.*

Based on an average seven verses per page the text must have filled c. 380 pages or 190 folios with many additional pages of illustrations and would have contained only the four books of Kings.[2] The texts became rubbed and soiled after they had been used as binding material. The original size of the leaves can be reconstructed approximately by adding the widest remaining margins to the text (height: 215 mm. text + 50 mm. top and 58 mm. bottom margins; width: 230 mm. text + 40 mm. outer margin and a 17 mm. (+) inner margin). These dimensions, ca. 323 × 287 (+) mm. reestablish the large and nearly square format of the codex.[3]

1. The following information summarizes the detailed reconstructions and descriptions of Degering, pp. 8, 86-102, 111-120. For a shorter description see Lowe, *CLA*, 8 (Oxford, 1959), p. 15, no. 1069.

2. According to Degering, pp. 119, 203.

3. Degering, pp. 116-18, noted that the parchment pictures were ca. 2 to 10 mm. smaller than the paint impressions on the bookcovers. The difference in size could have occurred when the parchment was first stretched and glued to the bindings. Later, the parchment could have shrunk when it was soaked to dissolve the glue so that the pages could be removed from the bookcovers.

PALEOGRAPHIC CHARACTERISTICS AND IDENTIFICATION OF HANDS

Clearly the TEXT on all extant folios was written by one skillful scribe; his uncial letter forms are consistent.[4] Since the fragments come from three of the four books of Kings this scribe most likely wrote the entire codex. The two corrections in smaller letters, *tu* on f. 2r and *in* on f. 5v, also appear to have been written by him.

M (and rarely *n*) at the end of a line may be abbreviated with a stroke; if there is an interpunctum at this point, the stroke stands above the interpunctum. The *nomina sacra* are $\overline{dns}$, $\overline{dni}$, $\overline{dno}$ and $\overline{dnm}$ for *dominus*, *domini*, *domino* and *dominum* and $\overline{ds}$, $\overline{dei}$, $\overline{deo}$ for *deus*, *dei* and *deo*. The ligatures AE, NT, UNT, OR, UM, UN, US, occur when there is lack of space at the end of a line. Israel is spelled *Istrahel*.

Fig. 1 — Quedlinburg Itala, gold labels (*a*, *b*, *c* from Picture 1, *d*, *e*, *f* from Picture 3, *g*, *h* from Picture 5, *i* from Picture 10, *j*, *k* from Picture 14). (Photo: Degering-Boeckler.)

Punctuation is placed at the end of sentences, of long complete passages, to separate a series of short phrases or the items of a list. It takes the form of an interpunctum (period) or of a space (or of an interpunctum followed by a space); there is no functional difference between these forms (see f. 1v, col. 2, lines 1-9 mainly spaces, lines 10-18 mainly interpuncta). Because ample room is left for the periods it is safe to conclude that they were written by the original scribe rather than by a later hand. Interpuncta are often put at the beginning and end of a quote, and thus serve the same functions as modern quotation marks (see: f. 1v, col. 2, line 19; f. 2v, 1 : 26 and 2 : 7; but spaces also occur with the same function, see f. 1v, 2 : 6). *Nomina sacra* are set off by interpuncta consistently even in the middle of a sentence (see: f. 2v, col. 2: 2, 12, 17, 25). Interpuncta separate a series of phrases or closely related short sentences in the same manner as does a modern comma (f. 1v, 2 : 10-18), and they also set off Roman numerals (f. 3r, 1 : 13).

GOLD LABELS identify important characters, activities and monuments. They are written in a small, rather informal uncial, which admits some alternative forms:[5] besides the *a* normal in uncial (pictures 1, 4, 13, 14), there is a slightly different form in *aga*, picture 7; there is a vertical *d* with a hooked staff (as in half-uncial) in *duo* and a half-uncial *r* in *uiri*, both in picture 1; an alternative *g* is found in picture 2, and the ligature *ns*, in cursive form, in *aloquens*, picture 12; the verticals of *p*, *q* and *h* are long, extending well beyond the line in accordance with the half-uncial form (see *quia*, *prophetarum* in pictures 1 and 3). The nomen sacrum $\overline{dm}$ for *deum* is in picture 2.

4. Also noted by Degering, pp. 86-87. Many of the following paleographic characteristics are also described by Degering, pp. 90-102; and Lowe, *CLA*, 8: no. 1069.

5. See Degering, pp. 106-110, for his description of the letter forms.

It is clear that the text and labels were written by different hands.[6] The eye of A is round and open in the labels, but sharp and almost closed in the text. The tongue of E is long and below the mid-line, and the shape of the letter is angular in the labels (figs. a, c, g, h); whereas in the text E is curved and its tongue is high, almost closing the eye of this letter. Hooks frequently appear on G, L, N, P and R in the labels (figs. e, f); but not in the text. G has a long, strong, hooked tail in the labels (pictures 5 and 7, fig. g), but is short and faint in the text. The first stroke of M is bowed in the labels (fig. f), but straight or barely curved in the text. The bow of R is very large, its first stroke descends below the line, and its last stroke is short and sharply angled in the labels (fig. f) in contrast to the small bow in the text which confines the letter to the line. S is made with three distinct strokes and has square proportions in the labels (fig. g, h) while it is flowing and narrow in the text. drew fine gold lines to highlight clothing, accessories, buildings and the tree, and then wrote the labels with the same gold paint. Unfortunately the variety of letter forms and the damage to the labels make it difficult to differentiate between the artists' personal writing styles; whatever subtle distinguishing differences there may have been are no longer evident.

The INSTRUCTIONS TO THE ARTISTS are written in rapid roman cursive using both cursive and uncial forms for several letters and numerous ligatures.[8] A has the uncial form with a pointed eye or the cursive form with an open eye when making a ligature with L, N, R, S and U. B is written only in cursive. C usually has a small tight form, but the beginning stroke can extend far to the right. Cursive D uses a straight vertical ascender, and both an open and closed eye. The very open uncial E has a long tongue placed in the center of the letter connecting with F, G, I, M, N, R, S and X to form ligatures; X also connects with the top stroke of E. Uncial F has a long descender and short tongues; the lower tongue forms ligatures with E and I. G occurs in uncial and cursive forms; the latter joins E and EN to form ligatures. I makes ligatures with E, F, and L. M occurs only as a cursive with a short middle stroke and forms a ligature with E. When written as an uncial, N forms ligatures with A, E and T. As a cursive N's last leg extends below the line. P and Q have small round eyes and long descenders; P also uses a closed eye. R occurs in a variety of forms: an uncial with large eye and small final leg; an old cursive and half-uncial form with long extended first stroke; and a cursive

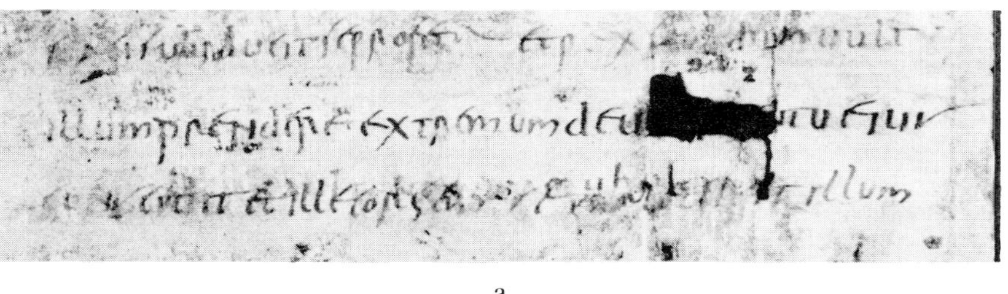

a

b

Fig. 2 — Quedlinburg Itala, instructions to the artist (*a* from Picture 6, *b* from Picture 8). (Photo: Degering-Boeckler.)

There are other differences in the metier and experience of text and label hands. The formation of the letters in the text is extremely regular. This scribe was able to repeat his beautiful letter forms with great care and precision and was without doubt a master of his craft. In contrast, the letters in the gold labels are definitely heterogeneous. The same letters can be made very differently, even when they are in the same phrase, and this would appear to indicate that they were not written by the experienced text scribe. Moreover, Hiram's name appears as *chiram* in the text but as *chiran* in the gold label in picture 13.[7]

It seems reasonable to assume that the labels were written by the artists, who, after they had finished painting each picture,

6. Schum, pp. 8-15; Schultze, pp. 32-34; and Degering, pp. 86-89, were aware of a difference in style between the text and labels. Schum thought that it took a lifetime to write the manuscript and that the labels came at the end of its production. Schultze thought that the scripts were contemporary. Degering, pp. 88-89, also rejected Schum's hypothesis and suggested that it took less than a year for one scribe to write the text. He explained that the difference in style should be attributed to the artist who probably wrote the labels.

7. These differences in orthography were also mentioned by Degering, pp. 79-82.

8. For a fuller description of the letter forms see Degering, pp. 102-106.

with final stroke extended far to the right, especially when making a ligature with A, E, I and O. S is sharp and angular with a pointed bottom bow and a final stroke extending far to the right. Uncial curved S never appears. Uncial T makes a ligature only with N. The same uncial form is used for U and V. The last stroke of uncial X descends below the line, and X forms a ligature with E.

Because the cursive writing is so radically different from the script of the text and labels it is not possible to attribute the instructions to the scribe or artists on a stylistic basis. Both the variety and the similarity of the letter forms used throughout the instructions make it difficult to determine whether they were written by more than one person. Even so, there are good reasons to believe that the artists did not write the directions on ff. 1r, 2r and 4r. Many directions begin with *facis ubi*, which seems to indicate that a second person was involved; the artist would not address himself in that way. Whereas, as will be demonstrated in subsequent chapters, the artists' repeated deviations from the text and instructions comply with the pictorial repertory of Roman art that was central to their professional practices, the instructions closely follow the sense of the text. Therefore it is probable that they were written by the programmer. As subsequent investigation will demonstrate, his responsibilities and training made him far more sensitive to the demands of the text than to methods of illustration. There are also differences in orthography between the instructions and the artists' labels. The spelling of *monimentum* (picture 1) and *samuhel* (picture 4) in the labels differs from the instructions, where they are spelled *monumentum* and *samuel*. Schum and Degering considered the scribe to be the author of the instructions, but J. P. Gumbert has questioned whether a well trained scribe would have used such coarse orthography and grammar.[9]

On the other hand, it seems reasonable to assume that on f. 3v the artist wrote the one word directions to identify his sketches. Moreover, the letter forms of P, U, and L in the instructions for picture 10 are very similar to those letters in the labels. Although the cursive writing on f. 3 is quick, broad and loose while the labels are small, tight and controlled, these variations in their execution could logically occur in the same hand given the different circumstances. In the first case, we are dealing with notes which were not meant to be seen, and so penmanship could be careless; however, in the gold labels care and control were essential.

DATE AND PROVENANCE OF THE THREE SCRIPTS

The Quedlinburg Itala text preserves one of the finest examples of mature uncial script surviving from the fourth and fifth centuries when it was especially popular for biblical, patristic and juristic texts.[10] Degering's attribution of the Quedlinburg Itala script to the school of Furius Dionysius Filocalus (active prior to 354 to ca. 380), the scribe of Pope Damasus, cannot be substantiated because no extant uncial texts can be attributed to him or his school for purposes of comparison.[11]

Nor can we accept Degering's romantic hypothesis that the manuscript may have been made for Pope Damasus who was so distressed by its inaccurate text that he commissioned Jerome to prepare a new translation of the Bible.[12] The text belongs to the group of Old Latin (Itala) translations of the Septuagint which preceded Jerome's Vulgate,[13] but the completion of Jerome's translation of Samuel and Kings prior to 395 cannot be used as a *terminus ante quem* for our manuscript because Old Latin texts remained popular and continued to be produced throughout the fifth century.[14]

The text script displays most of the principal paleographic characteristics of fourth and fifth-century manuscripts listed by E. A. Lowe in his 1922 study which served as a guide for his *Codices Latini Antiquiores* and other publications.[15]

9. In a letter written to me on July 9, 1982, Prof. Gumbert suggested that the designer of this manuscript, who was presumably the author and writer of the instructions, need not have been the scribe. Schum, pp. 13-15 and Degering, p. 104, considered the scribe to be the author of the instructions. Degering based his opinion partly on the execution of the letter F; yet this seems an unreliable basis for an attribution because F in particular exhibits the greatest variety of forms, even within the instructions for one picture.

10. For the history of uncial script see: Thompson, *Palaeography*, pp. 284-86; F. Muzika, *Die Schöne Schrift* (Hanau a. M., 1965), pp. 192-202; Lowe, *CLA*, supplement (Oxford, 1971), pp. viiff.; B. Bischoff, *Paläographie des römischen Altertums und des abendländischen Mittelalters*, Grundlagen der Germanistik, vol. 24 (Berlin, 1979), pp. 86-92; and for facsimiles, E. Chatelain, *Uncialis Scriptura* (Paris, 1901-1902), pls. 1-60.

11. See Degering, pp. 109-110, 203-204; moreover, there is no evidence to support his suggestion that the Quedlinburg Itala may have been part of a multivolume Bible made for Pope Damasus. Filocalus' work is discussed by T. N. Gray, 'Furius Dionysius Filocalus', *Enciclopedia dell'arte antica*, 3 (Rome, 1960), pp. 679-80; Stern, *Le Calendrier de 354*, pp. 7-12, 122-23; and Nordenfalk, *Zierbuchstaben*, pp. 83-88.

12. See Degering, pp. 203-204.

13. For a discussion of the early Latin translations of the Bible see B. J. Roberts, 'The Old Testament: Manuscripts, Texts and Versions', *Cambridge History of the Bible*, vol. 2 (Cambridge, 1969), pp. 1-27.

14. Both Old Latin and Vulgate texts continued to be produced from the fifth through the eighth centuries, and both versions were also conflated in several manuscripts and insular pandects during that period. The history of these Latin translations is discussed by: J. Chapman, *Notes on the Early History of the Vulgate Gospels* (Oxford, 1908); E. F. Sutcliffe, 'Jerome', *The Cambridge History of the Bible*, 2: 80-101; B. Fischer, 'Bibelausgaben des frühen Mittelalters', *La Bibbia nell'Alto Medioevo*, Settimane di Studio, vol. 10 (Spoleto, 1963), p. 523; and R. Loewe, 'The Medieval History of the Latin Vulgate', *Cambridge History of the Bible*, 2: 107-109.

15. The reader will note that my historical study of the paleography depends on Lowe's study of Late Antique manuscripts first published in the 1920's and reissued in 1972. Our manuscript contains twelve of the seventeen criteria (nos. 1-7, 10, 12-15) developed by E. A. Lowe and E. K. Rand, *A Sixth Century Fragment of the Letters of Pliny the Younger: A Study of Six Leaves of an Uncial Manuscript Preserved in the Pierpont Morgan Library, New York* (Washington, 1922), pp. 19-20; reprinted as 'The Paleography of the Morgan Fragment', in E. A. Lowe, *Palaeographical Papers, 1907-1965*, vol. 1 (Oxford, 1972), pp. 123-124. Lowe added other characteristics to this list in 'Some Facts about Our Oldest Manuscripts', *The Classical Quarterly*, 19 (1925): 197-208; and in 'More Facts about Our Oldest Latin Manuscripts', *The Classical Quarterly*, 22 (1928): 43-62. Both articles were reprinted in his *Palaeographical Papers* (Oxford, 1972), 1: 187-202 and 251-74. These and other criteria are frequently cited in Lowe's *CLA*.

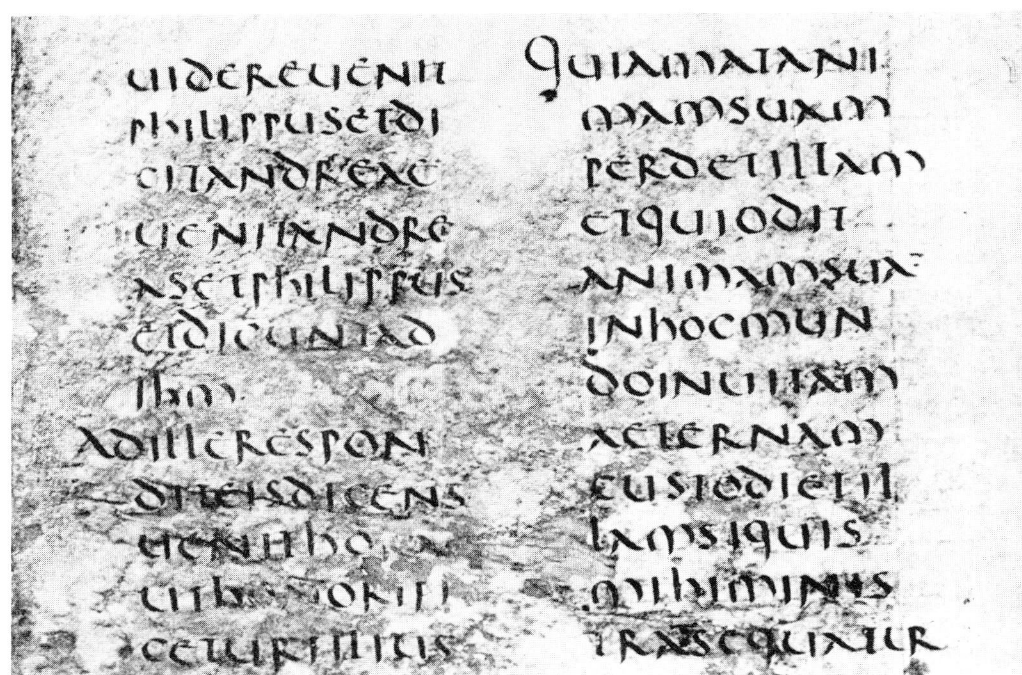

Fig. 3 — 'Codex Vercellensis': Vercelli, Bibl. cap. S.N., p. 267.

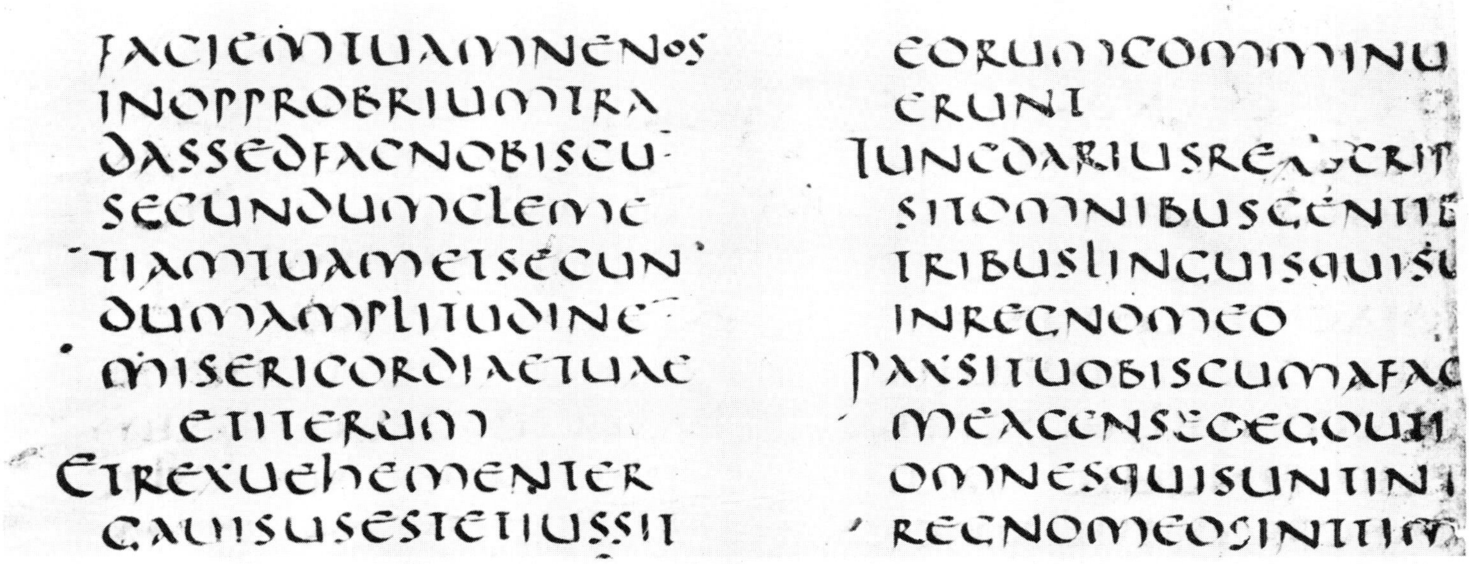

Fig. 4 — Cyprian, *Testimonia*: Brescia, Bibl. Queriniana, H. VI. 11, p. 7.

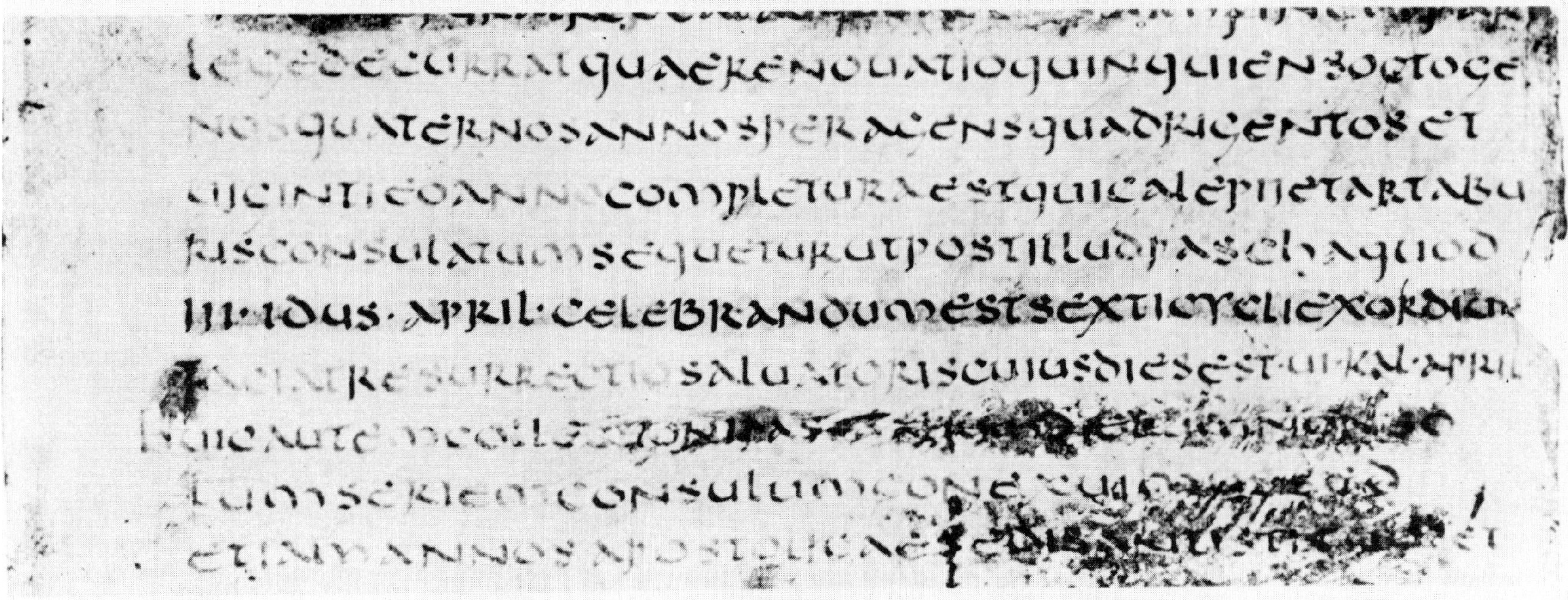

Fig. 5 — Liber Paschalis of 447: Berlin, Staatsbibliothek, lat. qu. 298, f. 1.

Fig. 6 — Jerome, *Epistulae*: Verona, Bibl. cap., XVII (15), f. 165.

The script can best be compared to the style of the uncial letter forms in the following manuscripts:

1. 'Codex Vercellensis', pre-Jerome *Gospels*, Vercelli, Bibl. Capitolare s.n. Italy, late 4th cent. The traditional attribution to Eusebius of Vercelli (died 371) is open to question. Cf. *CLA*, 4: no. 467 (fig. 3).

2. Cicero, *de Republica*, palimpsest, Vatican City, Bibl. Vat., Vat. lat. 5757. Italy, 4th-5th cent. Cf. *CLA*, 1: no. 35.

3. Constance-Weingarten *Prophets* fragments, Darmstadt, Landes- und Hochschulbibl. 895 + 3140 (olim in 896), Aa, la. The locations of other fragments are cited in *CLA*, 8: no. 1174. N. Italy, 5th cent.

4. *Scholia Bobiensia in Ciceronem*, palimpsest, Vatican City, Bibl. Vat., Vat. lat. 5750. Italy, 5th cent. Cf. *CLA*, 1: no. 28.

5. Cicero, *Pro Fonteio*, palimpsest, Vatican City, Bibl. Vat., Pal. lat. 24. Origin uncertain, poss. Italy, 5th cent. Cf. *CLA*, 1: no. 76.

6. Cyprian, *Testimonia*, Brescia, Bibl. Queriniana, H. VI. 11 (fly leaves). Italy, 5th cent. Cf. *CLA*, 3: no. 283 (fig. 4).

Although these codices do appear to have been written by different hands, they share with the Quedlinburg Itala certain stylistic characteristics which can be considered Italian. The roundness and fullness of the letters and the manner in which connections between separate strokes almost flow into each other to make a unified form are found in dozens of manuscripts which are attributed to Italy.[16] So little is known about the origin of manuscripts of this period that it has not been possible to assign them securely to particular schools, but based on its script style the Quedlinburg Itala was certainly written in an Italian center.

The dates that E. A. Lowe suggested for the six manuscripts whose script can be compared to our own text are spread between the late fourth and late fifth centuries, but none of these manuscripts are firmly dated. A reliable chronology has not been refined for the period due to the paucity of accurately dated manuscripts and the limited amount of comparative material; therefore a wide margin of error must be allowed.[17]

The letters in these manuscripts are shaded with precision in the regular alternation of stressed and unstressed strokes. The letters formed by curved strokes, namely C, D, E, G, M, O, begin at left of center so that the curved letters always have their axes tilted to the left. The strokes are often very short touches of the pen, as if they were merely brush strokes. The attack of fore and finishing strokes makes a very fine oblique hair line that is particularly apparent in the top joint of D, E, G, M, P, S, X. The upper and lower vertical shafts of H, L, P, Q project only slightly beyond the line; long ascending or descending strokes are avoided, and the letters lie between two lines. M, N and U are broad, but F, L, P, S and T are very narrow. The loop of A is sharply pointed and ends in a slightly open hair line. The loop of G fills the line, and its tail is barely indicated.

Several letters are distinctly different from uncial forms attributed to a later period. As in fourth/fifth-century examples, the tongue of E is a thin oblique stroke placed very high so that the eye is extremely narrow; in late fifth/sixth-century manuscripts the tongue is placed closer to the center of E (figs. 5, 6). In the Quedlinburg Itala and in many fourth/fifth century uncials the initial stroke of M tends to be almost straight or a barely curved arc (cf. figs. 3-4) instead of a well-rounded bow as it is in sixth-century uncial (figs. 5, 6). There are fifth-century examples of both types, but it is not certain when the change began. The loop of P is small and open in other fourth- and fifth-century manuscripts as are the top loops of B and R (cf. figs. 3-4) which become larger in the sixth century (figs. 5-6). S is formed of long shallow curves and is narrower than the sixth-century form (compare figs. 3-4 to 5-6). The small, sinuous top stroke of T may be extended in a thin flourish to the left when it begins the line.

Petrucci ascribed the letter X in the Quedlinburg Itala and the Vergilius Vaticanus to a new method of X formation in three parts and suggested that the similarities which he saw confirmed their strong interrelationship and permitted their attribution to the same school.[18] Thorough study of the Quedlinburg Itala has convinced me, however, that X was made with two strokes, not three. Moreover, the Itala's uncial cannot be compared with the capitalis rustica in the Vergil manuscript.[19]

The Quedlinburg Itala and the six manuscripts compared with it share many scribal practices typically found in fourth and fifth-century manuscripts which Lowe assigned to Italian as well as to North African and Eastern centers.[20] Their restricted use of abbreviations is typical of the period, and the Itala is partic-

16. In comparison see the scripts which Lowe assigned to North Africa, Egypt and the eastern Roman empire in *CLA*, Supplement, pp. viii-ix, pls. I-IV; and in *CLA*, 2: 137, 140, 206, 211.

17. In his January 25, 1977 response to my letter, Professor Bernhard Bischoff stressed the need for such caution in dating manuscripts of this period. He recalled that E. A. Lowe had often changed his mind about the dates and origins of several manuscripts, and he advised a certain scepticism about some of Lowe's dates. In his publications Bischoff suggested that the Quedlinburg Itala may have been the product of a professional scriptorium which produced Christian books at the end of the fourth century; he accepted the date of ca. 400 proposed for the illustrations by Nordenfalk, *Painting*, p. 93. See Bischoff, 'Scriptoria', pp. 485-86.

Degering, pp. 93-94, 109-110, compared our script to manuscripts 1, 2, 3 and 5 in my list, but he argued far too strenuously for a date in the third quarter of the fourth century for all of them. For his historical analysis of the letter forms see Degering, pp. 89-102.

18. Cf. A. Petrucci, 'Tratteggi e forme della lettera X nella scrittura latina', *Atti della Accademia Nazionale dei Lincei, Rendiconti*, ser. 8, vol. 16 (1961): 223-40.

19. Although the letters X, U and S in our manuscript are very similar to those in the Vergilius Vaticanus, Vatican City, Bibl. Vat., Vat. lat. 3225, it is not uncommon for manuscripts written by different hands to contain two or three nearly identical letter forms. If the Vergil scribe wrote other manuscripts in uncial, that would account for the similarities between them.

20. Many of the following characteristics were also cited by Lowe and Rand in *Pliny*, pp. 14-22 (cf. above note 15).

ularly sparing, limiting them to *nomina sacra* for forms of *dóminus* and *deus*: *dns*, *dni*, *dno*, *dnm* and *ds*, *dei*, *deo*, *dm*.[21] Lowe, following Ludwig Traube, noted that *dms* is the early form of *dominus* and occurs in fourth, fifth and sixth-century manuscripts, but *dns* is not found prior to the fifth century and becomes more frequent than *dms* in the sixth century, a view which he maintained in his last publication.[22] Statistically, however, Lowe's few dated examples do not provide a sufficient number of correlations to serve as a sound basis for his conclusion: only a handful of manuscripts listed in *CLA* are placed in the fourth century. In the dozens of manuscripts which he assigned to the fifth century, either *dms*, or *dns*, or both together can be found in so many manuscripts that a clear pattern does not emerge.

The codex format, nearly square proportions and many scribal techniques practiced in the Quedlinburg Itala, such as M and N omission, *scriptura continua*, significant punctuation, running titles, and two column text, do not suggest a precise date for our manuscript because they also occur in texts assigned within a range of dates extending from the late fourth through the entire fifth century.[23] Dates for the comparative manuscripts tend to be approximate, and they are rarely assigned to specific Italian centers, and then only tentatively. Under these conditions there is no substantive paleographic basis in the text script for determining whether the Quedlinburg Itala text was written in the late fourth century or sometime in the fifth century.[24]

The style of the letter forms in the instructions compares with cursive script in papyri and with inscriptions found in Roman catacombs from the fourth and fifth centuries.[25] Here also the wide range of dates suggested for the comparative material does not permit more precise dating of the Quedlinburg Itala's cursive script.

The style of the gold labels points to the fifth-century date of this manuscript. The letters have the round and upright form favored by Italian schools[26] rather than the styles found in African and Eastern scripts of the third to fifth centuries as they are classified in *CLA*.[27]

Attempts to classify and date this script raise several problems. Degering considered the labels half-uncials,[28] but Professor Bischoff, noting that most of the letters are written in uncial forms, thinks that the labels should be classified as uncials with a few half-uncial letters.[29] The use of only a limited number of half-uncial forms rather than the full complement is usually a symptom of the early stages of this style.[30] That might also explain the use of both half-uncial and uncial forms for the same letter; yet it is also possible that both phenomena are evidence of an inexperienced hand.

Dating matters are complicated because letters E, G, M, R and S in the gold labels possess the very characteristics of uncials in codices which Lowe placed in the second half of the fifth and early sixth centuries: the tongue of E is low and long; G has a long, curved, heavy tail; the first stroke of M is definitely curved; the eye of R is very large; and S has broad proportions[31] (figs. 5-6). It should be noted, however, that these letter shapes already appear in an Italian manuscript of A.D. 447, the Liber Paschalis, Berlin, Deutsche Staatsbibl. lat. qu. 298[32] (fig. 5).

The gold labels could have been added several decades after the manuscript was completed, but it is far more likely that they are contemporary with the text and paintings.[33] Although the text does not contain the letter style which Lowe associated with manuscripts made after the 440's, it may still be possible to explain the discrepancy. Whereas the text was obviously written by a mature and experienced scribe who may have continued to use the style he had developed earlier in his profession, the labels, written with uncial letters used by the 440's, if not earlier, could have been written in the newest style and

21. Discussed by Lowe in 'Some Facts', passim; 'More Facts', passim; and cited throughout his *CLA*.

22. See L. Traube, *Nomina Sacra* (Munich, 1907), pp. 189-191; Lowe, 'More Facts', pp. 60-61; and Lowe, *CLA*, vol. 2, rev. ed. (1972), p. xi.

23. For a discussion of these practices see Lowe, 'Some Facts', passim, 'More Facts', 45-46; Thompson, *Palaeography*, pp. 284-86; and Weitzmann, *Roll and Codex*, pp. 69ff. for the development of the codex.

24. In his description of the Quedlinburg Itala in *CLA*, 8: no. 1069, Lowe suggested that the manuscript was produced in an Italian center in the fourth or fifth century. In the late 1960's he told Professor Virginia Brown, who was his research assistant at the time, that the manuscript could have been written in the first half of the fifth century, and that Degering's attribution to Filocalus could not be substantiated. Professor Brown, now of the Pontifical Institute of Mediaeval Studies in Toronto, related this conversation to me in 1969. Cf. n. 17 for Professor Bischoff's opinion. Von Mülverstedt, p. 257, only guessed that the script might be fifth or sixth century, but he did not support his opinion with evidence from paleographic research. Schum, p. 14, Schultze, pp. 32-34 and Düning, passim, considered the text and script to be late fourth or fifth century.

25. Comparisons tend to be more general than exact and to fall within a wide range of dates. Degering, pp. 102-106, only compared the script to cursive inscriptions assigned to the period between 330-374 which were published by G. B. de Rossi, *Inscriptiones christianae urbis Romae*, vol. 1 (Rome, 1875), cf. nos. 37 (38) ca. 330; 43 (50), ca. 338; and 118 (243), ca. 374. The instructions, however, may also be compared to fifth-century cursive in an historical fragment in Manchester, John Rylands University Lib. Papyrus s.n. (*CLA*, Suppl., no. 1726) and to the Exercitatio Scribendi in Liverpool, Univ. Lib., POxy. 1314 (*CLA*, Suppl., no. 1701); while Marichal compares the instructions to cursive inscriptions in San Sebastiano which he places in the first half of the fourth century. See R. Marichal, *Scriptorium*, 18 (1964): 230.

26. Italian examples can be found in *CLA*, 4: no. 494; 4: no. 490; 3: no. 374a; and 4: no. 410a.

27. Examples of early half-uncial in African and Eastern manuscripts are in *CLA*, 2: no. 208 and suppl., pp. v-vi, 8; 1: no. 1a; 3: no. 287; 8: no. 1042; and 10: no. 1577.

28. Cf. Degering, pp. 106-110.

29. B. Bischoff in a letter written to me on January 25, 1977.

30. For a list of early half-uncial manuscripts see E. A. Lowe, 'A Hand List of Half-Uncial Manuscripts', *Miscellanea Fr. Ehrle*, 4 (1924), 34-35; and P. Schiaparelli, *La Scrittura Latina* (Como, 1921), p. 150.

31. See for example: *CLA*, 1: no. 27; 4: 489a (our fig. 6); 4: no. 418; and 3: nn. 281, 295 and 399.

32. See Lowe, *CLA*, 8: no. 1053.

33. Degering, pp. 86-89, was also of this opinion.

still be contemporary with the text. In any case, the labels would not have been written prior to the fifth century and probably not earlier than the second quarter of that century.

CONCLUSIONS

An analysis of its various scripts indicates that the manuscript was produced in a major Italian center in the fifth century, possibly at some time during the second quarter of that century. These conclusions must remain tentative in light of the wide margin of error in dating manuscripts copied between the fourth and sixth centuries. Such judgements must also be made in conjunction with the iconographic and stylistic evidence to be found in the illustrations.

CHAPTER TWO

The Illustrations

DESCRIPTION AND RECONSTRUCTION

The detailed descriptions provided in this chapter clarify the contents and style of the illustrations which would otherwise be difficult to understand without investing hours in patient study of the original material. Here Boeckler was the pioneer, and this chapter also incorporates his perceptive descriptions and reconstructions.[1]

My reconstruction drawings* provide the reader with convenient references. These drawings were made by tracing and combining the images on the parchment and impressions. Original elements in light lines reproduce tracings of similar figures in this manuscript whenever possible. This method of reconstruction is generally reliable because the artists constantly repeated a small number of pictorial topoi with scarcely any variation.

Assiduous examination of the illustrations, with the help of strong direct and raking light, reveals numerous details and small areas of modeling still in excellent condition. When the leaves were detached from the seventeenth-century book bindings, most of the final details, such as facial features, drapery folds, accessories and highlights, adhered to the binding and were hidden under the layers of transferred paint; while some of the paint disintegrated and was inevitably lost.[2] It is particularly difficult to disentangle the contents of the painted impressions of ff. 3v and 4r from the print of the discarded German Passion sermons pasted on the surface of the cardboard bookcover.

Most of the original content of the pictures can be reconstructed by comparing them with their impressions, but the mirror images on the paint impressions can be misleading if they are not read carefully. Although the labeled sketches on f. 3v provide reliable information, the instructions on the other folios must be used with particular caution because the artists often deviated from them or reinterpreted them, frequently adding other important elements.[3] The task of reconstruction is made simpler by the artists' addition of gold labels.[4] I have included my translation of Degering's transcriptions of the instructions and gold labels with the description of each picture. The words in parenthesis are his suggestions for missing and illegible passages.

DESCRIPTION OF F. 1R

The miniatures illustrate events from the selection of Saul as the first king of Israel in 1 Samuel 10. The first three pictures relate the fulfillment of Samuel's prophetic signs which prove to the sceptical Saul that God has chosen him; in the fourth

1. See Boeckler, pp. 123-50, for his detailed descriptions and reconstructions.

* These are my own reconstructions. The final drawings were made by Sharon Celestini. Solid lines are original elements found in the pictures and/or the paint impressions. Broken lines are my proposed reconstructions.

2. According to Degering, p. 3, in 1876 restorers removed the glue from the bare parchment, although the pictures are still covered with dark streaks of glue. Otherwise, the restorers limited themselves to conservation of the painted surfaces rather than attempting to clean and repaint them. The folios have been sealed between sheets of glass for several decades. In May 1977 I was informed in a letter sent by the State Library in Berlin that the folios were undergoing additional conservation.

3. See Degering's transcriptions of the instructions for each picture, pp. 65-77. Schum, pp. 10-12, and Schultze, pp. 12-19, deciphered very few words, but Degering, pp. 65-77, 102-106, read approximately seventy percent of the instructions with the aid of an arc lamp and a strong magnifying glass. He reconstructed missing letters and words by consulting the Septuagint, Vulgate, the Vetus Latina in the Margo Codicis Legionensis and J. Wellhausen, *Der Text der Bücher Samuelis* (Göttingen, 1871).

I was only able to verify ninety percent of Degering's reading because I was limited to the use of a simple table lamp and a strong magnifying glass. The reconstructions of the Instructions and Labels use the following conventions: [ ] include text destroyed and reconstructed, ( ) include abbreviations expanded.

4. All gold labels and later glosses are quoted from Degering's transcriptions, pp. 77-81. See also, pp. 15-16, 83-84.

Reconstruction of Quedlinburg Itala, f. 1r = Pictures 1-4.

picture Samuel presents the king to the Israelites. Faint remains of an earlier set of instructions, barely visible at the top of pictures 1 and 2, were erased by the scribe, who then wrote a second set of instructions which the artist followed. Facial features are badly damaged and the white paint on clothing and Rachel's monument has disintegrated. The blue background on pictures 1 and 2 is paler than that of 3 and 4 because more color from the first two pictures adhered to the bookbinding.

Picture 1

SUMMARY: Saul and his young companion stand next to Rachel's tomb. They are addressed by two messengers, standing before three large holes in the ground, who tell Saul that his father's asses have been found. (1 Sam. 10: 2.)

INSTRUCTIONS: *Facis monumentum* [*adsunt*] *saul et puer eius et du*[*o*] *viri fossas s*[*uper*]*silientes locuntur illi et a*[*nnunciant quod asinae sint*] *inventae*. The words after 'illi' are illegible. 'You make a tomb, [nearby] are Saul and his attendant and two men leaping above pits speak to him and [announce that the asses are] found'. This latter part, though destroyed in the instructions, is found in the labels.

GOLD LABELS: *Monimentum rachel; saul; duo viri nunciantes saul quia inventae sunt asinae*: 'Rachel's tomb; Saul; two men announcing to Saul that the asses have been found'. Later glosses in black ink: above the three holes, *fovea* 'pit', and to the right of the two soldiers, *salie*(*n*)*s foveas* 'jumping the pits'.

Saul wears the full dress uniform of a Late Roman emperor: short white tunic decorated with colored bands near the hem, cuirass, red-purple paludamentum clasped by a round gem-encircled fibula, gold spear, and simple gold band diadem with its ribbon ends fluttering behind his head. The same uniform is worn consistently by all the kings in this series of miniatures. Other details of this uniform, which are more clearly legible in pictures 2 and 5, are: soft white boots tied with dark laces, a square decoration on the chest, fringed leather straps on the upper arm and skirt and a belt tied at the waist.

Saul stands in stiff frontality with only a strongly directed side glance showing his awareness of the messengers. He is clearly taller than all other figures in every picture, with the exception of Samuel on f. 2. His purpose in holding his right hand before his chest is uncertain; he may be making a speaking gesture or holding the edge of his mantle. Here, as in almost every picture, his left hand, wrapped in his cloak, holds a spear.

The young traveling companion at the left is mentioned in the instructions and in 1 Sam. 9. He wears a long-sleeved yellow tunic decorated with an orbiculum on the skirt and an orange chlamys on which brown and gold lines indicate folds and highlights. His posture and gestures are identical to those of Saul. The peculiar drape of their mantles is a cliché repeated in almost all of the miniatures. Their cloaks are pulled at an oblique angle across the chest, then wrapped tautly around the left hand, falling straight at the side to reveal much of their tunics.

The messengers, with right arms raised in speaking gestures, are also carbon copies of each other. Although the text, instructions and labels refer to them simply as messengers, they are dressed as soldiers. Their blue helmets, long-sleeved tunics covered with hooks to represent mail armor and laced boots are typical of Late Roman soldier's uniforms. Both men carry orange oval shields emblazoned with large gold crosses drawn with flared arms.

Rachel's tomb is a tall, round, multistoried shaft capped by a double-tiered conical roof; two rows of small quadratic patches may be windows or decorations. The tomb sits on a low round base amidst clumps of dry, dark green grass and bushes rendered in a sketchy manner. Three large irregular patches in the right corner, two of which are dark brown and one a dark lilac grey, are the large pits in the ground over which the messengers should be jumping according to the 'fossas supersilientes' of the instructions. Because there is no indication of solid ground the holes seem to float against the sky blue background color extending upward from the lower frame. Near the top of the picture a schematic pink strip represents the sunset glow painted in all of the miniatures.

Picture 2

SUMMARY: Saul and his young companion stand next to the Oak of Thabor where they are greeted by three pilgrims going to Bethel. Only one of the three remains, the other two having been cut off. (1 Sam. 10: 3-4.)

INSTRUCTIONS: *F*[*acis*] *saul ad arborem glandiferenntem et puer*[*um eius et viros tres qui locu*]*ntur cum eo unus portat tres aedos unu*[*s portat tres tortas panis unus portat*] *utrem vini*.[5] 'You make Saul near an oak tree and [his] attendant [and three men who speak] with him, one carries three goats, one [carries three loaves of bread and one carries] a skin of wine'.

GOLD LABELS: *Arbor glandi*[*s electae*] (I can only read 'arbor'); *saul; viri tres* [*in bethel*] *ad* $\overline{dm}$ (= 'deum') *eg*[*redientes*]: '[oak] tree; Saul; three men [going] to the Lord [in Bethel]'. Fifteenth-century glosses[6] in black ink: *ad quercum thabor* 'at the oak of Thabor' near the tree, and *rex d*(*omi*)*ne* 'Lord King!' above the hand of the first pilgrim.

This time Saul assumes a disjointed, flattened contrapposto pose with his weight thrust forward on his left leg and his right leg and arm bent at sharp angles for balance. His boy attendant,

5. In a letter written to me on January 4, 1976, Bonifatius Fischer stated that Degering, pp. 66-67, incorrectly completed the instructions as 'tres tortas panis' when the phrase should read 'tria vasa panum'. Degering's reading was based on the Vulgate, but Fischer's is taken from the Old Latin marginalia in the Margo Cod. Goth. Leg.; see the copy of 1587 in Vatican City, Bibl. Vat., Vat. lat. 4859, edited by C. Vercellone, *Variae lectiones vulgatae latinae bibliorum editionis*, vol. 2 (Rome, 1862), p. 224.

6. Discussed by Degering, pp. 15-16, 83-84.

still wearing a yellow tunic and orange mantle, stands in an equally flattened contrapposto much like Saul's but with his weight on his right leg and his left knee slightly bent. The details of Saul's armor are clearer: a large square red decoration and a long gold strap on his chest, a round orbiculum on his shoulder, a bright cingulum at his waist, a spear clasped in his mantle-covered left hand and the ribbon ends of his diadem fluttering behind his head. Here the oak of Thabor is a dead, leafless tree.

The sole surviving pilgrim of the original three runs toward Saul and stretches out his exaggeratedly large hand in a speaking gesture. He wears a grey-green short tunic with long tight sleeves and is bare legged. The grey mass above his shoulders is scarcely legible, but his grasping gesture indicates that he holds a ram in the familiar manner of ancient shepherds and not the three animals mentioned in the text and instructions.

Drawing based on Picture 2. Large figure: pilgrim carrying a ram in the final painted version; small figure: pentimento of the earlier painting of a pilgrim holding a vessel.

My observation of the miniature revealed that this pilgrim was painted over an earlier figure which has been stripped off the parchment and transferred onto the surface of the paint impression. Only the upper part of this earlier figure is visible on the ram bearer's tunic, and it is a small figure, approximately the size of Saul's boy. His eyes, nose, mouth and hair are clearly indicated, and he holds an object in his outstretched hands that could be the bread platter carried by the second pilgrim in verse 4. The specks of blue paint over the outline of this small figure indicate that it was drawn and painted after the blue background was applied over the instructions.[7]

Picture 3

SUMMARY: As the third sign of his divine election as king, Saul prophesies with a chorus of three prophets who play musical instruments. He is still accompanied by his boy companion. (1 Sam. 10: 5-6.)

INSTRUCTIONS: *Facis pofetas* (sic, for 'profetas') *unum cum citara ali[um cum] tibia [tertium cum tympano et pro]fetantem [saul et puerum illius cum psal]terio.* I can see only the *t* of 'tibia', and I cannot read the words after '[pro]fetantem'. 'You make prophets, one with a lyre, the other [with] a flute, [the third with a drum and Saul] prophesying [and his attendant with a psal]ter'.

GOLD LABELS: *Puer saul; saul; chorus prophetarum*: 'Saul's attendant; Saul; a chorus of prophets'.

Three young beardless prophets wear white tunics decorated with dark red-brown clavi, white pallia and sandals. Each holds a gold musical instrument in his pallium-covered left hand. The first prophet at the right holds a lyre and the second a double flute. The third prophet's instrument is no longer identifiable, but according to the text it must have been a tympanum. Although the text implies that the four instruments were carried by four prophets, the triangular psalterium was given to the boy. Nonetheless, the cluster of rocks separating him from Saul indicates that only the king prophesies with the three seers.

Saul stands in a frontal pose with his weight on his right leg and his hand on his hip. The right side of his cloak is pulled in a taut triangle across his lower body and grasped in his left hand. Much of the gold network of highlight lines on the cloak is exceptionally well preserved, and gold also highlights the details of his armor and spear, the round fibula surrounded with gems (represented as gold circles), his diadem and the musical instruments. The prophets' clothing is covered with many fine white fold lines; gold decoration is never used on white clothing.

Unfortunately, colored photographs give the false impression of a defined foreground which does not exist in the original where remains of the blue background color clearly extend to the lower frame. The ruined streaks of grey in the pink strip most likely represent the housetops of Gibeathelohim since they serve a similar function in the better preserved miniatures 7 and 8 on f. 2r. Dark brown rocks are clustered between Saul and his companion and are aligned in front of the prophets.

Picture 4

SUMMARY: Samuel introduces Saul to the Israelites at Mizpeh as their first king. (1 Sam. 10: 23-24.)

INSTRUCTIONS: *Facis ubi samuel profeta et sau[l conveniunt in maspha] et populo lo[cuntur].* 'You make where the prophet Samuel and Saul [assemble in Mizpeh] and sp[eak] to the people'.

GOLD LABELS: *Saul; fil[* (the rest was cut away, but it probably read 'filii istrahel'): 'Saul; sons (of Israel, i.e., Israelites)'.

7. This change is discussed further in chapter 4.

Samuel and Saul stand in the same flattened three-quarter pose and raise their right hands in identical speaking gestures directed at a group of Israelites. Samuel wears a prophet's white tunic, pallium and sandals as he does in the picture on f. 2. The dark area under Saul's chin must be a smudge from the paint outlining his face because he is young, beardless and has short dark hair in all the miniatures.

Originally there was room for three Israelites in the foreground and two heads behind their shoulders, a common Late Antique schematic formula for representing crowds which was used as well in pictures 10, 12 and 14. Here the five men signify the multitudes assembled at Mizpeh to await Samuel's presentation of their king. Only the first man is fully preserved; standing in stiff frontality he wears a bright orange calf-length, belted tunic decorated with orbicula on the shoulders and knees. His light yellow-brown mantle is pulled to the side and covers his left hand in keeping with this artist's favorite drapery convention. All that can be seen of the man who stands behind him is a damaged head and the upper part of a red mantle.

A few damaged patches of grey in the pink sky strip are the remains of the housetops and hills of Mizpeh which must have resembled those in pictures 7 and 8. Once again the blue sky extends down to the bottom edge of the frame.

DESCRIPTION OF F. 2R

In these miniatures Samuel tells Saul that God has rejected his kingship because he did not destroy all the Amalechites as God had commanded but had spared their king, Agag. Samuel renounces Saul, and after a final prayer together the prophet slays Agag. (1 Sam. 15: 13-34.) The bookcover's spine defaced a strip running through pictures 6 and 8. The painted surface is well preserved on picture 5 but severely damaged on the other pictures.

Picture 5

SUMMARY: After conquering the Amalekites, Saul, in the company of two young bodyguards, pours a libation on a burning altar. Samuel approaches riding in a biga with his right arm extended in a speaking gesture as he denounces the king. (1 Sam. 15: 10-15.)

INSTRUCTIONS: *Facis profetam [de curru] loquente contra regem saul sacrificante et pueros [regis duos].* 'You make the prophet speaking [from his biga] facing King Saul sacrificing, and [the king's two] attendants'.

GOLD LABELS: *Samuhel descendens in galgala*: 'Samuel going down to Gilgal'; and *saul offerens holocaustum*: 'Saul making a burnt offering'.

In the center of the picture Saul pours a libation rom a patera into the flames on a rectangular altar according to a long established formula in Roman art for a sacrificing emperor[8] instead of performing the burnt animal offering required by the text and Hebraic rite. The artist obviously consulted the text when he labeled the scene 'holocaustum'.[9]

The original paint surface is well preserved. Details of Saul's military dress are now clearly legible. (See the descriptions of pictures 1 and 2). Note, in particular, the gold decorated green bands above and below his waist and on the hem of his tunic. Clothing folds and details of his uniform are first drawn with fine brown lines, then accented with gold highlights.

The two boys at the right are not mentioned in the text, but they are required by the instructions. The first of these attendants wears a dull green short tunic and orange chlamys, the second wears the same colors in reverse.

Following the Septuagint, the Itala text places Samuel in a 'currum' (cart). Only his head and enlarged right hand stretched out in a speaking gesture are still visible. Two toylike, prancing horses pull his 'biga'; the first horse is rust brown, the second is grey, and their reins and harnesses are outlined in gold.

A monumental grey arch rises behind Samuel; its attic and arched opening are still clearly visible, and the remains of a large gold decoration can still be seen on the front of the right pylon. It is no longer possible to tell whether the artist indicated the rest of the arch summarily and left it afloat against the blue background, or whether he elongated the arch in order to place it on the tan ground line which ends behind the horses' hooves. Both alternatives occur in Roman art[10] (figs. 26, 36). A long row of marks in the attic may be windows if the arch is the city gate of Gilgal or they may be intended to resemble an inscription if it is a triumphal arch. The artist's reliance on established military imagery makes it more likely, however, that he has represented a tall triumphal arch like the one depicted on the Triumph panel of Marcus Aurelius[11] (fig. 36).

8. For similar representations of emperors and generals pouring libations see Ryberg, *Rites*, pp. 120-41, figs. 45e, 51, 61b, 90, 91.

9. 'Holocaustum' is found in other Old Latin versions of 1 Sam. 15: 12. Cf. R. Weber, 'Les interpolations de Samuel dans les mss. de la Vulgate', *Miscellanea Giovanni Mercati*, vol. 1, Studi e Testi, 121 (Vatican City, 1956), pp. 19ff.; and P. Sabatier, ed., *Bibliorum Sacrorum Latinae Versiones Antiquae seu Vetus Italica*, vol. 1 (Reims, 1743), p. 1. The 'ôlâh' of the hebraic rite was a burnt animal sacrifice and sufficiently close to the pagan 'holocaustum' to enable it to be designated by a word in the same family in the Septuagint and in patristic studies. See, S. Daniel, *Recherches sur le vocabulaire du culte dans la Septante* (Paris, 1966), pp. 253, 257-58; and A. V. Billen, *The Old Latin Texts of the Heptateuch* (Cambridge, 1927), pp. 1, 199.

10. See the elongated arch on Marcus Aurelius' Triumph panel in Ryberg, *Panel Reliefs*, pl. 9a, and the city which seems to float in the air in Vatican Vergil min. 18; cf. de Wit, pl. 11 (our figs. 26, 36).

11. Schultze, *Quedlinburger Itala*, p. 17, suggested that this structure is either the city gate of Gilgal, or a building meant to signify a place of distinction. Boeckler, pp. 130, 156, wondered whether it was a house representing the city of Gilgal. Those houses, however, are confined to the pink strip, and they have defined roofs; whereas the structure in picture 5 is clearly a large arch which extends well below the pink strip.

Reconstruction of Quedlinburg Itala, f. 2r = Pictures 5-8.

Picture 6

SUMMARY: As Samuel turns away to leave him, Saul grasps the prophet's mantle and it tears. Samuel's speaking gesture illustrates his prophecy that God will renounce the house of Saul. (1 Sam. 15:27-28.)

INSTRUCTIONS: *Facis ubi ducit se profeta et rex saul dum vult illum prendere extremum de v*[*estim*]*ento eius conscidit et ille corgens semul ducit illum*. 'You make where the prophet goes off, and King Saul, while he wishes to grasp him, tears the outer edge from his garment, and he running at the same time leads him'.

GOLD LABEL: *Saul tenens samuhelem*: 'Saul grasping Samuel'.

Saul chases Samuel, and holds the torn edge of the prophet's pallium in his right hand as Samuel, running to the right, turns his head back and makes a speaking gesture. Their feet almost touch the frame, and the blue background color extends to its bottom edge. A few red and brown patches of paint to the right of Samuel are all that remain of the altar and fire, best preserved in picture 5. Specks of dark grey in the pink sky strip are the remnants of the housetops of Gilgal which can be seen more clearly on the bookcover impressions and in pictures 7 and 8.

Picture 7

SUMMARY: Agag, defeated king of the Amalechites, begs Samuel for clemency. Samuel prays with Saul for the last time. (1 Sam. 15:30-33.)

INSTRUCTIONS: *Facis ubi rex saul profetam* (added: *iratum*) *rogat ut in se rogent deum et orantem* [*agag sibi ign*]*osc*[*ere*]. The text is illegible after 'orantem'. 'You make where King Saul entreats the (enraged) prophet that they beseech God on his behalf, and [Agag] begging [to be] forgiven'.

GOLD LABELS: *Aga rex; samuhel; saul; samuhel*: 'King Agag; Samuel; Saul; Samuel'.

Two scenes are represented. Agag, extending his left hand in submission and placing his right hand on his chin in an ancient gesture of anxiety or sorrow, begs Samuel for clemency. At the right Samuel and Saul raise their arms in an orans gesture as they pray together for the last time.

The artist has not adhered strictly to the instructions which request three scenes: Saul begging Samuel to pray with him; both men praying together (which is not in the text); and Agag beseeching Samuel for mercy. Instead the artist omitted the first scene and reversed the order of the last two. Both kings wear

Proposed composition of Picture 7 provided the artist had followed the instructions.

identical costumes, and therefore can only be distinguished by the gold labels.

The impressionistic rendering of the hilltops and housetops in the pink strip is clearly preserved here. The yellow tan foreground extends from the lower frame to a little above the men's feet and then abruptly changes to the sky-blue and pink background.

Picture 8

SUMMARY: Samuel slays Agag in the presence of Saul and his attendants outside the walls of Gilgal. (1 Sam. 15: 33.)

INSTRUCTIONS: *Facis civitatem et extra civitatem ubi profeta asta cocidit regem alienum dexreta* (sic, for 'dextera') [*facis*] *saul ubi in contra est* [*cum p*]*ueris du*[*obus*]. 'You make a city, and outside the city where the prophet killed the foreign king with a spear, to the right [you make] where Saul is opposite [with] his two attendants'.

GOLD LABELS: *Samuhel interficiens regem amalechitarum*: 'Samuel killing the king of the Amalechites'.

Samuel leans forward and grasps Agag by the hair. His weapon is totally destroyed, but his gesture would suggest that he was killing Agag with a spear in accordance with the instructions.[12] Agag has fallen, his cloak still flows out behind him, and his weight is momentarily balanced on his arms in a common fallen warrior position.[13] Saul and his two young attendants, standing in stiff frontal poses, observe the death of Agag. Saul appears to place his right hand before his chest, and he pulls a triangular corner of his paludamentum across his tunic as he did in picture 3.

The row of housetops and hilltops in the pink strip are not mentioned in the instructions, but they continue the landscape cliché used to represent a series of cities in pictures 3 through 7. Here, however, the instructions specifically ask that the artist represent a city and place the death of Agag outside its walls, 'facis civitatem et extra civitatem ...'. The artist selected a vignette of a six-sided fortified city which has no buildings within its walls; fragments of the bright brown walls, a few corner towers and a red portal in the right side wall are partially preserved above Samuel's right shoulder.

DESCRIPTION OF F. 3V

The pictures illustrate 2 Sam. 3: 6-39, the story of Abner, a military commander who changed his allegiance to David during the civil war with Saul's heirs, but who was assassinated by Joab and buried and mourned by David.

Instead of detailed instructions, quick line sketches, which are visible above the painted figures, were drawn on the bare parchment to indicate the placement of the figures in the compositions with circles for their heads and single lines for their gestures. Here the written instructions were limited to short titles denoting the status of each person rather than his name.

Picture 9

SUMMARY: In an angry confrontation, Abner renounces his allegiance to Saul's heir, king Ishboseth. (2 Sam. 3: 6-11.)

INSTRUCTION AND SKETCHES: *Dux* 'general', written in large letters in rapid cursive, appears above Abner's head. The figure of Ishboseth and the accompanying instructions were cut away in 1618 by the binder, Reitel. Single lines, indicating the angle of a seated figure's legs, are all that remain of the preliminary sketch of the king.

GOLD LABEL: *Abner* 'Abner', above his head.

Abner wears a long-sleeved, short, white tunic belted low and decorated with rose-colored patches on the shoulder, chest and wrists; such richly embroidered garments are frequently depicted in late Roman art. His clothing should be compared with the costume worn by the so-called Stilicho on the diptych in Monza (fig. 44). A brownish-green mantle, held on Abner's right shoulder by a large gold cross-bow fibula, hangs heavily to mid-calf and completes his official costume. His two young

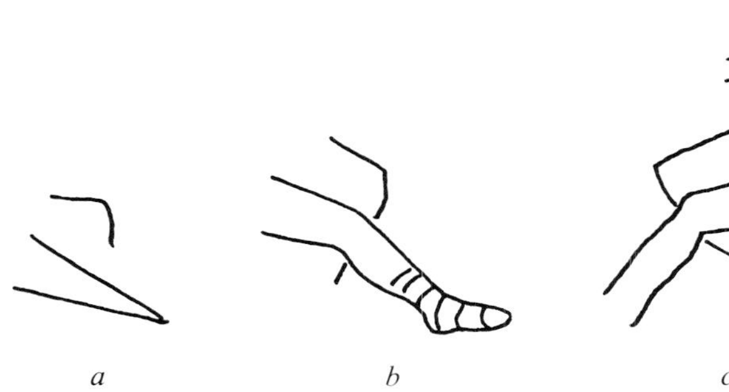

Drawings based on Picture 9; *a*. underdrawing of the seated figure, *b*. painted remains on the parchment, *c*. paint impression on the book-cover.

12. Other versions of this text indicate that 'Samuel hewed Agag in pieces' with a sword. It is possible that the lost passage in the Quedlinburg Itala text might have made a spear seem like a plausible choice since it is required in the instructions. Boeckler, pp. 132-33, assumed that the text called for a sword, as did Delbrück, who suggested that the artist settled on a spear instead because he was following a pictorial model. Delbrück overlooked the word 'asta' in the instructions. See Delbrück, *Lipsanothek*, p. 88. The model was, presumably, generic to the repertory of soldiers in combat widely used in Roman art.

13. For examples of this pose see Boeckler, p. 133; S. Reinach, *Répertoire de reliefs grecs et romains* (Paris, 1909), 1: 434; 2: 666 and 3: 443; and the fallen man in the lower right corner of the boar hunt in the Small Hunt mosaic at Piazza Armerina, illustrated by Dorigo, *Late Roman Painting*, fig. 106.

Reconstruction of Quedlinburg Itala, f. 3v = Pictures 9-12.

escorts are identical in pose and dress to Saul's attendants in picture 8; the first wears a short orange tunic and dull green mantle, the other wears a rose-purple cloak over his white tunic.

Abner makes a speaking gesture, but only the bent knee and extended leg of the seated person whom he addresses remain. The white laced boot indicates that this person was dressed in the armor worn by all the kings in the extant illustrations. According to the outline of this figure appearing as a mirror image on the impression, he is seated with his right arm extended in what was probably a speaking gesture. Presumably this is Ishboseth enthroned. He would have been accompanied by one or more bodyguards, much like King Hiram in picture 13 because in Roman art kings and emperors always have standing attendants.

Picture 10

SUMMARY: Abner announces to the elders of Israel that he has changed his allegiance from Ishboseth to David. (2 Sam. 3: 17-19.)
INSTRUCTIONS AND SKETCHES: The title *dux* 'general' is written above Abner and below it are sketched a circle for his head and a wide V-shaped line for his speaking gesture. Above the circles for the Israelites' heads is the word *populus* 'people'.[14]
GOLD LABELS: *Abner* 'Abner' above him; *praesbyteri* 'elders' above the Israelites.

Abner stands at the left in the company of a young attendant and addresses a group of Israelites. His stance and speaking gesture are similar to those of Saul and Samuel in picture 4. Once again his escort wears a dark orange tunic and green cloak. The elders are dressed as court dignitaries in calf-length bluish-white tunics and long cloaks of rose, green, brown and purple enlivened with gold highlights. There are four men in the first row facing Abner in a slight three-quarter turn, and the heads of two more men appear behind their shoulders. Their leader answers Abner with a speaking gesture. It is important to recognize that on pictures 10 to 12 flecks of blue paint on the lower portions of the miniatures indicate that the blue background continued down to the lower frame, and that blue was painted over the pink strip in pictures 11 and 12. Therefore, the beige color now seen in the lower portion of these miniatures is actually bare parchment.

Picture 11

SUMMARY: David accepts Abner's pledge of allegiance and they part in peace, but Joab, David's general, lures Abner back to Hebron and slays him to avenge the death of his brother Asahel. (2 Sam. 3: 20-27.)

INSTRUCTION AND SKETCHES: In the upper scene *dux* 'general' is seen to the left of the gold label 'abner'. The right-angle line signifies his speaking gesture, and two circles at the right indicate his escorts.
GOLD LABELS: *Abner* 'Abner' above his head in the upper scene;]*et joab* '... and Joab' above the left figure in the lower scene.

Two scenes are arranged in registers. In the upper level, Abner, accompanied by two attendants, once again makes a speaking gesture. The left half of the picture is destroyed except for a foot which probably belonged to the lost seated figure of King David. Given this artist's penchant for repeating com-

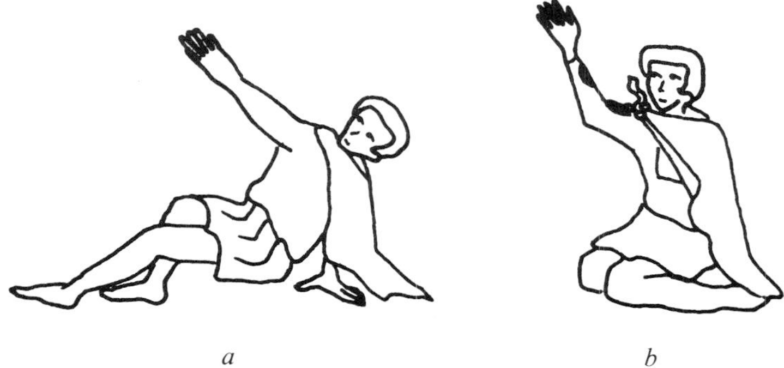

Reconstruction drawings of Abner's fallen figure on Picture 11: *a*. underdrawing, *b*. painted figure.

positional schemes, the composition was most likely identical to the court scene reconstructed for picture 9. Abner wears an orange tunic under a brownish-green cloak which is fastened by a gold, long-staffed, crossbow fibula. Boeckler thought that the two spear bearing escorts who accompany him are two of the twenty men which the text placed in Abner's entourage,[15] but their short stature indicates that they are the young armsbearers who appear with him in every miniature.

In the lower scene the helmeted Joab lunges at Abner, stabbing him with his javelin. Abner has fallen to the ground; the two shields behind him must have been placed aside as a peace gesture. 'et joab' written above his head indicates that he had a companion in the space cut away at the left; it may have been his brother, Abishai.

The preliminary drawing shows Abner fallen on his back with his legs extended in front of him. Boeckler did not recognize that Abner's posture is very different on the impression; there his torso is more vertical, and his legs are tucked under and behind him. Extensive damage has obliterated part of his arms and legs in the sketched and painted versions making it impossible to reconstruct either one of them in complete detail,

14. The small 's' to the right of the first Israelite's head was reconstructed to read 'senior' by Degering and Boeckler, pp. 72-73, 137, but it is not in the same script as the instructions, and a single letter seems an insufficient basis for inserting this word. Degering, p. 72, incorrectly associated the instruction 'populus' with picture 11, but it is found in this picture.

15. Boeckler, p. 137.

but sufficient information remains to suggest that both poses repeat conventional representations of fallen warriors in ancient art.

The beige color is not ground but bare parchment. The blue sky once extended from the top to bottom frame and even covered the pink strip.

Picture 12

SUMMARY: King David heads the procession following Abner's funeral bier. When the Israelites come to ask David to break his fast they are pleased to see that he truly mourns Abner. (2 Sam. 3: 31-39.)

INSTRUCTION AND SKETCHES: A small circle for the head and five simple straight or bent lines to show the angle of the back, arms and legs, place each figure in the composition and establish principal movements and gestures. Above the top scene *dux* 'general' is written over Abner's bier.[16]

GOLD LABELS: *Corpus abner* 'Abner's body' is seen above the bier in the upper scene. In the lower scene *david alloquens suos* 'David speaks to his men' is to the right of David's hand across the center of the composition.

Here as well, blue paint once extended from the top to bottom frame. In the upper scene, David leads four other men in a funeral procession behind Abner's bier. In the sketch (under the pink strip) David puts his hand to his mouth in a gesture of emotional distress that recalls Agag's gesture in picture 7. The sketch for Abner's body is a circle and a line on a rectangular pallet drawn in perspective. The four pallbearers bend under the weight of the bier, but they appear to have a springy step and almost seem to be running both in the sketch and in the painting.

In the lower scene, David addresses a group of five men whose leader urges the king to break his fast. The composition is a repetition of picture 10. The Bible relates that David is in mourning and dresses in sackcloth, but the impression reveals that he wears a military uniform as do the kings in all of the miniatures. He is accompanied by two tall, fully armed bodyguards carrying spears and shields. The gold inscription, 'david alloquens suos', would indicate that the five men to the right, who are best seen on the bookcover impressions, are members of his household, formally dressed in tunics and long mantles.

DESCRIPTION OF F. 4R

This page is divided into two rectangular pictures, the lower one twice the height of the upper frieze. The illustrations depict the building of the Temple in Jerusalem from Solomon's first request to king Hiram for materials and skilled workers to the final dedication. The related text begins on the verso with 1 Kings 5: 2-9 and would have continued through chapter 8.

Picture 13

SUMMARY: King Solomon sends a message to Hiram of Tyre requesting cedars, cypresses and skilled carpenters to build the temple in Jerusalem. (1 Kings 5: 2-9.)

INSTRUCTIONS: *T*[*rip*]*licem facis facis ubi misit rex salomon* [*ad chiram regem nuntium pe*]*tentem ut mitteret ei tignarios ad domum aedificanda*. (Only the *t* in 'triplicem' is still legible, but Degering expanded it to read 'triplicem' in accordance with the three components in this miniature. Although his restoration cannot be verified, it cannot be dismissed categorically.) 'You make [a triplet], you make where King Solomon sent [a messenger] requesting [King Hiram] to send him carpenters to build the house'.

GOLD LABELS: *Salomon* 'Solomon' over the seated figure at the left, and *chiran rex* 'King Hiram' above the second seated figure near the center of the picture.

Three separate events are condensed and appear as simultaneously occurring aspects of one event. Solomon dispatches a messenger who is received by Hiram. The three workers signify the carpenters who will be sent to build the temple.

A spear-carrying bodyguard at the far left was damaged by the bookbinding. Solomon's figure was destroyed, but the gold label above identifies him, and his projecting foot, which appears on the impression, indicates that he was seated, presumably in the same manner as Hiram. A second spear-bearing guard, standing in front of Solomon gestures to dispatch the king's envoy whose cloak swings out behind him as he moves swiftly forward. The messenger extends a roll in his left hand and makes a speaking gesture with his raised right hand and is thus simultaneously sent from the court of Solomon and received by Hiram.

As we have now come to expect, the king of Tyre wears the same military uniform established for all kings in these miniatures. Hiram rests his left hand on the seat of his rectangular stool on which the cross bars and horizontal supports are clearly marked, and he extends his right arm to welcome the messenger. A guard, standing behind the king, holds a red shield rimmed in gold; he leans forward and extends his arm, but it is no longer possible to determine whether his lost hand was meant to receive the message roll or to hold a spear. The episode is completed

16. Degering, p. 73, assumed that the instructions were more detailed and read 'dux occisus' or 'dux in feretro', but there is no remaining evidence to support his conjectures.

Reconstruction of Quedlinburg Itala, f. 4r = Pictures 13-14.

by the third scene on the right where three men wearing the typical Roman laborer's exomis stand ready to be dispatched to Jerusalem. The clothing in this miniature is painted in the colors: light orange, light green, greenish-brown, pink, rose, light red and purplish red.

Picture 14

SUMMARY: The building of the Temple in Jerusalem and its dedication by Solomon before the elders of Israel. (1 Kings, chapters 5-8.)

INSTRUCTIONS: *F[ab]ricam facis ubi fabri regis salomon et [chirae re]gis [faciunt domum] auream et columnas aereas et infra a columnas et su[pra] facis mall[og]ranato[rum ordi]nes [d]uplices et facis m[are] aen[eum] et facis baccas aereas xii et in quattuor partes [cae]li facis illas [f]ronta[ta]s s. intuentem respicientes et posteriora earum in domo sint et leones aereos et coronulas [et cherubim et plectas] et facis ubi sacrificabit salomon ante dom* (= 'dominum') *et ingeniculans expansis manibus orabit et omnis populus [cum illo] orans stetit ante [dominum]*. 'You make a workshop where the workmen of king Solomon and king [Hiram make] a golden [house] and brazen columns, and below the columns and above you make double [rows] of pomegranates; and you make a brazen [sea], and you make twelve brazen oxen and you make them fronting the four parts of the heavens and looking at the beholder and their hind quarters are inward; and brazen lions and borders [and cherubim and 'plectas']. And you make where Solomon will sacrifice before the Lord, and he will pray on his knees with his hands outstretched, and all the people praying [with him] stand before [the Lord]'.

GOLD LABELS: *Templum* 'temple', found in the upper blue strip 5 cm. from the left side of the frame; and *salomon orans* 'Solomon praying' above the kneeling king's head.

The picture lost more than half its paint; much of it adheres to the bookcover, but the colored impression has enough essential evidence to permit reconstruction.

The instructions tell the artist to portray the workers of King Solomon and King Hiram building the golden temple and to show some of the large bronze ornaments, namely, the twin columns covered with pomegranate vines, the brazen sea supported by twelve oxen gazing at the heavens, and the bronze basins decorated with lions, 'plectas' and cherubim. He was given no other clues.

The scribe who wrote the instructions and the artist who illustrated them were of different minds. Whereas the former stressed the temple's decorations, the artist emphasized an extensive building scene whose elements were popular in Roman art. It is difficult to determine whether the temple decorations requested by the instructions were ever painted. Their most likely location should have been in the upper left corner above the wall, where irregularly shaped patches of paint remain. Boeckler suggested that the forequarters of a lion from a bronze basin might be seen there, but even he conceded that the area was too damaged to permit a secure identification.[17] On the contrary, it seems to me that this area would have been too small to permit the artist to include the details described in the text and instructions, and the artist may have decided not to represent the temple decorations at all.

The original shape of the large red-brown smudge in the left end of the pink strip is no longer intelligible, but it is doubtful that the artist would have made the temple so small, or that he would have placed it outside the confines of the fortified walls. The gold label 'templum' may actually designate the sacred area under construction rather than an actual building; in Ancient art religious precincts are often surrounded by fortified walls. At present, there is no trace of a structure which could have represented a building in any part of the picture, and the double colonnade along the inner perimeter of the wall is too irregular to correspond to a building of a preconceived plan. The workers fill most of the area, leaving no room for other structures or temple decorations described in the instructions.

Construction activities take place within the wide perimeters of an eight-sided city wall seen in bird's-eye view. The wall is built of large rectangular blocks of tan stone outlined in gold. The double colonnade is simply drawn in vertical lines with short cross bars on the top and bottom to indicate capitals and bases. Gold lines remain on a few of the columns and on a long golden beam, or possibly it is the top edge of the wall running above the upper row of columns.

The three fortified towers, still visible at the angles of the wall in the foreground, are in proportion to the wall, but an enormous fourth tower rises high above the wall to the right of center. This tower is further distinguished by its light salmon color, a gabled roof topped by a round finial, decorations in gold lines, and a large double-valved window which fills the upper half of the tower. There may have been a flat wall behind Solomon and the courtiers where the blue sky ends in a straight horizontal line that can be drawn to the same height as his head, but the area has been too deprived of its paint to make it possible to determine whether there was a structure or an empty space.

Six workers, dressed in the exomis, engage in building activities. The worker just above the second tower wears a pink exomis decorated with gold highlights; he is running with his arms outstretched, and seems to have held an object which has since been destroyed. At the right, two men saw a plank of wood resting on a sawhorse; one man stands on top of the sawhorse, leans forward, and grasps the end of the saw with both hands as the man standing below him to the left raises his arms to work its other end. On the upper left a man bends over to lift a large rectangular object which may be a building block. He

17. See Boeckler, p. 137.

looks to the right at a kneeling man who raises his arms to hold a large object on his back; a sixth worker standing behind this man leans forward to help him steady his heavy load.[18]

The dedication ceremony performed outside the walls, follows the instructions quite closely. King Solomon kneels before the large tower with his arms spread in an orans gesture, his lower body turned to the right and his upper body frontal. The gold label 'salomon orans' lies between his head and left hand. Traces of red, brown and gold color found between the king and his dignitaries are the remains of an altar and its fire.

The five dignitaries, who stand in two rows at the right and turn toward Solomon, wear long-sleeved, calf-length tunics and long cloaks pulled to the side and grasped in their covered hands. Some of the colors can still be distinguished in patches of paint which remain on their clothes: soft rose, pink, lilac, peach, dull orange and light green with drapery folds drawn in local colors and highlighted with many fine gold lines. One can still see that a gold decoration was embroidered on the tunic shoulder of the first man and that a large gold rectangular tablion was sewn near the front edge of his long mantle.

NARRATIVE TECHNIQUES

The designer, working closely with the scribe, and the master artist each made their own important contributions to the narrative structure of this cycle of illustrations. The programmer directed the scribe to divide the text into meaningful narrative sections, each preceded by one side of a folio left free for illustrations.[19] The divisions cannot be compared with any known ancient systems, and they do not correspond with modern chapters, which were devised in the thirteenth century.[20] The length of these units varies widely, with f. 2r illustrating a story on as few as four pages of text, and f. 4r followed by as many as twenty-four pages.

The pictures act as visual introductions to their units, thereby enabling the reader to locate and differentiate parts of the text in a manuscript which appears to have otherwise limited its division and identification of the text to numbering each of the four books. Apparently all pictures were placed in closest possible proximity to the beginning of their narrative units, and the first miniatures of ff. 2, 3 and 4 illustrate verses on the following page. On f. 3 the scribe ended the text on the recto with 2 Sam. 3: 5, using only twenty-two lines rather than the usual twenty-six, so that 2 Sam. 3: 6, which is illustrated in the first picture on f. 3v, could directly follow it on the lost facing recto.

The pictures were not always meant to illustrate the entire text; they could also depict one or more of the stories from within it. A few densely clustered verses are represented in the miniatures on f. 1r; whereas, on f. 4r, the pictures relate to events widely dispersed through twenty-four pages. Although the four miniatures on f. 1r directly precede the text of 1 Sam. 9: 1, they actually illustrate the story in chapter ten, but they must have prefaced chapters nine through eleven which recount a unified story, the divine election of Saul and his acceptance by the Israelites as their first king. Therefore f. 1r also adheres to the rule that illustrations immediately precede their relevant textual units.

To a considerable degree, the programmer influenced the narrative techniques used in the illustrations by his choice of episodes to be depicted on each page. He conceived of the cycle as the episodic illustration of closely related series of verses. In his disposition of the instructions on the subdivided pages no scene was given greater significance than any other, unessential connective events were omitted and use of descriptive detail in the text was reduced so that the pictures could focus on the interaction of a few figures. Through his instructions the programmer stipulated the activities, which are frequently dialogs, and he established the narrative unity between miniatures gathered on each page.

All activities illustrated on a folio belong to a coherent story. Cause and effect are often implied in closely linked events compressed within a few representative incidents, just as they are evoked in six scenes on f. 3: Ishboseth's accusation and Abner's angry response (9) lead to the latter's disaffection. This he announces to his followers (10) when he asks them to join him in a change of allegiance to the house of David, thus weakening Saul's dynasty. When Abner offers his loyalty to David in the top scene in picture 11 he becomes vulnerable to Joab's plotted revenge for the death of his brother. Abner's assassination below is followed by his burial in the upper scene in picture 12. In the last episode, David establishes his innocence and strengthens his claim to the throne by leading the funeral procession and explaining to his followers why he mourns Abner (12).

When the illustrations relate events found far apart in the text, the programmer must have expected the viewer to supply the missing links from his knowledge of the text. This would have been the circumstance for f. 4r, which begins with Solomon asking Hiram to send him workers and materials, develops through a construction scene, and ends with the dedication of the temple.

18. Victor Schultze, *Quedlinburger Itala*, p. 26, did not decipher the instructions. He assumed that the temple was complete and located in the left corner, and he thought that the workers were bringing service vessels to the temple. The exact shapes of their burdens are not always certain, but they were probably meant to resemble heavy building materials.

19. Degering, pp. 86-87, 111-20, attributed the design and program to the scribe.

20. For a discussion of chapter and verse divisions used in Late Antique and Medieval Bibles see, D. De Bruyne, *Sommaires, divisions et rubriques de la Bible latine* (Namur, 1914); E. Mangenot, 'Chapitre de la Bible', *Dictionnaire de la Bible*, ed. F. Vigoroux, vol. 2 (Paris, 1899), p. 562; and E. Jacquier, *Le Nouveau Testament dans l'Église chrétienne*, vol. 2 (Paris, 1913), pp. 44-59.

Several compositions represent only one specific incident, but in others the artists condensed distinct actions into one pregnant moment. In picture 5, for example, four separate moments appear to occur simultaneously: Saul sacrifices the animals of the Amalechites in contravention of God's command; Samuel arrives in a biga; with a speaking gesture he asks Saul why he has disobeyed God's commands; and he pronounces God's rejection of Saul and his house. In picture 6 Samuel turns to leave; Saul chases him and asks him to stay; the king grasps the prophet's pallium and tears the hem; and Samuel's gesture prophesies that the nation will be rent into two parts.

The artists interpreted their instructions through a variety of well established narrative compositions. The classic panel containing one incident was their most frequent choice, but two or more actions were also accomodated in short friezes (7 and 13), or double registers (11 and 12), and in a panoramic scene (14). Continuous narration, with its repetition of key figures in double scenes, permitted the artist to depict the passage of time in a limited space (7, 11 and 12). The artist of f. 4 knew that his viewers were accustomed to seeing one figure serve for two scenes, and he represented the messenger sent by Solomon and received by Hiram only once in picture 13. Limitations of available space also prompted him to condense three events in that picture so that they appear to occur simultaneously. In the last picture (14) he used an annular wall to separate two distinct historical incidents and incorporated a variety of building activities in a large space seen in bird's-eye view.

DESCRIPTION OF THE STYLE AND TECHNIQUE[21]

The simplicity of the compositions and their placement in outdoor settings before a blue sky streaked with a glowing pink band of color make the most vivid impressions. Closer examination reveals the coloristic variety and subtlety of these miniatures and provides new insights into the workshop's practices through careful analysis of the painting techniques and style.

Each step in the execution of the miniatures can be recognized. The programmer established the layout of ff. 1r, 2r and 4r by lightly drawing the multipartite frames with a fine black line (seen faintly under the final painted frames on ff. 1r and 2r), then he wrote the instructions for each picture across the upper part of each framed area. The artist of f. 3v also used this ink to draw the frame and sketches and to indicate the titles of the figures.

The artists painted the background and ground colors, then the architecture and figures, and applied gold highlights and labels. As a final step they added the colored frames. This progression is apparent on pictures 1 and 12 where the loss of paint reveals blue background color underneath the red frame, and on picture 7 where the frame overlaps the edge of Agag's cloak and foot. Because the frames are painted freehand in a careless manner the width of every miniature varies noticeably from top to bottom. A thin black outline defines the inner edge of each red frame. On f. 2r gold lozenges still decorate the red border at the four corners of every miniature, and presumably once decorated the frames on the other folios.

The artists first painted the pale pink glow in the sky and then the blue color, often blending its edges into the pink strip to soften the transitions. Differences in the intensity of the background color, which now varies within each miniature and between miniatures, are most likely due to damage. The two shades of blue, well preserved on pictures 3 and 4 where the sky above the pink strip is a shade darker than the blue sky below, may have been standard in all pictures.

By rendering the background in three broad bands of color and by making the pink strip uniform in height, width and color in every picture, the artists achieved decorative unity, but the sky became a schematic convention, a flat backdrop placed directly behind the scenes with its blue color often descending to the lower frame, thus totally omitting the horizon. Originally the garments, warm pastel colors, linear details and the network of gold highlights stood in clear contrast against the cool blue sky.

Several scholars have had the mistaken impression that the artists bathed the figures in an atmospheric haze and that the lower level of blue sky served as a middleground and extended back to a pink horizon.[22] This, however, is a false impression. When the folios were pulled away from the bookbindings, not only was much of the blue background exposed, but a great deal of the blue paint adhered to the cardboard, thus covering over the figures. Therefore, blue dominates over all other colors in a manner that was never intended. Furthermore, the overlay of brown glue muddies colors and blurs forms.[23]

Strong similarities in the artists' figure style and painting techniques have given their work a homogeneous appearance. Their figures are tall, long-legged and well proportioned, but lack a sense of organic connection and clear articulation. Many passages leave us uncertain of the form, angle and action of parts of the body. The full figure was never painted, but only those areas of flesh which would be exposed, as is clearly seen in pictures 1 and 2 where skirt hems overlap truncated thighs; this accounts, to some extent, for the flat, disjointed appearance

21. Most of the description of the style is my own, but this discussion also incorporates Boeckler's perceptive comments, pp. 154-65, about the colors, the decorative gold highlights, the paratactic compositions and the ambivalence which occurs when artists working in a Late Antique schematic style incorporate elements borrowed from earlier classicizing, illusionistic traditions.

22. See Boeckler, p. 155; Bianchi Bandinelli, *Miniatures of the Iliad*, p. 141; Byvanck, 'Antike Buchmalerei: I.', p. 246; and Nordenfalk, *Painting*, p. 91; for a corrected translation of Nordenfalk's German text see, D. Wright, 'Review of Grabar and Nordenfalk, Early Medieval Painting', in the *Art Bull.* 43 (1961): 245-55.

23. The overlay of brown glue and the domination of the blue background caused by the stripping away of the final paint layers may have led Boeckler, pp. 121 ff., to incorrectly characterize many of the colors as dull and dirty.

of most figures. Attempts at modelling the figures in color values generally fail to create truly solid forms, as, for example, in picture 5 where Saul's legs remain flat because the artist only juxtaposed vertical strokes of three separate values of the flesh color (ranging from light salmon to brick red), then highlighted the legs with a bright streak of white paint down the center and added dark outlines.

The garments hang in straight heavy folds without conveying any sense of body movement or structure. Even when cloaks swing out behind swiftly moving figures in pictures 6, 7 and 13, the stiff fabric only emphasizes the body's schematic structure. Furthermore, this flatness is also accentuated because major details, such as facial features and principal drapery folds, are drawn in thin brown lines. Occasionally, fine outlines can still be seen on either one or both sides of limbs and garments. Although some figures seem not to have been outlined in this way, it is difficult to determine how consistently contours were drawn, and to what extent they may have further flattened other figures.

Garments painted in a variety of harmonious pastel colors further enliven the miniatures, but only a few small fragments remain to reveal their former coloristic richness and subtlety. The grouped Israelites in picture 10, for example, wear soft shades of rose, drab green, tan and lilac, and the dignitaries and workmen in picture 14 dress in light rose, lilac, peach, pink, green and dull orange garments. Kings wear white tunics decorated with colored bands and dark red (purple) paludamenta.

A lighter value of the garments' principal color usually indicates the major folds, as on the boy's yellow-tan tunic in picture 1 and on the central courtier's light purple cloak in picture 14, but clothing can also be modeled in contrasting colors. Long strokes of brown-green and red-brown represent the shadows on the folds of Abner's drab green cloaks in pictures 9 and 11, and blue shadows and rose-colored embroidery enliven his white tunics. Delicate nuances of pale yellow, pink and blue provide warmth and life to the white clothing worn by the prophets and kings.

The abundance of fine gold highlights on every colored garment far outnumbers the actual drapery folds. These metallic accents correlate with similar decorative effects made by the profusion of white lines describing the many fine folds on white drapery. Gold highlights are well preserved only on pictures 3 and 8, but, from the fragmentary remains on other pictures, it is possible to imagine how lavishly the artists spun this network of lines over the clothing. Gold paint also outlines the lances, musical instruments, horses' harnesses, architectural details, trees and altars, indeed, everything solid except flesh and white clothing. The total effect must have made a scintillating surface of bright patterns worked in a decorative linearism which threatened to dissolve the solidity of every form.

Until now no one has recognized that more than one artist painted the four extant folios. The miniaturists achieved stylistic unity by repeating the same schematic sky, a common palette of colors and a very limited number of compositional formulas based on a small repertory of figure types, poses, gestures and costume arrangements.

Despite these common stylistic traits and the alterations caused by later damage, we can, nonetheless, differentiate between the work of two and possibly three individuals. Ff. 1 and 2 can be assigned to the first artist; f. 3 to a second painter, who was possibly the master, and f. 4 may be the work of a third person.

The figures on ff. 1 and 2 have stiffer and more angular movements than those of ff. 3 and 4 and are seemingly weightless and frozen within their rectilinear silhouettes. Their three-quarter profiles have been flattened to the broadest possible extension. Occasional frontality evidently stems from this artist's technical difficulties rather than from any hieratic intention since his figures generally move in a lateral direction. In numerous passages, the function and movements of his figures are uncertain due to the joining of inconsistent viewpoints which shift between frontal, profile and three-quarter views for different parts of the same individual. That is why, at first glance, Saul and Samuel appear to stride vigorously to the right in picture 4, but the impression is unintentional. They were actually meant to stand in a contrapposto pose while making a conventional Roman Adlocutio gesture. Here, however, as in so many other miniatures, certain parts of the body have been subordinated to other parts to emphasize the meaning of oratorical gestures, while all movements have been channeled into a single layer of depth parallel to the picture plane.

It had long been accepted practice for Late Antique artists to combine a pastiche of conventions ultimately derived from varied figure styles. The Itala workshop was no exception. The first artist, for example, used an exaggerated, flattened contrapposto pose for Saul in picture 2, along with stiff, frontal figures confined by rectilinear outlines for the Israelites in picture 4, as well as sinuously curving and graceful movements for the profile view of Samuel in pictures 4 and 7. In contrast, Samuel in the first episode of picture 7 is a frozen angular figure.

The bodies painted by the second artist on folio 3 contrast with the broad figures on ff. 1 and 2 with their wide, square shoulders and hips and curved thighs and calves. The slender figures on f. 3 have narrow shoulders sloping down in a curved line and straight, thin, shapeless legs. Although both artists used the same Adlocutio topos in pictures 4, 10 and 12, their figures differ considerably in physical structure. Those in pictures 10 and 12 assume a true three-quarter turn and gesture directly at each other. The chlamyes and paludamenta of f. 3 hang with straight heavy folds which partially obscure the figures, but the first artist pulled his cloaks sharply to one side to reveal more of the body. Even when the second painter shows a cloak drawn to the side, it is not at the sharp angle used by the first artist. The gold lines on f. 3 are also heavier than those of the first painter. In addition, the latter used small barefoot boys for Saul's attendants, while Abner's taller bodyguards wear short boots.

On f. 4 the figures have a wider variety of movements and

gestures as well as more weight and stature than those on ff. 1-3. The builders in picture 14 and the messenger and court attendants in picture 13 turn in various directions; they are more lithe and more convincingly articulated than the figures on the first three folios. The people on f. 4 interact with and gesture at each other, and several builders are drawn in foreshortening. Smoothly curving outlines accent the suppleness of active men; nevertheless, they also belong to the same class of weightless bodies lacking true self-motivation which dominate in all the miniatures. Damage, distortions and limited evidence now make it difficult to determine with any certainty whether ff. 3 and 4 were painted by the same person, but the modest differences evident in their figure styles suggest that f. 4 is the work of a third artist.

The heads on all four folios share a common structure: a smooth oval shape, wide at the temples with broad cheekbones curving softly inward to a small rounded chin (figs. 53, 54, 56). The faces are always pleasant and sweet smiling, which makes them seem particularly simple-minded when the episode is tragic or solemn. The artists prefer high, broad foreheads, short, straight noses and small, full mouths. All heads turn slightly, but their strongly side-directed glances usually aim only in the general direction of the opposite party. Every king wears a high roll of hair above his forehead and a loose full fringe at the nape of the neck. Other men wear a short cap of hair brushed forward into a fringe of bangs with a wisp curving forward at the side-locks.

The faces reveal differences in the painting techniques of the artists. The miniaturist of the first two folios drew the features with thin brown lines and without modeling. Instead, the artist of f. 3 constructed heads as solid forms with planes defined by strong highlights and shadows, and he made eyes gleam in deep pools of shadow. Unfortunately, damage has made his tonal contrasts appear so harsh, that several faces dissolve into layers of flat dark and light color patches, as does Abner's head in picture 9 (fig. 54). Where, however, the fine modelling survives intact, as in picture 10 and in the head of the boy accompanying Abner in picture 9, the heads remain solid and attractively formed (fig. 56). The courtiers' heads (14) are also modeled in soft gradations of highlight and shadow, and their features are drawn with fine brown lines.

Despite the strong stylistic unity consciously achieved in this workshop product, the consistency of the artists' personal stylistic and technical characteristics enables us to differentiate between their work. These subtle differences cannot be attributed to a change in models or modes because, to the contrary, in miniature after miniature the workshop repeated a remarkably limited range of topoi.

The artist rarely provided a foreground or any rational or measurable indication of pictorial depth. Tan paint only defines the foreground in pictures 5, 7, 8 and 14, and, even then, only as a shallow area that stops just behind the figures, providing them with a narrow stage space cut off by the sky. On all other miniatures, however, the blue background extends down to the lower frame, effectively eliminating a foreground. In the double register pictures, 11 and 12, the artist even covered the pink strips with blue paint. Therefore, in ten miniatures, all the figures are projected against a continuous flat sky. Because the men have broad body structures they do not appear to float, and stylized cast shadows represented by short strokes of grey paint also help to keep the figures grounded. The prominent 'fossae' in picture 1, on the other hand, never approximate holes in a solid ground, but remain large smudges of color floating against the blue background.

The artists usually confined individuals and landscape elements to the same shallow foreground. When two scenes occur one above the other, as in pictures 11 and 12, they both appear to be limited to the same shallow space as upper and lower registers closed in by a continuous backdrop. Every figure stands isolated without integration in a spatial ambient. Static vertical forms are stressed, gestures and movements are kept parallel to the surface, and oblique lines in depth are avoided. Undoubtedly, when the gold highlights were intact they further emphasized this sense of flatness and isolation and diminished the effectiveness of modelling in highlight and shadow.

Basically, the pictures are extremely simple; they contain only essential characters and narrative elements to the exclusion of unnecessary details. Because the same limited number of compositional conventions characterize the extant miniatures of three artists, these formulas surely prevailed in most of the pictures when the codex was intact.

Two basic compositional structures dominate. In one, conventionalized figures stand in isocephalic and paratactic alignment. The second type, which is a minor variation of the first, arranges the figures to face each other in simple, bilateral groups. On ff. 1 and 2 the schematic flat compositions of the first artist often confuse the meaning of the biblical narrative, as in picture 3 where the figures stand in a paratactic row, isolated in stiff frontality, and the prophets mindlessly direct their emphatic glances to their left, outside the picture, rather than towards Saul with whom they are supposed to be spiritually united. In picture 4 the purpose of the Adlocutio becomes ambiguous because both leaders appear to walk, gesture and stare past the Israelites, who remain isolated from them in a schematic crowd of stiff, frontal figures confined to a rear plane. The second artist, however, was able to use the convention more effectively as a dialog. By turning the figures in pictures 10 and 12 toward each other, he made them communicate directly across a space meaningfully charged by their emphatic gestures and glances.

The illusion of depth established in one miniature can be totally negated in its neighbor by an abrupt change in the scale and placement of the figures. In miniature 5, for example, the frame defines a classic Roman picture window composition opening onto a stage space inhabited by figures standing before a tall arch and a banded sky. The space in picture 6, however, dissolves and flattens because the unusually large figures of

Samuel and Saul fill the area; moreover, both men and the sky backdrop extend down to the bottom edge of the frame.

To balance visual weight within their compositions the artists altered the natural comparative scale of the components, as in picture 5 where the size of Samuel and his horses are radically reduced to adjust them to the pictorial weight of Saul and his attendants. For similar reasons, in picture 14 the artist decided to make the builders smaller than Solomon and his courtiers. He may not have even considered their size in terms of aerial perspective. The change in scale was determined as much by the available space within the walls as by the necessity to create a balance between two equally important scenes, particularly since the construction of the temple occupies two-thirds of the area. The resulting differences in figure scale may have also been intended to clarify the time separation between events and, at the same time to give hieratic importance to the king and his court. By enlarging the tower, the artist related it visually to the dedication rather than to the wall which surrounds the building scene. All of these compositional methods had long been associated with Roman paintings and reliefs and were common in Late Antique art.

For a number of reasons, landscape motifs and buildings painted by the first artist, in particular, fail to define pictorial depth. In addition to their frontal orientation, these motifs remain confined to the same shallow space as the biblical characters, i.e. in alignment between an imaginary frontal plane and a schematic backdrop. Moreover, the oak tree and the buildings in pictures 1, 2, 5 and 8 have the same size and compositional weight as the figures. Not even the city of Gilgal adds depth to picture 8 because it is limited to a small, empty vignette of a fortified city floating against the blue sky above the scene. The first artist treated the city of Gilgal, the oak of Thabor and Rachel's tomb essentially as place signs that identify sites important to the story rather than as spatial components. In keeping with this planar approach, he flattened the large arch in picture 5 against the background and kept it in strict alignment with the pink strip.

The rhythmic organization of hilltops and housetops stretching across the pink strip in pictures 3, 4, and 8 conforms to this artist's decidedly stylized and decorative treatment of all compositional components. He turned the hills and houses into flat weightless forms that lack supporting understructures. Divorced from any contact with the ground, they float high in the sky above the figures rather than at a distance.[24] Although the artist used two contrasting values of grey to indicate that forward planes lie in sunlight and the sides recede into shadow, his broad, impressionistic brushstrokes and linear details only serve to emphasize the flat and weightless character of these forms.

The fortified wall surrounding the construction of the temple presents a third and very different approach to architecture. It represents the only extant example in this manuscript of an architecturally defined space. The artist painted a bird's-eye view of a wall enclosing a space rising steeply to a high horizon; he then shifted to a straight-on view of the large tower and all the people.

All the forms, no matter how badly damaged, have now been identified because they derive from established topoi maintained through a long artistic tradition. By analyzing the sources of the Itala's imagery and by comparing its style to other works of art in the next chapters we will lay the foundations for determining the origin and date of this pictorial cycle.

24. Boeckler, p. 155, incorrectly described them as sitting on the distant horizon line.

CHAPTER THREE

Pictorial Traditions

It is profitable to inquire into the sources and methods used to construct the Quedlinburg Itala's pictorial cycle. Many of the specific elements in the miniatures were already established in first and second-century painting and relief sculpture, as Boeckler has demonstrated.[1] Until now the circumstances which made particular early Roman repertories of formal and thematic elements accessible and attractive to these late Roman artists have not been investigated.

The relationship of the illustrations to late Roman art has never been fully examined. Although Boeckler described in considerable detail the striking similarity of the style and imagery of the Itala miniatures to a contemporary pagan codex, the Vatican Vergil, and to the nave mosaics in S. Maria Maggiore, by miscalculating the date of all three cycles he failed to compare the Itala's illustrations to other art of the late fourth and fifth centuries.[2]

On first sight the illustrations make three vivid impressions; we immediately note their richly episodic character, their incorporation of landscape motifs found in early Roman illusionistic frescoes and their extensive use of imperial imagery, particularly of conventions found in second and third-century triumphal reliefs. Herein lies the key to the Itala's pictorial sources. Contextual analysis indicates that the cycle was formulated primarily from three traditional modes: landscape painting, narrative illustration and imperial imagery.[3]

THE LANDSCAPE STYLE

The Quedlinburg Itala artists clearly wanted their illustrations to capture the appearance of illusionistic paintings within frames opening like picture windows to reveal narrative scenes. The blue sky aglow with soft rosy light, the harmony of warm and varied pastel colors, the modeling of forms with colored highlights and shadows deliberately evoke early Roman painting traditions so well represented by frescoes in Pompeii and Herculaneum. The oak of Thabor is, presumably, a live tree in the Bible, but in picture 2 it is curiously dead and leafless. Apparently the artist decided that the dead trees found occasionally in sacral-idyllic painting provided the most suitable model for this venerable oak.

This interest in classical motifs appears most vividly in the treatment of architecture. Impressionistically rendered hilltops and housetops painted in monochromatic grey across the upper background in ff. 1 and 2 ultimately refer to the hazy distant buildings and hills so often found in first-century layered coulisse landscapes[4] (fig. 7).

In picture 8, for example, the death of Agag bears a remarkable resemblance to the composition depicting the punishment of Dirce in a lost fresco from Herculaneum (fig. 14): the action is also confined to the foreground, the walled city is placed in a space veering ambiguously between middleground and back-

1. Boeckler, pp. 150-54.

2. Boeckler, pp. 123-202; note that many of the dates which he suggested for comparative manuscripts and mosaics are no longer accepted.

3. For a discussion of workshops using various modes see: Meyer Schapiro's review of C. R. Morey's *Early Christian Art* in *Review of Religion*, 8 (1944): 181-182; E. Kitzinger, 'Byzantine Art in the Period between Justinian and Iconoclasm', *Berichte zum XI. internationalen Byzantinisten-Kongress* (Munich, 1958): 1: 36ff., 47ff.; Brendel, *Prolegomena*, pp. 72-73; and J. Bialostocki, 'Das Modusproblem in den bildenden Künsten', *Zeitschrift für Kunstgeschichte*, 24 (1961): 128ff.

4. Boeckler, pp. 156ff. compared these illusionistic characteristics to landscape paintings in Pompeii, but he did not explain how they were able to influence the Itala's style. For particularly good comparisons between first-century frescoes and the Itala's landscape features see: G. E. Rizzo, *La pittura ellenistica-romana* (Milan, 1929), pls. 97, 174; K. Schefold, *Vergessenes Pompeji* (Bern and Munich, 1972), pls. 8, 38, 39; W. J. T. Peters, *Landscape in Romano-Campanian Painting* (Assen, 1963), figs. 63-71; and Rostovtzeff, 'Architekturlandschaft', figs. 10, 12, pp. 33-34, 85ff., 132-34.

ground, and small irregular buildings perch atop the rim of steep hills to form an irregular skyline.[5] Although the Itala artist modeled his picture on a similar composition, his buildings are weightless.

The temple scene in picture 14 uses a walled city convention which can be traced back to late Hellenistic and early Roman art. It appears in the Fall of Icarus, a Pompeian fresco panel in the House of Sacerdos Amandus (fig. 11), as well as on the first-century Capitoline Iliac Tablet.

Each of the early Roman architectural motifs used by the Itala artists reappears during the intervening centuries in paintings and reliefs on a miniature and a monumental scale. Large spaces enclosed by fortified walls occur in reliefs on the Column of Trajan and on the Arch of Septimius Severus in Rome as well as in Late Antique paintings such as the third-century Hypogaeum of the Aurelii frescoes in Viale Manzoni in Rome, and in the Vatican Vergil, Milan Iliad and Vienna Genesis miniatures[6] (figs. 10, 13, 29, 32). Pictures 14 and 49 of the Vatican Vergil come closest to the open space and viewing angle of Itala miniature 14.

The fortified city in picture 8 represents a later simplification of the conventionalized city formula used in the Herculaneum Dirce fresco (fig. 14). In this miniature, however, the walled city becomes a schematic vignette, a hexagonal, frontal, symmetrical enclosure of an empty space seen from an elevated view. Third-century coins struck in eastern mints for Philippus the Arab (244-49 A.D.) bear the earliest example of this schematic type.[7] In the West it first survives on a Constantinian coin representing Trier[8] (fig. 15). With remarkable speed the formula became canonical in Late Antique art and endured in paintings for many centuries. It appears in Vatican Vergil picture 49, and, most notably, in cartographic contexts in Medieval copies of such Late Antique manuscripts as the 'Tabula Peutingeriana', the 'Notitia Dignitatum', and the 'Corpus Agrimensorum Romanorum'[9] (fig. 29).

Boeckler recognized that Rachel's tomb (picture 1) sits in the midst of dry grass and bushes in a manner resembling other tall multistoried shaft tombs and sacred buildings found in first-century sacral-idyllic frescoes[10] (fig. 9). Such round tombs had a long history in the Mediterranean, and they continued to be built during the fifth century.[11] Rachel's grave has been compared by de Wit to Polydorus' monument in nearly contemporary miniature 18 in the Vatican Vergil and to similar tombs on fourth and fifth-century sarcophagi[12] (fig. 26).

The Itala artists need not have consulted first-century paintings to obtain classical ideas since far more recent examples were available. While the evidence is too fragmentary to permit us to postulate an unbroken tradition continuing from the first and second centuries, examples of classicizing paintings have also survived from the third, fourth and fifth centuries, albeit transformed in a Late Antique manner.

One of the finest examples of this illusionistic style has been preserved in a series of labors of the months frescoes painted in the second quarter of the third century on the walls of an ancient cortile under S. Maria Maggiore in Rome.[13] These large fresco panels feature panoramic landscapes teeming with activity, bird's-eye views into walled enclosures and monochromatic grey and white buildings in the background.[14] They represent with remarkable faithfulness the early Roman pictorial heritage from which the Itala artists ultimately derived their motifs.

Scenic settings are also preserved in some fourth-century paintings. Trees and bushes surround the goddess Diana in frescoes discovered under Via Livenza in Rome. Here too, a vivid pink sunset illuminates the brilliant blue sky. Outdoor scenes also occur in several Via Latina Christian catacomb paintings[15] (figs. 8, 12). In each instance a few landscape motifs have been used

5. A drawing of this lost fresco from Herculaneum is illustrated in Dawson, *Landscape Painting*, p. 95, pl. 12, no. 32.

6. The history of the walled city convention has recently been discussed by Ehrensperger-Katz, 'Villes fortifiées'; and Carder, *Land Surveying Manuscript*, pp. 189-95. For illustrations see my Bibliography for Works of Art Most Often Cited.

7. Cf. Carder, *op. cit.*, p. 191, fig. 220.

8. Ehrensperger-Katz, *op. cit.*, pp. 1-2, fig. 2.

9. Discussed and illustrated by Carder, *loc. cit.*, pp. 192-195; Ehrensperger-Katz, *op. cit.*, pp. 1-27; G. Mansuelli, 'La rappresentazione della città nell'arte tardo romana e bizantina', *Corsi di Cultura*, 19 (1972): 239-42; and Seeck, *Notitia Dignitatum*.

10. Boeckler, p. 125.

11. See Rostovtzeff, 'Architekturlandschaft', passim, esp. figs. 10-12 for tall, round buildings pierced by rows of small windows and capped by shallow cupolas, and for a study of architecture in sacral-idyllic landscape painting. Round pagan and Christian tombs are discussed by A. Grabar, *Martyrium, recherches sur le culte des reliques et l'art chrétien antique*, 2 vols. (Paris, 1946). Ancient round buildings are discussed by W. Altmann, *Die italischen Rundbauten* (Berlin, 1906); and P. Grimal, 'Les maisons tour hellénistiques et romaines', *Mélanges d'archéologie et d'histoire*, 56 (1939): 28-59.

Charles Rufus Morey, in mimeographed lecture notes from his course in Early Latin Illustrated Manuscripts given at New York University (n.d. but in the 1920's), pp. 11, 14, compared this monument to an Egyptian altar of Isis. He used this as an argument that the artist was influenced by Septuagint illustrations from Alexandria. The study of A. M. Smith, which Morey cited, does not support his argument. See A. M. Smith, 'The Iconography of the Sacrifice of Isaac in Early Christian Art', *AJA*, 2nd ser., 26 (1922): 159-73. The studies cited above disprove Morey's theory that round sacral buildings denote Egyptian sources, as does V. Spinazzola and S. Aurigemma, *Pompei alla luce degli scavi nuovi di Via dell'Abbondanza*, 2 vols. (Rome, 1953), 2: 795, fig. 870.

12. De Wit, pp. 65-67, related a conversation with Boeckler in which the latter suggested that the tomb on the San Celso, Milan sarcophagus would make a good comparison with Rachel's tomb. The sarcophagus is illustrated in J. Wilpert, *I sarcophagi cristiani antichi*, 3 vols. (Rome, 1929-36), 2: pls. 243-246. The shaft tomb in Vatican Vergil picture 18 is inappropriate to the story, which describes a burial mound. The Late Antique artist may have decided that a shaft tomb would be better understood by a contemporary audience than a mound of earth.

13. I place these frescoes in the third century in my article, 'A Reconsideration of the Date of the Esquiline Calendar and of Its Political Festivals', *AJA* (1982): 429-35.

14. The labors of the months frescoes were first published by Magi, 'Il calendario dipinto'.

15. For illustrations see the Bibliography for Works of Art Most Often Cited.

sparingly in shallow compositions. The glass panels recently discovered at Kenchreae contain perspective views of nilotic landscapes and seaside villas which recall first-century painting. Shortly before 375 A.D. the panels were probably shipped from Alexandria where they may have been recently manufactured.[16] An idyllic landscape based on a later phase of Pompeiian second style can still be seen on the fragment of a fresco painted in the early fourth century on a narthex wall in Basilica A in Dion.[17] Had more non-funerary paintings survived from the fourth century they might have testified to extensive landscape painting practices.

The landscape settings in the Itala can best be compared with those in the fifth-century Vatican Vergil miniatures and in the S. Maria Maggiore nave mosaics. Because their close relationship has been carefully described by Boeckler and numerous other scholars, it need only be summarized here.[18] In these three cycles red and black borders frame scenes placed before pink and blue banded skies in shallow stage-like spaces or in steeply rising panoramas. Small antique buildings, annular city walls and trees identify locations and define settings more regularly in the mosaics and the Vergil miniatures than in our manuscript (figs. 16-18, 20, 21, 23, 26, 27, 29).

It is most likely accidental that the Quedlinburg Itala and Vatican Vergil represent the earliest surviving evidence of landscape painting in illustrated manuscripts. The Vergil miniatures, in particular, incorporate such a wide range of landscape motifs and compositions that they would seem to reflect workshop experience accumulated by more than one generation of manuscript artists. Such landscapes may not have been included in manuscript illustration prior to the fourth century. It was then that the codex became more popular than the roll and stimulated the development of more complex framed compositions and illusionistic painting techniques for the page format.[19]

This landscape style continued to influence workshops producing lavishly illustrated pagan and Christian manuscripts in the eastern and western empire until the sixth century, when it was used by the artists painting the Iliad in Milan and the Cotton and Vienna Genesis.

When the Itala's illustrations are viewed within the larger context of late fourth and fifth-century silver, ivories, marble reliefs and sarcophagi, it becomes apparent that their classicizing style conforms with prevailing tastes in luxury arts made for imperial, pagan and Christian patrons.[20] Yet the classicizing influence on our manuscript is actually limited to a thin veneer of stylish quotations transformed through the more linear, flat and schematic tendencies so common in Late Antique art.

THE NARRATIVE TRADITION

A tradition of illustrated classical literature provided the necessary experience and probably even the inspiration for the development of our manuscript's narrative cycle. Unfortunately we can only guess at the original extent of those earlier achievements because few manuscript fragments have survived from the late Hellenistic and Roman periods. Nevertheless, Kurt Weitzmann has been able to suggest the considerable dimensions of this earlier history through his study of the sources of Late Antique, Medieval and Byzantine manuscript illustration.[21]

Between the late fourth and sixth centuries, scriptoria were producing deluxe editions of Vergil and Homer along with a wide range of other literary and scientific texts. They illuminated these codices with newly devised programs or with revisions and expansions of older cycles.[22] This activity may have been stimulated by the contemporary flowering of Latin literature and by the desire of aristocratic pagans to preserve the classical heritage of their religion and culture from steady erosion.[23] Lavishly illustrated manuscripts delighted the aesthetic tastes of bibliophiles and art collectors whose patronage gave impetus to this production.

After the Peace of the Church Christianity attracted a growing number of wealthy and prominent converts who, like the pagan members of their class, also commissioned luxury editions of texts; in this case, selected biblical texts.[24] The Quedlinburg Itala was a product of this artistic environment.

It is surely an historical accident that the Quedlinburg Itala

16. L. Ibrahim, R. Scranton and R. Brill, *Kenchreai, Eastern Port of Corinth*, vol. 2, *The Panels of Opus Sectile in Glass* (Leiden, 1976), pp. 30ff., figs. 80ff.

17. This fresco is discussed by S. Pelekanidis, 'Die Malerei der Konstantinischen Zeit', *Akten des VII. Internationalen Kongresses für christliche Archäologie*, 1965, 2 vols. (Vatican City, 1968), 1: 221-224, 2: fig. 15.

18. Boeckler, pp. 123-202; Brenk, *Mosaiken*, pp. 149-51; Kitzinger, *Byzantine Art in the Making*, pp. 67-69; and de Wit, pp. 151-57.

19. The stylistic changes in the style and format of manuscript illumination which were generated by the replacement of the papyrus roll by the codex have been discussed by Weitzmann, 'Book Illustration', pp. 96-125.

20. For a recent discussion of the classicism in this period see Kitzinger, *Byzantine Art in the Making*, pp. 22-69.

21. See in particular his collected articles in Weitzmann, *Studies in Classical and Byzantine Manuscript Illumination*, ed. H. L. Kessler (Chicago, 1971). He has long argued for the extensive illustration of the most popular pagan texts during the Hellenistic and Roman periods; cf. his *Ancient Book Illumination*. De Wit, p. 209, and R. Bianchi Bandinelli, 'Continuità ellenistica nella pittura di età medio-e-tarda-romana', *RINASA*, n.s., 2 (1953): 368-72, were reluctant to place the development of illustrations in ancient literary texts much before the late Roman period, but they fail to offer convincing arguments in opposition to Weitzmann's theories.

22. See, for example, the Vatican Vergil, Roman Vergil and Milan Iliad, in my Bibliography. See Weitzmann's studies in *Ancient Book Illumination*, *Roll and Codex*, and *Studies* for a discussion of later copies (7th to 17th cent.) of ancient texts. Numerous deluxe pagan manuscripts without illustrations are catalogued in Lowe's *CLA*.

23. Their desire to preserve their classical traditions is discussed by H. Bloch, 'The Pagan Revival in the West', *The Conflict between Paganism and Christianity in the Fourth Century*, ed. A. Momigliano (Oxford, 1963); Cameron, *Claudian*; and P. Brown, *The World of Late Antiquity* (London, 1971), chap. 9, esp. p. 116.

24. An opinion also shared by Kitzinger, *Byzantine Art in the Making*, p. 68. Lowe's *CLA* contains descriptions and detailed photographs of Christian manuscripts and fragments which can be considered deluxe editions although they do not contain illustrations. Cf., for example, *CLA*, 4, nn. 437, 481; 5, no. 572; and 9, no. 1613. Jerome's caustic criticism of large and lavish Christian codices did not halt their production. Cf. Jerome, *Praefatio in librum Job*, Migne, *PL*, 28: 1083.

fragments are the sole surviving examples of Christian illuminated manuscripts predating the late fifth/sixth century. The loss of most Early Christian manuscripts misrepresents the real dimension of their production. For a fuller assessment of their original status during the fourth and fifth centuries, we must turn to studies of Medieval and Byzantine art. Time and time again scholars studying biblical codices illustrated between the ninth and thirteenth centuries have identified a large core of material that must have dated back to this earlier period.[25]

Additional evidence of such illustration is suggested by studying narrative biblical art in other media. Series of Old and New Testament scenes decorate an ivory casket in Brescia made during the last third of the fourth century. Painters working sporadically in the Via Latina catacombs during that century depicted scenes taken from many books of the Bible. The narrative character of several of these frescoes indicates that they derive from a class of pictorial art that sets them apart from the symbolic and signative approach of most third and fourth-century funerary imagery. It is questionable whether churches were decorated with extensive narrative cycles prior to 400 A.D.;[26] instead the Via Latina artists may have taken their scenes from manuscripts or ivory and silver objects possibly owned by the wealthy patrons of that burial complex.[27] Whatever their direct sources may have been, these frescoes and the Lipsanothek of Brescia provide evidence that Christians commissioned narrative Old and New Testament art by the second half of the fourth century.

The earliest period and circumstances for the development of Old Testament narrative still remain a matter of speculation.[28] The Synagogue frescoes at Dura Europos (ca. 245-56) preserve the oldest biblical cycles, but the artists working in that provincial Syrian town must have depended on polycyclic programs developed for wall paintings, and perhaps even for manuscripts, in more important hellenized Jewish cultural centers by the early third century.[29]

Evidence of the illustration of Jewish manuscripts in Late Antiquity is indirect; none of them have survived prior to the Gothic period. They might have provided the missing link between the iconography of Dura Europos and the reappearance of some of its scenes in Medieval manuscripts.[30] Several scholars have suggested that the rabbinic legends repeatedly appearing in Early Christian and Medieval manuscript illustrations were first developed for lost Jewish manuscripts,[31] however, others argue that Christian knowledge of rabbinic literature was a more likely intermediary.[32]

Examples of a systematic effort to develop Christian art only began to appear in the early third century. Our view of this period is distorted because most Christian art surviving from the third and fourth centuries was made for a funerary context in which the biblical themes are isolated, simple images lacking narrative qualities. This limited approach could not satisfy the growing number of aristocratic converts accustomed to more highly evolved pictorial art. These new patrons stimulated the development of more complex and varied religious imagery such as we find in the Quedlinburg Itala.[33]

THE NARRATIVE MODE

The instructions to the artists in our manuscript provide us with rare insights into the programmer's contribution to its narrative program. As was noted in the preceding chapter, he divided the text into thematic units and he determined the physical and thematic relationship of the pictures to the text, the episodic character of the cycle and the narrative unity of scenes gathered on each page.

He did not use the Vatican Vergil's traditional system of

25. There are many Medieval and Byzantine manuscripts which by their style or iconography appear to have copied at least part of their cycles from archetypes devised prior to the sixth century. See, for example, the studies by Weitzmann on the early sources of the Octateuch, Psalter and Septuagint pictorial cycles in 'The Illustration of the Septuagint', *Studies*, 45-75; 'Jewish Pictorial Sources', *Studies*, 76-95; and in 'Book Illustration', *Studies*, 96-125. Also see H. L. Kessler, 'Hic Homo Formatur: The Genesis Frontispieces of the Carolingian Bibles', *Art Bull.*, 53 (1971): 143-60. In his study of the Carolingian Bible of San Paolo f.l.m. in Rome, Joachim Gaehde points to the abundant use of Roman imperial imagery. He thinks this imagery was most likely in the biblical exemplar which probably dated from the Theodosian period. Cf. Gaehde, 'Carolingian Bible of San Paolo', pp. 351-84, esp. 381-84.

26. Paulinus of Nola and Prudentius indicate that their decision to decorate their early fifth-century churches with Old and New Testament scenes was an innovation. See Paulinus of Nola, *Carmina*, 27: 512-95, translated by Davis-Weyer, *Early Medieval Art*, pp. 17-23; and Prudentius, *Forty-Nine Lines to be Inscribed under Scenes from History*, transl. by Davis-Weyer, *loc. cit.*, pp. 25-33.

27. Kötzsche-Breitenbruch, *Via Latina*, pp. 15-37, 103-109, discusses the iconography and sources of these frescoes. The early development of Christian art is discussed by Grabar, *Christian Iconography*.

28. Kurt Weitzmann has proposed that the Septuagint was illustrated by Hellenistic Jews soon after its translation in the third century B.C. Cf. Weitzmann, 'Jewish Pictorial Sources', pp. 85 ff., and in 'Illustrations of the Septuagint', p. 75. Grabar, *Christian Iconography*, passim, does not accept this theory, nor does Hempel, 'Anfänge der AT-Illustration', pp. 123-24. The earliest extant Jewish and Christian art does not predate the late second to early third century. On the whole, the style and iconography of these works have a Late Antique character, which was most likely true of their archetypes.

29. The two basic studies of the Dura Synagogue were written by Goodenough, *Dura Synagogue*; and by Kraeling, *The Synagogue*, esp. pp. 365, 388-98, for his theories on their sources. More recent studies which discuss the possible sources of these frescoes are found in J. Gutmann, ed., *The Dura Europos Synagogue: A Re-Evaluation (1932-72)* (Missoula, Mont., 1973). The Dura frescoes are unique survivors of Jewish narrative cycles which were developed in Late Antiquity despite rabbinic injunctions against figurative arts.

30. Illustrated manuscripts have been postulated as the source of the Dura Synagogue frescoes by Kraeling, *Synagogue*, pp. 388-98; and Weitzmann, 'The Illustration of the Septuagint', pp. 71-75; and 'Jewish Pictorial Sources', pp. 76-79. Jewish wall paintings are proposed as a far more likely source than manuscripts by Joseph Gutmann, 'Programmatic Painting in the Dura Synagogue', *The Dura Europos Synagogue*, pp. 137-54.

31. This opinion is proposed by Hempel, 'Anfänge AT-Illus.', pp. 109-24; and by Weitzmann, 'Jewish Pictorial Sources', pp. 76-95; but it is challenged by J. Gutmann, 'The Illustrated Jewish Manuscript in Antiquity: The Present State of the Question', *Gesta*, 5 (1966): pp. 39-44.

32. Many articles on the controversial issues relating to the origins and character of early Jewish art are collected in J. Gutmann, ed., *No Graven Images. Studies in Art and the Hebrew Bible* (New York, 1970).

33. See the discussion of iconographic developments in Grabar, *Christian Iconography*, pp. 40-51, 94-95.

placing individual pictures within the text immediately preceding their related verses. Instead he decided to group the pictures together as a pictorial preface to larger textual units which can encompass several pages and even chapters. Of course, this system fails to maintain close physical unity between each picture and its own text, however, even in the Vatican Vergil such proximity is lost in those pictures which include two or more scenes illustrating an entire story that extends over many of the following pages. In other instances, a single scene in the Vergil manuscript may focus on a distinct episode in the midst of a long course of events. Under both circumstances the same number of pages often follow one of the Vergil's miniatures as would follow all of the pictures grouped on one page in the Quedlinburg Itala.

Had the Itala used the traditional system of placing pictures within the columns of text, pictures 1 to 3 would have been placed very close to each other preceding verses 2, 3 and 5 in chapter 10, but the last picture would have been placed after a three page interval before page 24, thus losing its present impact as the conclusion of a story. Moreover, the scribe would have also lost his opportunity to vividly demonstrate that what we now designate as chapters 9 through 11 actually constitute a narrative unit. Because f. 4r illustrates a few verses clustered at the beginning, middle and end of four chapters, the narrative relationship between the scenes grouped on one page would have been lost had they been dispersed as individual pictures through twenty-four pages of text.

Grouping miniatures on one page may have been a recent invention; it would not have been suitable for the roll format which had dominated manuscript production prior to the fourth century. From then on workshops increasingly came to prefer the codex over the roll. The individual page format of the codex motivated fourth-century scriptoria to develop new designs to replace the simple individual compositions placed in the columns of rolls.[34] The Itala's grid framework was only one of the solutions.

It is difficult to tell how often this grid system was used because few comparative examples survive. Only one of the preserved folios in the Vatican Vergil employs the subdivided frame, picture 1, which prefaces book 3 of Georgics, but its six-part frame shares the page with text, and its illustrations do not relate to one unified story.[35] The only other extant examples of the grid scheme come from the sixth century or later.[36] The older system of placing a picture within the column of text continued to outweigh the Itala's system in popularity. Even so, it is interesting to see that series of episodes joined together in double frames were introduced within the columns of text in an extensively illustrated Byzantine book of Kings, Vatican City, Bibl. Vat. gr. 333.[37] The possibility of its relationship with our manuscript will be examined in the next chapter.

The close relationship between literature and art which is seen in the Itala and Vergil manuscripts has a long history in Antiquity, as has been shown in studies of Hellenistic Homeric cups.[38] Indeed, classical literature had a considerable impact on the subject matter of Greek and Roman art in its narrative techniques and formal structures.

The labeling of the pictures in both manuscripts is symptomatic of their text-centered character. There is, of course, a long if somewhat sporadic tradition of such labels in ancient painting, but the names of characters and objects so liberally supplied in the Itala and Vergil illustrations are particularly pedantic in their persistent clarification of the content of each miniature. Itala picture 1 even quotes lines of the text. It is as if the labels were trying to say, 'Here is an illustration of an episode in the text precisely identified by naming its characters and their actions'.

Artists working in other media during this period also relied heavily on textual sources. The nave mosaics of S. Maria Maggiore depict closely related series of verses in Old Testament texts. Whether or not those mosaics were actually copied from illustrated manuscripts is still a matter of controversy, but scholars generally agree that the mosaics follow an established narrative mode also used in manuscript illustrations.[39]

Ernst Kitzinger has recently discussed a more extreme example in the Samson mosaics in Mopsuestia.[40] The narrative cycle in these floor mosaics (ca. 5th cent.) is accompanied by extensive paraphrases from the text of Judges. The Bible was also the direct source of wall paintings for a church according to a passage in the *History of the Franks* written by Gregory of Tours, who relates that the wife of Bishop Namatius (446-62) sat in the middle of her husband's church and directed the artists to paint pictures on the walls based on her selections from the Bible which she held on her lap. The passage implies that she used an unillustrated text.[41] The tituli and verse inscriptions related to the early fifth-century wall paintings of Paulinus of Nola and Prudentius offer yet another example of the correlation

34. Weitzmann, 'Book Illustration'.

35. Described by de Wit, pp. 17-19.

36. For examples see the bird illustrations on f. 483v of the early sixth-century Dioscurides in Vienna, Nat. Bibl., cod. med. gr. 1; the frontispiece to Luke in the late sixth-century Italian S. Augustine Gospels, Cambridge, C.C.C., ms. 286, f. 125r; and the busts of months arranged in a frame in a Medieval copy of the Alexandrian World Chronicle (after 392 A.D.) in Moscow, Pushkin Museum. For illustrations see: Gerstinger, *Wiener Dioscurides*, pl. 1; F. Wormald, *Miniatures in the Gospels of St. Augustine, CCC ms. 286* (Cambridge, 1954), pl. 1; C. Lewine, 'Vulpes Fossa Habent or the Miracle of the Bent Woman in the Gospels of St. Augustine, CCC, Cambridge ms. 286', *Art Bull.*, 66 (1974): 502; and Bauer and Strzygowski, *Alexandrinische Weltchronik*, pp. 144ff.

37. See, for example, ff. 7r, 84, 15v, et al. in Lassus, *Livre des rois*.

38. They were discussed by C. Robert, *Homerische Becher*, 50. Winckelmanns-programm (Berlin, 1890); and Weitzmann, *Roll and Codex*, pp. 35ff.

39. Morey, *Early Christian Art*, pp. 151-52, and Cecchelli, *Mosaici*, p. 89, proposed that the mosaics in the nave copied miniatures from an illuminated Septuagint. This theory has been challenged by Brenk, *Mosaiken*, p. 180; and by Kitzinger, 'Role of Miniature Paintings', pp. 122ff.

40. Kitzinger, 'Role of Miniature Painting', pp. 138-40; and the same in 'Observations on the Samson Floor at Mopsuestia', *DOP*, 27 (1973): pp. 133ff.

41. St. Gregory of Tours, *The History of the Franks*, ed. and trans. by O. M. Dalton (Oxford, 1927), pp. 58-59; cf. Davis-Weyer, *Early Medieval Art*, pp. 57-59.

of texts and paintings.[42] The expressed emphasis on the textual origins of these cycles may be a sign of the times.

The densely episodic character of the Quedlinburg Itala's cycle and its choice of narrative techniques had been used by Roman artists for centuries to develop historical and mythological cycles.[43] To facilitate the dramatic interaction of individuals and to create the impression of a sequential flow of events the Itala artists avoided the hieratic centralized compositions and frontality which otherwise dominated so much Late Antique art (fig. 40). Instead they used three-quarter profiles and lateral movement of figures.[44] As an example, Samuel and Saul (7) pray in a profile pose because they offer a specific prayer integrated within a series of events in the continuous stream of historical time; as does Anchises in Vergil min. 16, Noah in the S. Paolo f.l.m. frescoes and Moses observing the fall of the quails at S. Maria Maggiore[45] (figs. 19, 24). Their artists avoided the frontal orant so popular in funeral art because it stood as an isolated image of piety and of the eternal prayers of the deceased and would have negated the flow of narrative time.[46] Working within the same principle, in the Itala's court scenes kings and their audiences are presented in side views (figs. 18, 22, 28). Just two generations later, gods and kings sit in frontal poses in centralized compositions in the Iliad Ambrosiana.

The changes in scale and viewpoint and the combination of bird's-eye and straight-on views in Itala picture 14 also occur within other illustrated manuscripts. These compositional practices were fairly common in painting and relief sculpture because Roman artists were interested in detailed narrative accounts for which they willingly sacrificed coherent and logical spatial organization (figs. 13, 16, 20, 21, 23, 27, 29, 30, 32, 33).

Both the concept of narrative time and the representational methods used in the Quedlinburg Itala applied equally well in fifth and sixth-century pagan and Christian manuscripts.[47] The Vatican Vergil's framed panels frequently contain only one episode, but its artists also depicted two or more actions in short friezes (pictures 13, 18) and double registers (pictures 4, 33), and they used panoramic views (pictures 23, 50) (figs. 23, 24, 26, 29). Key figures are repeated in continuous narration, and the second artist used one figure of Ascanius to function simultaneously in two adjacent scenes (11) (fig. 22),[48] just as one messenger belongs to two consecutive events in Itala picture 13.

IMPERIAL IMAGERY

The Itala's reliance on imperial imagery is one of its most outstanding characteristics. The Roman epic mode had been extensively developed on the second-century Columns of Trajan and Marcus Aurelius, and for the next three centuries it continued to provide models for reliefs on Severan, Tetrarchic, Constantinian and Theodosianic triumphal monuments.[49] The Itala shares with these official reliefs an interest in densely episodic depiction of historical events in continuous narration presented in friezes, registers and bird's-eye panoramas, and like them it interweaves representations of official acts and ceremonies with military ventures[50] (figs. 13, 30-35, 37, 38).

An analysis of picture 5 demonstrates how thoroughly the official mode was integrated into the Itala's program. An emperor pouring a libation and riding in a chariot and a monumental arch had been the basic elements of triumphal iconography for many centuries prior to the Constantinian period, and precisely those elements were used to construct picture 5 (figs. 36, 37).[51]

Saul pours a libation from a patera onto a low rectangular altar according to a long-established representation of a Roman emperor making a sacrifice.[52] This scene can be compared to the sacrificing Tetrarch on the Arch of Galerius in Salonica and to generals performing this rite on second-century biographical

42. These passages are translated by Davis-Weyer, *op. cit.*, pp. 17-23 and 25-33.

43. Roman and Early Christian narrative art are discussed by P. H. von Blanckenhagen, 'Narration in Hellenistic and Roman Art', *AJA*, 61 (1957): 78-83; K. Weitzmann, 'Narration in Early Christendom', *AJA*, 61 (1957): 83-91; and K. Weitzmann, 'The Selection of Texts for Cyclic Illustration in Byzantine Manuscripts', *Byzantine Books and Bookmen* (Washington, D.C., 1975), pp. 69-99.

44. Although the artist of ff. 1 and 2 selected models using a contrapposto pose and three-quarter viewpoint; unfortunately his flat, schematic style makes his figures seem frontal.

45. Restorations of the Moses panel are discussed by Brenk, *Mosaiken*, pp. 87-88. The lost S. Paolo frescoes were restored by Cavallini and are known through seventeenth-century drawings; cf. Vatican City, Bibl. Vat., Barberini, lat. 4406, f. 33; illustrated by Waetzoldt, *Kopien*, fig. 338.

46. According to T. Klauser, 'Studien zur Entstehungsgeschichte der christlichen Kunst', *JbAC*, 2 (1959): 115-30, the orans had a double meaning and use in pagan art, as a personification of 'pietas' and as the deceased in an attitude of prayer. For another interpretation of the orans, see Lucien de Bruyne, 'Les "Lois" de l'art paléochrétien', *Riv. Archeol. Christ.*, 35 (1959), 164-75; and the 'Adunanza pubblica del 2 giugno 1960', *Atti d. Pont. Acc. Rom. d. Arch.*, *Rendiconti*, 32 (1959-60), 7.

47. See the Vatican Vergil, Milan Iliad, Cotton Genesis and Vienna Genesis in my Bibliography; and Brenk, *Mosaiken*, pp. 125ff. for the narrative style of the mosaics.

48. Vatican Vergil min. 11 is discussed by Buchthal, 'A Note on the Vatican Vergil'.

49. See the Arches of Septimius Severus, Galerius and Constantine and the Columns of Trajan, Marcus Aurelius, Theodosius and Arcadius in my Bibliography.

50. For representations of the passage of time in Roman narrative art see R. Hinks, 'Raum als Fläche in spätantiken Reliefs', *Archäol. Anz.*, 51 (1936): 238-51; R. Brilliant in 'Temporal Aspects in Late Roman Art', *L'Arte*, 10 (1970): 65-87; and Brilliant, *Septimius Severus*, pp. 220-231.

51. For a discussion of the Roman triumph and representations of 'Triumphus' and 'adventus' in art and literature see: Ryberg, *Panel Reliefs*, pp. 21-24, 66-70; Koeppel, 'Profectio und Adventus'. For representations of this iconography over preceding centuries see a Roman-Etruscan Cista, now in the Ehem. Staatl. Mus., Berlin, Antikenabteilung 6238 in Larissa Bonfante-Warren, 'A Latin Triumph on a Praenestine Cista', *AJA*, 68 (1964): 35-42, pls. 13-14; her suggested date is ca. 100 B.C. The Arch of Titus panels in G. M. A. Hanfmann, *Roman Art* (New York, 1964), pls. 108-109; the Marcus Aurelius panel in Ryberg, *Panel Reliefs*, pl. 9; Septimius Severius' Arch in Leptis Magna in Brilliant, *Gesture and Rank*, fig. 4.40; the Arch of Galerius (the upper register, northeast side of the southwest pillar) in Laubscher, *Galeriusbogen*, pl. 46; Constantine's Arch in L'Orange and von Gerkan, *Konstantinsbogen* 2: pl. 3b.

52. For a discussion and illustrations of official sacrifices in art, see Ryberg, *Rites*, pp. 104-119, and 174-189, pls. 25-50; and Hamberg, *Studies*, pp. 94-99.

sarcophagi (fig. 37).[53] A burnt animal offering would have been more accurate, but the artist did not understand the meaning of the term 'holocaustum' in Hebrew ritual or its particular significance in this story.

The prophet's speaking gesture and biga scarcely modify the conventions for an emperor raising his right hand in a gesture of power and his victorious entrance in a quadriga. Throughout the fourth century the chariot continued to be associated with other ceremonies that had taken on the aura of triumphs, even though the old triumphal entry and its sacrifices had ceased to be celebrated due to their pagan associations.[54]

The structure rising behind Samuel represents a Roman triumphal or commemorative arch. Its inclusion in this composition must have seemed quite natural to the artist for many reasons. Representations of the triumphal chariot and sacrifice suggested by the instructions were often depicted with a monumental arch[55] (fig. 36). The city of Rome and the empire were filled with monumental arches commemorating victories. An arch was erected in Rome as late as 405 in honor of a Theodosian victory; and the meaning of the Porta Triumphalis was still a recent memory.[56] If, as I suspect, the Itala artist found the arch associated with the other elements of this composition in a model taken from official art, it might not have occurred to him to omit the arch simply because it was not requested in the instructions.

His method of composition is not unusual. Artists frequently failed to eliminate from their models those elements which were not required by or suitable to their new context; a circumstance which also occurred frequently in the Vatican Vergil, S. Maria Maggiore and Iliad Ambrosiana cycles.[57]

The artist who composed picture 5 did not recognize that discredited pagan triumphal ceremonies were unsuitable for representing the history of Old Testament kings. Public monuments and carefully preserved pictorial traditions continued to provide him and his contemporaries with official models for illustrating biblical, mythological and historical scenes.

It is instructive to see how many of the Itala's individual figures, poses and drapery motifs can be continuously traced back through centuries of official art. Agag's plea for clemency with bowed back and extended arm (7) recalls the submission of foreign nationals before an emperor or general repeatedly occurring on coins and reliefs between the second and fifth centuries[58] (figs. 20, 31, 40).

To depict the death of Agag and Abner (8, 11) the artists borrowed stock fighting figures paired in combat from the popular repertory of military combat scenes. The poses assumed by the Itala's combatants appear so often in Roman art that comparisons are almost too numerous to mention.[59] The enthroned kings accompanied by bodyguards (9, 11, 13) copy compositions used for centuries to depict emperors and magistrates in court (figs. 31, 38).[60]

The youthfulness of the armed guards in pictures 11 and 12, where they are somewhat shorter in stature than Abner and David, corresponds with court custom of the period recorded on Theodosius's Missorium and Obelisk Base (figs. 39, 40). It is puzzling, however, to see that small boys consistently accompany Saul and attend Abner in pictures 9 and 10. Although Saul's young companion in pictures 1-3 can be explained by the text and instructions, the spear-carrying attendants on ff. 2 and 3 are uncommonly young and small for the traditional bodyguards of kings, generals and emperors. Their shorter height cannot be explained as a hieratic reduction because all other characters have full adult stature. Perhaps the artists were mechanically

53. Laubscher, *Galeriusbogen*, pl. 40.1; Ryberg, *Rites*, pp. 120, 141, 163, and figs. 45e, 51, 61b, 90, 91.

54. For examples of fourth-century triumphal entries see the description of Constantius II's entrance into Rome by Ammianus Marcellinus, 16.10; and the marble intarsia depicting the consul Junius Bassus in a quadriga in Dorigo, *Late Roman Painting*, fig. 113. For a discussion of the modification of the old Roman triumph with its pagan associations and the need to devise a format more acceptable to Christian sensitivities, see: Koeppel, 'Profectio und Adventus', 130-195; Stern, *Calendrier de 354*, pp. 136ff., 161-163; and H. P. L'Orange, 'The Adventus Ceremony and the Slaying of Pentheus as Represented in Two Mosaics of about A.D. 300', *Late Classical and Mediaeval Studies in Honor of A. M. Friend, Jr.*, ed. K. Weitzmann (Princeton, 1955), pp. 7-14.

55. The chariot and the arch appear on the reliefs in the Arch of Titus, in Josephus' description of Vespasian's entry into Rome, on the Marcus Aurelius Triumph panel and on the reliefs just mentioned on the third and fourth-century Arches in Leptis Magna, Salonica and Rome; see n. 51. Beginning with Antonine Art the Adventus and Profectio typically included the Porta Triumphalis on reliefs and coins. Cf. Ryberg, *Panel Reliefs*, pp. 28-37.

56. Commemorative triumphal arches continued to be built in the late Roman period. Diocletian's Arch stood near S. Maria in Via Lata, and the Arches of Septimius Severus and Constantine still flank the extreme ends of the forum area. A marble arch was erected by the Senate at the West end of the Pons Neronianus after the victory of Stilicho over the Goths at Pollentia in 405 A.D. It was dedicated in honor of Theodosius, Arcadius and Honorius and was still standing in the fifteenth century, but it had been stripped of its marble facing; cf. *CIL*, 6: 1196; and Platner and Ashby, *A Topographical Dictionary of Ancient Rome* (London, 1929), p. 34.

57. For a discussion of the transfer of unnecessary details from a model to another context, see: Weitzmann, *Roll and Codex*, pp. 130-181; de Wit, pp. 31-33; Buchthal, 'A Note on the Vatican Vergil', pp. 167-172, and Buchthal's review of de Wit's *Miniaturen* in *Art Bull.*, 45 (1963): 372-75.

58. The comparison of Agag's pose to second-century submissions was first made by Boeckler, p. 153. For other examples see Ryberg, *Rites*, p. 164, pl. 58; and Brilliant, *Gesture and Rank*, pp. 156-59, figs. 3.132, 4.86. For examples on the Obelisk Base of Theodosius see Bruns, *Obelisk*, pl. 37; and drawings of the Column of Arcadius published by Freshfield, 'Notes', pls. 7, 20.

59. For examples see Boeckler, pp. 138 and 152.

60. Boeckler, pp. 150f., recognized that this schema appeared in Antique art. Note the seated emperor on the Gemma Augustea and the Boscoreale cup which depict Augustinus; the Anaglypha Traiani; and the Severan relief in the Palazzo Sacchetti, Rome; illustrated in Brilliant, *Septimius Severus*, figs. 2.58, 2.61, 3.6 and 4.19. The continuation of this formula in Early Christian and Medieval art for the highest powers of state is discussed by Weitzmann, *Roll and Codex*, p. 156. For other examples see Volbach, *Art*, pls. 85, 87, 89, 100, and 234; Vergil 34, 41, 42; and S. Maria Maggiore, Cecchelli, *Mosaici*, pls. 26 and 28; Karpp, *S. Maria Maggiore*, pls. 79, 82.

Bodyguards in attendance in Roman official ceremonies are discussed by T. Mommsen, *Römisches Staatsrecht*, 3 vols. (Leipzig, 1887-88), 1: 762; Alföldi, 'Mon. Zeremoniell', 44 (1934): 103ff.; and R. I. Frank, *Scholae Palatinae, The Palace Guards of the Later Roman Empire* (Rome, 1969).

repeating a convention originally inspired by the text and instructions when an Old Testament king was first represented on f. 1.[61]

Boeckler recognized that the speech and dialog conventions pervading these miniatures first appeared in official art in the Adlocutio scenes and formal conversations of the emperors on the Columns of Trajan and Marcus Aurelius[62] (figs. 30, 33, 35). The full Adlocutio scheme, which featured the emperor addressing his troops, had been simplified for unofficial art by eliminating the suggestum, limiting the size of the audience and by placing all figures on the same ground level. In a recent study of the S. Maria Maggiore mosaics, Beat Brenk carefully described the repertory of very specific poses and gestures commonly shared by the artists of the nave mosaics, the Quedlinburg Itala and Vatican Vergil (figs. 16-20, 22, 23, 25, 27, 28). He also traced their dialog conventions back to the second-century columns.[63]

Three of these conventions for representing a standing speaker are prominent in the Itala. Saul and David (4, 12) stand in a flattened three-quarter profile with their weight thrust onto the forward leg without raising their back leg from the ground (compare figs. 30, 33). Their right arms are projected in a speaking gesture, and their left hands, swathed in the paludamenta which they pull at a sharp angle across their chests, also hold spears. Samuel strikes the same pose in picture 4, and nearly identical conventions apply to Saul and Abner in pictures 2 and 10.[64] In another topos, Saul (1) raises his hand before his chest in a speaking gesture and assumes a frontal pose with a slight inclination of his body to one side.[65] The third convention used in pictures 9 through 12 and for the soldiers in picture 1 places the speaker at the right side of the composition in a three-quarter pose with his weight evenly distributed on both feet and right arm thrust forward at a sharply bent angle. On f. 3 the left hand, once again, is hidden under the cloak which it grasps and pulls to one side.[66] Brenk recognized that these speaking conventions were used in the Itala, Vergil miniatures and nave mosaics as generalized topoi freely applied to persons of every rank from leaders to servants.[67]

Actually the three topoi had entered the mainstream of Roman art much earlier. They had already achieved widespread use in Christian and pagan art of the fourth century, particularly in narrative painting and reliefs. These formulas also achieved popularity in other Late Antique manuscript cycles and in official art.[68] The second topos, for example, appears on the Arch of Galerius in Salonica.[69] The speaking gesture, in which the right hand is held before the chest with the palm facing outward or with two projecting fingers, occurs frequently in court and courtly art of the Theodosianic period[70] (figs. 39, 42, 43, 45).

The influence of official art on the Quedlinburg Itala was so pervasive that we are scarcely surprised to see the extent to which military costume and official insignia predominate throughout the miniatures. The preliminary sketches on f. 3 even furnish titles indicating the figures' social rank to guide the artist in the appropriate choice of official costumes rather than providing the names of the biblical characters.

All the kings wear the full-dress military costume of Roman emperors: short tunic, cuirass, cingulum, and red-purple paludamentum. The details of their dress and their laced white boots often appear in third to fifth-century representations of kings

61. The classical meaning of the word 'puer' in the instructions is boy, but in Late Antiquity it often means attendant. Small attendants are represented with the consul on the Probianus diptych, on the consular diptych of Bourges and on the diptych of Asturias in Darmstadt, but they are probably men reduced in size for hierarchical or compositional reasons. For illustrations see Volbach, *Elfenbeinarbeiten*, figs. 3, 36 and 52. In the Vatican Vergil the attendants at the sacrifices in pictures 18, 22, 32 and 40 are smaller than the principal characters; the builders in picture 10 are smaller than the overseers, and the figures in the caves in pictures 8, 33 and 34 are smaller than Orpheus and Aeneas with his guide, but the builders and the dead are not children or young men.

62. Boeckler, pp. 128, 150-51. For the Adlocutio in Roman art see, Brilliant, *Gesture and Rank*, pp. 118-22, 165-70; and Hamberg, *Studies*, pp. 135-49.

63. Brenk, *Mosaiken*, pp. 146-48 thought that the Itala, Vergil and mosaic artists had taken the dialog topoi directly from modelbooks based on Roman imperial art.

64. This convention also appears in Vatican Vergil pictures 18, 31, 34, 37, 41, 42; and in the nave mosaics, cf. Cecchelli, *Mosaici*, pls. 25, 34, 40, 41; Karpp, *S. Maria Maggiore*, pls. 74, 108, 128, 133.

65. Also see Vatican Vergil pict. 37, 49 and the mosaics in Cecchelli, *Mosaici*, pls. 25, 33; Karpp, *S. Maria Maggiore*, pls. 74, 103.

66. Also see Vergil mins. 11, 24, 31, 33, 40; and the mosaics in Cecchelli, *Mosaici*, pls. 20, 22, 25, 28; Karpp, *S. Maria Maggiore*, pls. 61, 66, 74, 82.

67. Brenk, *Mosaiken*, pp. 146-48.

68. The first and third speaking conventions which I have described in Itala miniatures 2, 4 and 9 through 12 also occur on the third-century Arch of Galerius in Salonica. These topoi are found more frequently in the fourth century: on frescoes in the Hypogea of Trebius Justus and of Vibia; in the Via Latina catacomb in Rome; on the ivory Lipsanothek of Brescia; as well as in the fifth century: on the doors at S. Sabina in Rome, and on the christological scenes on the ivory diptych in Milan. For illustrations see: Arch of Galerius in Grabar, *Christian Art*, fig. 153; Hyp. Vibia in J. Wilpert, *Die Malereien der Katakomben Roms*, Freiburg i.Br., 1903, 2: pls. 132, 224; T. Justus in Casalone, *Cah. Arch.*, 12 (1962): 53-64; Via Latina in Ferrua, *Via Latina*, pls. 92, 72, and 81; Brescia ivory, Roman door reliefs and the Milan ivory in Volbach, *Art*, pls. 88-89, 103, 100-101.

In his study of the models of the Vatican Vergil miniatures, de Wit, p. 154, mistakenly maintained that this arrangement of the spear and cloak only rose to popularity in the first third of the fifth century. For this convention see Vatican Vergil: 10, 18, 24, 33-37, 40-41, 49-50; and Cecchelli, *Mosaici*, pls. 41-43; Karpp, *S. Maria Maggiore*, pls. 133, 138, 143.

69. The second topos for a standing speaker used in Itala miniature 1 as well as in the Vergil illustrations and nave mosaics has been discussed by Brenk, *Mosaiken*, pp. 146-48, who noted that the gesture also appears in the Columns of Trajan and Marcus Aurelius, the Arch of Galerius and in the Ilias Ambrosiana miniatures. For the column of Trajan see Lehmann-Hartleben, *Trajanssäule*, sections 125, 130, 137, 140, 141. On the Marcus Aurelius Column the emperor stands in a more frontal pose and the type appears more frequently than on Trajan's Column. See Petersen et al., *Markus-Säule*, pls. 10b, 16a, 22a, 29b, 34a, 84a, 92a, 97a, 109a and 110a. On the Arch of Galerius see Laubscher, *Galeriusbogen*, pls. 30.2, 34 and 36.1. See miniatures 14, 24, 31 and 33 in the Ilias Ambrosiana in Bianchi Bandinelli, *Miniatures of the Iliad*, figs. 50, 60, 67, 69.

70. The degree to which this is a speaking, teaching or power gesture varies according to the context. For various examples see the following works illustrated in Volbach, *Art*, pls. 62, 53, 95, 113, 115: the boy on the left valve of the ivory diptych in Monza; Arcadius on the Missorium of Theodosius; Christ on the ivory pyxis in Berlin; and Joseph and Solomon on the San Nazaro silver reliquary (although its authenticity is questionable).

and emperors wearing formal military dress[71] (figs. 37, 41). The square chest decoration on Saul's cuirass can also be seen on Galerius's armor on the Arch reliefs in Salonica and in the Vatican Vergil and Milan Iliad miniatures.[72] The soldiers' mail tunics and crested helmets (1) were typical of that period (figs. 29, 33).

Abner's short, belted tunic and long, heavy chlamys copy the field costume of Roman emperors, generals and soldiers whose social and legal rank were differentiated by special insignia. His important status (he was the king's leading general) is defined by the embroidered patches on his clothing, the large, gold crossbow fibula on his chlamys and by his right to have attendants. The details of his costume can be compared to those worn by the official on the ivory diptych in Monza (fig. 44). The exceptionally long vertical staff of his gold fibula was an attribute of high ranking courtiers from the early fourth to seventh centuries.[73]

The young bodyguards wear the same short belted tunic and long chlamys with paired orbicula on the skirt as Abner because this was the accepted military field costume, but, as we would expect, they do not wear the long fibula or the large embroidered patches.

Contemporary fashion also dictated the dress of the Israelite elders (4, 10, 12, 14) who wear the long-sleeved, mid-calf length tunics and long, heavy chlamyes that were typical of civilian garb in Late Antiquity[74] (figs. 18, 42, 43). The insignia worn by the central Israelite in the temple dedication scene (14) designated him as a high official; like the consuls on the fifth-century Halberstadt and Felix diptychs he wears a decorative patch on the shoulder of his tunic and a large rectangular tablion sewn at the chest level of his chlamys near the vertical border[75] (fig. 42).

The important role which the official mode plays in the Itala cycle reflects, to a considerable extent, the Roman custom of illustrating historical and mythological scenes from current pictorial repertories. Imperial models offered the closest correlations for representing Old Testament kings.

Even when we take such working methods into consideration they still fail to explain fully the extraordinary impact of triumphal imagery on our manuscript. We must first understand that the art of the late fourth and fifth century was decisively influenced by the court's art, which, in turn, primarily concerned itself with the depiction of official ceremony, status symbols and imperial triumphs.[76] Emphasis on victory was at the heart of late Roman political ideology, as it had been since the end of the first century, because Rome was repeatedly at war with external enemies and her own insurgents. Therefore victory became a major theme in official art.[77]

Our direct knowledge of this imagery is limited, on the whole, to a few surviving reliefs, but there is good reason to believe that the imperial narrative mode, which we see reflected in the Itala, had been extensively developed in large scale triumphal and historical painting.[78] Unfortunately very few examples of official painting survive, and they are scattered over four centuries, from a Republican tomb painting found on the Esquiline to the lost Tetrarchic frescoes at Luxor.[79] Nonetheless, from the third century B.C. to the fifth century A.D. Roman literature contains numerous references to paintings officially displayed to commemorate important victories.[80]

The custom of carrying paintings depicting battles and conquered countries, towns and peoples in triumphal processions extended over many centuries. According to a description by Josephus, these paintings were numerous, and they afforded the spectators with a vivid, detailed and emotionally affective representation of devastating wars.[81] Livy, Cicero and Pliny the Elder stated that after the paintings were used in triumphs they were

71. Some of the most interesting studies of imperial costume are by Delbrück, 'Kaiserornat'; Alföldi, 'Insignien'. Also compare Saul in Itala 3 and 8 to Aeneas in Vatican Vergil 11 and 31 and to other figures in Santa Maria Maggiore, Cecchelli, *Mosaici*, pls. 28 and 43; Karpp, *S. Maria Maggiore*, pls. 82, 143.

72. See Itala 3, 5 and 14; Vatican Vergil 16 and 40; and Iliad miniatures 13 and 14. For the Iliad see Bianchi-Bandinelli, *Miniatures of the Iliad*, figs. 128, 131. For Galerius see Laubscher, *Galeriusbogen*, pls. 41.2, 53.1 and 59.2.

73. Late Roman clothing and insignia of rank are discussed by Alföldi, 'Insignien', passim; and Delbrück, *Consulardiptychen*, pp. 244-47, esp. nn. 3, 64. See studies of these fibulas by Heurgon, 'Le tresor de Ténès'; and Noll, 'Kaiserfibel von 316'.

74. For a discussion of Roman civilian clothing see: Rinaldi, 'Il costume romano', pp. 230-32; L. M. Wilson, *Clothing of Ancient Romans* (Baltimore, 1938); F. Kolb, 'Römische Mäntel', *Röm. Mitt.*, 80 (1973): 69-172, esp. 158-162; J. B. Wild, 'Clothing in the Northwest Provinces of the Roman Empire', *Bonner Jahrbücher*, 168 (1968): 222; and Brenk, *Mosaiken*, p. 161.

75. For the consular diptych of 417 in Halberstadt and the lost valve from the Consul Felix diptych of 428 see Delbrück, *Consulardiptychen*, 1: 32-40, 2: pls. 2-3. The imperial family wears this costume and these insignia on the Missorium of Theodosius. Young Moses dresses as a nobleman in the same apparel in the S. Maria Maggiore nave mosaics; cf. Cecchelli, *Mosaiken*, pl. 29; Karpp, *S. Maria Maggiore*, pls. 85, 87. I suspect that the nobleman in picture 14 also wore the same long fibula worn by Abner on f. 3, but that it has been destroyed. The other men accompanying him (14) may have also worn the same high ranking insignia. The tablion is discussed by Rinaldi, 'Costume romano', p. 224.

76. The influence of imperial art is discussed by: Kollwitz, *Oström. Plastik*, pp. 81ff.; and Grabar, *L'empereur*, esp. pp. 209ff.

77. Triumphal formulas were used with increasing frequency in representations of the emperors, particularly after the late second century. See the comments of Alföldi, 'Insignien', pp. 43-68; Brilliant, *Gesture and Rank*, p. 216; and Grabar, *L'empereur*, pp. 126-27.

78. The principal reliefs are the Columns of Trajan and Marcus Aurelius and the Arches of Septimius Severus and Constantine in Rome and the drawings of the Arcadius Column in Constantinople. For a discussion of the probable influence of triumphal painting on official sculpture see Brilliant, *Septimius Severus*, pp. 223-26; Lehmann-Hartleben, *Trajanssäule*, cf. index: Triumphalmalerei; and W. Zwikker, *Studien zur Markus-Säule*, 2 vols. (Amsterdam, 1941), 1: 7-11.

79. The Republican fresco of Q. Fabius and M. Fannius, found on the Esquiline hill and now kept in the Conservatori Museum in Rome, may be an early reflection of triumphal painting; cf. the illustration in M. Swindler, *Ancient Painting* (New Haven, 1929), fig. 568. For the frescoes in Luxor see Kalavrezou-Maxeiner, 'Imperial Chamber at Luxor'.

80. For an excellent bibliography of ancient citations see Zwikker, *Markus-Säule*, pp. 7-11.

81. Cf. Josephus, *Jewish Wars* 7, 138ff.

often exhibited in temples.[82] Other types of public displays are recorded, and the texts imply that the paintings were executed both inside and outside major official buildings often at the express command of the emperors.[83]

In 165 A.D. Emperor Lucius Verus despatched pictures along with detailed written descriptions of a military campaign to guide M. Cornelius Fronto in writing an account of the Parthian wars.[84] It is tempting to speculate that Lucius Verus assumed that the pictures would also serve as sources for illustrating the final text.

During the late Roman period the Tetrarchs and the emperors from the houses of Constantine and Theodosius erected many triumphal monuments with sculptured reliefs relying on second and third-century traditions. It is likely that they also continued to support heavily the more economical medium of triumphal and commemorative painting.[85] According to Eunapius, such paintings were carried in the early fifth century as part of the triumphal entry of Honorius.[86] Evidently we are dealing with highly developed pictorial traditions which continued to be practiced when the Quedlinburg Itala was illustrated.

Aristocrats and wealthy patrons traditionally followed trends set in official art. Representations of pagan and secular themes, particularly in the luxury arts, also responded to the influence of imperial imagery and the epic mode so closely linked with it.[87]

After the Peace of the Church imperial iconography served as an important source for representing the triumph of Christ over death and of Christianity over its pagan enemies. Rich patrons from Rome's ruling class, and possibly even the government itself, encouraged these trends. This influence is largely reflected after the first third of the fourth century in Christian catacomb paintings and sarcophagi, on ivories and silver as well as on wooden doors, mosaics and frescoes in fifth-century churches.[88]

Official imagery appears in both narrative and non-narrative illustrated manuscripts of the period such as the Itala, Vatican Vergil, Iliad Ambrosiana, Calendar of 354 and Notitia Dignitatum of ca. 425 (figs. 28, 29). Such imagery also occurs in a number of Medieval and Byzantine manuscripts which obviously acquired those iconographic characteristics from fourth/fifth century sources.[89]

When the workshops which produced the Itala, Vergil and Milan Iliad drew liberally from the rich storehouse of ideas found in official narrative art, they were reflecting the tastes and interests of their patrons' social class. Because they shared so many pictorial conventions it seems reasonable to suppose that official, pagan and Christian manuscripts could have been made side by side in the same scriptoria where they would have been able to influence each other at a time when imperial iconography was enjoying prominence in the figurative arts.[90]

If scriptoria specializing in the production of deluxe manuscripts were regularly patronized by the courts, they would have developed and maintained a repertory of images which suited the ideology and tastes of their ruling class clientele.[91] After all, we know that fourth and fifth-century courts patronized poets, panegyrists and historians, and that they supported the production of deluxe books.[92]

82. See Livy, 24, 16: 16-19 and 41, 28: 8-10 where he mentions commemorative paintings which honored the victories of Ti. Sempronius Gracchus in 214 B.C. and of his namesake in 174 B.C. Triumphal paintings were often erected in temples according to Livy, 41, 28: 8-10; Cicero, *in Verr.*, 6, 55.122 and Pliny, *Nat. Hist.*, 35, 10: 27-28. For citations of paintings carried in triumphal processions see: Josephus, *Jewish Wars*, 7, 138ff.; Pliny, *Nat. Hist.*, 5, 5: 36-37; 22, 6: 12; and Tacitus, *Annals*, 2, 41.

83. See the preceding footnote. After conquering the Parthians, Septimius Severus dispatched a report to the Senate and the people of Rome and ordered them to make and publicly exhibit paintings of his battles and victories; cf. Herodian, 3, 9: 12; Historia Augusta, *Vita Severi*, 21, 12; and *Vita Caracallae*, 9, 6. Emperor Maximinus ordered that huge pictures of his victories over the Germans in 235/236 A.D. be painted and set up before the Senate house in Rome; cf. Herodian, 7, 2: 8.

84. See the letter in Fronto, 2, 194-95.

85. For a discussion of these monuments see Laubscher, *Galeriusbogen*; Brilliant, *Septimius Severus*; L'Orange, *Konstantinsbogen*; and Bruns, *Obelisk*.

86. Eunapius, fragm. 78.28. See the discussion of the fourth and fifth-century imperial ceremonies which came to be treated as triumphs in Kollwitz, *Oström. Plastik*, pp. 65ff.

87. For a discussion of these trends see Kollwitz, *Oström. Plastik*, pp. 81ff.; Grabar, *Christian Iconography*, pp. 125ff., 139ff.; and Weitzmann, 'Book Illustration', pp. 120-25. Numerous examples are illustrated in Volbach, *Art*, passim.

88. See, for example, the wooden doors at S. Ambrogio in Milan and at S. Sabina in Rome; the church mosaics at S. Pudenziana, S. Maria Maggiore and S. Sabina in Rome; the Junius Bassus sarcophagus and numerous works in ivory and silver illustrated in Volbach, *Art*, passim.

89. For examples see: Stern, *Calendrier de 354*, pp. 119-68; and Berger, *Notitia Dignitatum*, pp. 153-56, 165-68.

For Medieval illustrations using imperial, military imagery which they probably took from fourth/fifth century manuscript models see studies of: the Solomon cycle in the Carolingian Bible of San Paolo in Gaehde, 'Carolingian Bible of San Paolo', pp. 381-84; the Julian the Apostate cycle in the Homilies of Gregory of Nazianzus, Paris, Bibl. Nat., cod. gr. 510, f. 374 in Weitzmann, 'Chronicles'; the heroic David cycles in the Cyprus silver plates and in Byzantine psalters in Weitzmann, 'Prolegomena'; and the Joshua Roll, in Weitzmann, *Joshua Roll*.

90. This theory was proposed by Weitzmann, 'Book Illustration', pp. 123-125.

91. Weitzmann, *op. cit.*, pp. 123-25 recognized this principle. Many of Rome's leaders from Julius Caesar through Marcus Aurelius, as well as Gordian I and Julian the Apostate wrote historical, biographical or poetic works. Deluxe editions of these texts must have been made, but we do not know whether they were illustrated or if they were usually produced in scriptoria supported by imperial courts. For a discussion of the emperors' literary interests see O. A. W. Dilke, 'The Literary Output of the Roman Emperors', *Greece and Rome*, ser. 2, 4 (1957): 78-97; A. Momigliano, 'Pagan and Christian Historiography in the Fourth Century A.D.', *The Conflict between Paganism and Christianity in the Fourth Century*, ed. A. Momigliano (Oxford, 1963), pp. 79-99; and L. Bonfante-Warren, 'Emperor, God and Man in the Fourth Century. Julian the Apostate and Ammianus Marcellinus', *La Parola del Passato*, 19 (1964): 403ff.

92. Scattered evidence suggests that imperial scriptoria may have been established by the fourth/fifth centuries if not earlier. Porphyrius, a fourth-century panegyrist and poet, wrote in his *Praefatio*, 2 after his exile from Constantine's court that, whereas he once wrote his poetry in silver and gold on purple vellum, he must now content himself with black and red script on plain parchment. Cf. a discussion of this passage in Nordenfalk, *Zierbuchstaben*, pp. 57ff.

According to tradition, the emperor Valens had a particular center for copying manuscripts and an imperial library; cf. J. Irigoin, 'Centres de copie et bibliothèques', *Byzantine Books and Bookmen* (Washington, D.C., 1975), p. 24. The emperor Theodosius II (408-450) was called 'o kalligraphos', and manuscripts were attributed to his hand; cf. Bischoff, 'Scriptoria'. This emperor's

THREE RELATED CYCLES

Throughout this chapter a significant number of very specific comparisons have been made between the Itala, Vatican Vergil and S. Maria Maggiore mosaics. The correlation of their style and imagery extends to their sharing of an extraordinary number of precisely repeated figural conventions including details of pose, gesture, weight, viewpoint and costume, even in its precise arrangement, as well as in the grouping of figures. Boeckler, and more recently, Beat Brenk have described these numerous correlations, and they need not be repeated here.[93] A selection will suffice to demonstrate the close relationship which can be seen by comparing Aeneas and Joshua (figs. 16, 21) with Saul, Abner and David (pictures 4, 10, 12), and by comparing Aeneas to Abner (picture 11, fig. 25).

Official art provided topoi for all three cycles. Aeneas, for example, wears either the military field costume or cuirass of an emperor; many of his activities are reinterpreted according to imperial formulas.[94] When the mosaic artists represented Joshua conquering the Holy Land, they relied heavily on triumphal imagery (figs. 16, 20). For Abraham's meeting with Melchisedec the artist used a variation of an Adventus as did the painter of our manuscript's picture 5.[95]

In essence all three modes which played such an important role in the formation of the Quedlinburg Itala's illustrations had a strong impact on the Vergil miniatures and the nave mosaics. Their figures move before pink and blue striped skies in landscape settings which frequently include individual buildings or walled cities. Moreover, they all illustrate closely related series of verses in episodic narration.

The conditions which led the artists of these three cycles to use so many of the same pictorial ideas remain open to question. It has often been suggested that the Vergil and Itala should be attributed to a single workshop which produced Christian and pagan manuscripts side by side.[96] The most frequent explanation offered for the resemblance of the nave mosaics to both manuscript cycles assumes, or, at the very least, implies, that the mosaicists copied a manuscript illustrating the Pentateuch and Joshua in this style.[97] This theory is enhanced when we consider that the placement of the mosaics high above the spectator makes their small scale and busy compositions difficult to see. While most of the compositions would have been appropriate in a manuscript they are unsuitable decoration in a large church.

If the Vergil and Itala cycles and the hypothetical manuscript model for the mosaics were actually products of the same atelier, then their similarities would be easy to explain, but the issues are more complex, and the immediate sources of the mosaics remain hotly debated. Recently Beat Brenk has presented a number of cogent arguments disputing the theory that the mosaic cycle was directly copied from an illustrated manuscript model.[98] Ernst Kitzinger shares some of his doubts, but he rightly cautions that any attempt to solve this problem must still take into account the extent to which the mosaics evoke the style of manuscript illumination.[99]

An assessment of the relationship of these cycles must also consider their differences. The Vergil miniatures and the mosaics have many more conventions in common than either one of them shares with the Itala miniatures; although, if all of the Itala miniatures had survived, perhaps their correlations would have been more numerous. Many of the mosaic panels have far more spatial complexity than we find in any surviving Itala composition; while other panels are self-consciously reminiscent of a monumental mode. The schematic backdrops in our manuscript are a far cry from the coloristic richness of the mosaic backgrounds whose shimmering gold light patterns belong to mosaic traditions which are absent from manuscript painting.[100]

When compared with our manuscript, the Vatican Vergil exhibits a deeper understanding of classical sources with a richer and more subtle range of atmospheric effects, compositional structures and perspective motifs of considerable complexity.[101] The color transitions in the Vatican Vergil skies are, on the whole, more gradual and softer, and the pink sky glow is placed on the horizon as an intermediary between the ground color and the blue sky rising above. The horizon line is usually very high, in contrast to the Itala, where the horizon is low or totally lacking when blue paint continues down to the lower frame.

The closest correlations in technique and style between these two manuscripts occur with the first and third group of Vergil miniatures (1-9 and 26-50). Even so, in the Vergil manuscript figures have longer proportions, particularly in the torso, more rounded and three-dimensional forms, and smoother and more organically articulated joints in contrast to the disjointed angular-

wife, Eudocia, also composed poetry, panegyrics and paraphrases of biblical and Christian texts according to Sozomenos, *Praefatio*. For a study of court patronage of poets in this period see Cameron, *Claudian*. For studies of scriptoria and libraries in Antiquity and the Early Christian period see: C. Wendel, 'Bibliothek', *RAC* (1954), 2: 244-54; T. Kleberg, *Buchhandel und Verlagswesen in der Antike* (1967), pp. 26-67; E. D. Roberts, 'Notes on Early Christian Libraries in Rome', *Speculum*, 9 (1934): 190-94; and F. G. Kenyon, *Books and Readers in Ancient Greece and Rome*, 2nd ed. (Oxford, 1970), pp. 81-84.

93. See Boeckler, pp. 121-65; Brenk, *Mosaiken*, passim, has added several more precise comparisons; and of course de Wit, passim, discussed many of the correlations of their pictorial formulas.

94. This influence was also recognized by de Wit, pp. 146ff., 159ff.

95. The fullest discussions of triumphal imagery in the mosaics can be found in Grabar, *L'empereur*, pp. 45-54; and Brenk, *Mosaiken*, pp. 53-56, 97-107, 165-78.

96. This has been suggested by Boeckler, pp. 166-68; Cecchelli, *Mosaici*, pp. 89-91; and Nordenfalk, *Painting*, p. 93.

97. See Cecchelli, *Mosaici*, pp. 88-90; Byvanck, 'Sta. Maria Maggiore', pp. 15-27; and J. G. Deckers, *Der Alttestamentliche Zyklus von S. Maria Maggiore in Rom* (Bonn, 1976), pp. 1ff.; among others.

98. Brenk, *Mosaiken*, pp. 178-81.

99. Kitzinger, 'Role of Miniature Painting', pp. 122-34.

100. Gold is used in the mosaic sky in San Aquilino, Milan; in S. Giovanni in Fonte in Naples; and in S. Pudenziana, Rome.

101. The rich variety of sources used by the Vergil miniaturists has been discussed by de Wit, pp. 16ff., 159-74, 205-10.

ity of the Itala's figure style (compare ff. 1r, 2r with figs. 27, 28). Although the painting technique of the second Vergil artist (mins. 10-25) is far more expressive and moves away from the interest in classicism found in the other miniatures and in the Itala, this artist still shares with them the same repertory of pictorial conventions (compare figs. 21-23, 25 and 27-29).

If both manuscripts were, after all, products of the same workshop, in the case of the Vergil manuscript the artist of pictures 1-9 and 26-50 was far more adept in capturing the classicism in his sources than were the Itala painters.

The appearance of this style in two different media, in the S. Maria Maggiore nave mosaics and in our two manuscripts, one pagan, the other Christian, testifies to its contemporary stature. This style with its banded skies and distinctive figural conventions is also reflected in several Carolingian and Ottonian codices whose artists must have had access to comparable manuscripts.[102] We must then wonder whether the models of those Medieval manuscripts were actually made in a single workshop along with the Quedlinburg Itala and Vatican Vergil. It may also be possible that more than one atelier located in the same artistic center worked in this style. The means by which these manuscript and mosaic artists selected and shared so many motifs will be explored at the end of this chapter.

PICTORIAL SOURCES

It is important to recognize the Itala's position in relation to other art of its generation. A few telling comparisons will further establish both the antiquity and the currency of its formulas within late fourth/fifth-century art in the city of Rome.

Individual workers and teams of laborers lifting heavy building blocks to construct the temple walls in picture 14 recall the builders represented in frescoes from a first-century Esquiline columbarium depicting the legendary history of Rome; on Trajan's Column reliefs; and in the fourth-century Hypogaeum frescoes of Trebius Justus[103] (fig. 32). The chase topos in picture six had been repeated in centuries of bacchic art, and it became equally useful in the Late Antique illustrated Comedies of Terence[104] (fig. 48).

Precise comparisons can often be made with other narrative paintings produced by the same generation of artists working in Rome. The pallbearers in picture 12 recall numerous examples of men carrying litters in Roman art dating back to the first century, but they bear an even more remarkable resemblance in their exact pose and in the relationship of the figures to each other when compared with the men carrying the Ark of the Covenant at S. Maria Maggiore and with the four bearers recorded in a drawing of a lost fifth-century fresco at San Paolo f.l.m.[105] (fig. 16). Solomon's messenger (13) is almost identical to Ascanius and Cupid in Vatican Vergil pictures 11 and 12; to Jacob meeting Laban in the S. Maria Maggiore mosaics; and to October in the Calendar of 354 (figs. 17, 22, 23, 47). As already noted, the profile pose of figures in prayer used in Itala picture 7 was also preferred by the artists of the Vatican Vergil (16), S. Maria Maggiore and San Paolo f.l.m. cycles[106] (figs. 19, 24).

Despite access to a wide variety of sources evidently available to contemporary artists working in Rome, the evidence in the extant miniatures consistently indicates that the Quedlinburg Itala artists limited themselves to the repetition of a few topoi. In eleven of the fourteen miniatures the instructions and sketches restricted the narrative action to speeches and dialogs which the artists illustrated by repeating a remarkably small number of figural and compositional conventions. Boeckler recognized that most of the scenes consisted simply of a leader speaking to a group of people with very minor variations such as whether the listener was one or more persons standing or sitting. Otherwise the compositional principle of two confronted groups was always the same.[107]

The mechanical nature of this approach to illustration becomes evident when we recognize the basic similarities between pictures 9 and 11, 10, 12 and 4. Their artists employed the same selection of: paired speakers making identical gestures; speakers accompanied by escorts; listeners standing tightly packed in double rows; and seated leaders with bodyguards. Even more striking is the way their artists repeated the same viewpoints, emphatic side glances, angles of the gesturing arm, drapery arrangements, poses and shifts of body weight and stance. For example, paired figures, such as the two soldiers in picture 1, are carbon copies of each other, just as are Samuel and Saul in picture 4.

So many scenes have interchangeable parts that, were it not for the gold labels and distinctive costumes, the viewer would often find it difficult to identify specific episodes. Had an effort been made to represent other types of activities, they would have given the viewer a more vivid and informative impression

102. Boeckler, p. 200, noted that the similarities to the Itala and Vergil style could be found in Carolingian and Ottonian manuscripts: the Vivian and Grandval Bibles, the Gospel of Prüm, the Stuttgart Gospels and Codex Egberti. Also see Weitzmann's discussion in 'Book Illustration', pp. 96-125. The proposal by Koehler, *Schule von Tours*, 1: 164ff., 212, that the Grandval Bible copied a hypothetical manuscript made for Pope Leo I (440-460) in a style similar to the Itala and Vergil has been refuted; cf. Kessler, *Bibles from Tours*, pp. 139ff. For the Codex Egberti cf. H. Schiel, *Codex Egberti der Stadtbibliothek Trier*, 2 vols. (Basel, 1960).

103. The Esquiline frescoes are illustrated by M. Borda, *La pittura romana* (Milan, 1958), color pl. opp. p. 176. Also see Lehmann-Hartleben, *Trajanssäule*, pls. 11-12, 19, 20, 39, 60, 65. The tomb of Trebius Justus is discussed by C. Casalone, 'Note sulle pitture del Ipogeo di Trebio Giusto a Rome', *Cah. Arch.*, 12 (1962): 53-64.

104. The best comparisons are in the Medieval copies of the lost Late Antique illustrated *Comedies* of Terence, particularly in Paris, Bibl. nat., ms. lat. 7899. See the *Andria*, ff. 9v, 18, 26 and *Eunuchus*, ff. 40, 60 illustrated in Jones and Morey, *Manuscripts of Terence*, figs. 42-45, 91, 125, 179, 261, 275.

105. Examples are provided by Boeckler, pp. 145-46. For S. Paolo see Waetzoldt, *Kopien*, p. 762.

106. See Moses and the Fall of the Quail, and Noah's prayer in S. Paolo in Waetzoldt, *Kopien*, fig. 338.

107. Boeckler, pp. 150-51.

of the story than seeing the characters speak about those events in undifferentiated compositions.

This predilection for representing conversations which describe events rather than depicting them in action has been recognized by Friedrich Mehmel as a distinctive characteristic of Late Antique art and literature. As part of his evidence he cited the preponderance of conversational schemes in the Vatican Vergil miniatures and in the S. Maria Maggiore nave mosaics as well as in the dialogs and rhetorical structure of the pagan poet Claudius Claudianus and the Christian Prudentius[108] (figs. 17-20, 22, 25, 27, 28). Speeches also dominate in the copies of the Late Antique illustrated Comedies of Terence, and dialogs are considered a late intrusion into the pictorial cycle of the Iliad Ambrosiana.[109]

The actual proportion of dialogs in the complete Quedlinburg Itala can never be known, but it was probably considerable given this workshop's propensity for repeating a small repertory of models and its acceptance of the contemporary preference for static dialogs over dramatic action in narrative art and literature.

Apparently the Itala artists were just as unwilling to seek out more interesting pictorial variations and solutions for other types of scenes. The stiff, frontal, staccato alignment of figures which prevails in most of the miniatures (such as Saul among the prophets in picture 3, and the workers awaiting their departure in picture 13) stands as clear evidence of this workshop's unimaginative reliance on simple conventions. The three workers (13), for instance, represent the larger labor force requested by Solomon. The artist might have shown the summoning of, preparations for, or the embarcation of the builders, but, instead, the three men signify rather than enact the fulfillment of Solomon's request to Hiram.

It is true that a large percentage of the original illustrations has been lost, and it is reasonable to assume that had the entire cycle survived it certainly would have contained a few more types of figures. Still, I venture to propose that the workshop's pattern of confining itself to a highly repetitive and limited repertory held true throughout the manuscript. After all, these patterns are repeated in the four preserved folios which represent the work of three artists and come from three of the four books of Kings that survive from this codex.

One might have expected these artists to have been more receptive to a wider variety of models. The manuscript does, in actuality, belong to a category of deluxe works of art, and other ateliers working under those circumstances and producing fine silver, ivories and illuminated manuscripts for Christian and pagan clients, still used the large repertory of imagery available in the older classical tradition, as did the Vatican Vergil miniatures and the S. Maria Maggiore nave mosaics.

At all events, the Itala's atelier does not stand alone in its self-imposed limitations. For generations, numerous Late Antique and Early Christian artists had sacrificed individuality and variety to stereotyped and schematic formulas.

The recurrent appearance of identical stereotyped figures and motifs in the Quedlinburg Itala, Vatican Vergil and S. Maria Maggiore mosaics raises several questions about their sources. We must still account for the transfer of triumphal imagery from official art to these manuscripts and Christian mosaics. It is unlikely, if their artists set out independently to study and glean ideas from imperial reliefs and paintings, that they would have selected identical topoi from the hundreds of images on these monuments.[110] If pictorial motif books containing triumphal imagery were available to these artists, this might explain the close relationship between these three cycles.[111]

The individual images and compositional groupings which they used occurred in diverse contexts over several generations. Perhaps compendia of pictorial ideas were especially compiled for the use of some Roman workshops. By making a few minor changes their artists would then have been able to adapt generalized conventions to their particular needs. Such compendia would have also facilitated the transmission of ideas between workshops and from one generation to another.

Unfortunately it is difficult to define the nature and use of these hypothetical motif books because only a few disparate and fragmentary drawings survive from Antiquity which might be interpreted as portions of modelbooks.[112] Such fragmentary evidence does not permit us to draw firm conclusions about the availability or contents of such technical aids or how they may have functioned.

Nonetheless, we need not rule out the possibility that motif books were available in workshops simply because adequate examples have failed to survive. After all, such books, by their very nature, would have been submitted to much wear and tear and then would have been discarded when they were no longer

108. Mehmel recognized that the stress on dialog was a negation of action. See F. Mehmel, *Virgil und Apollonius Rhodius. Untersuchungen über die Zeitvorstellung in der antiken epischen Erzählung* (n.p., 1940), pp. 99-127. His arguments are summarized by Franz Dölger and A. M. Schneider, *Byzanz* (Bern, 1952), p. 292. Brenk, *Mosaiken*, 126-28, 146-49 expands on Mehmel's study in his discussion of dialog scenes in the S. Maria Maggiore nave mosaics, and cites many more examples of this emphasis in art and literature of the third to fifth centuries. Boeckler, pp. 150-151, and de Wit, p. 87, in their respective manuscript studies, recognized the stress on dialog scenes and their inherent similarity, but they did not discuss the larger artistic and cultural manifestations of this trend which Brenk describes in great detail.

109. This is a suggestion of Bianchi Bandinelli, *Miniatures of the Iliad*, pp. 129-130. See a discussion of this theory by Kurt Weitzmann in his review of Bianchi Bandinelli's book in *Gnomon* 29 (1957): 606-16.

110. Weitzmann, 'Book Illustration', p. 123 has made this observation.

111. This is the theory of Brenk, *Mosaiken*, pp. 178ff.

112. The evidence is discussed by Scheller, *Survey of Model Books*, pp. 1ff., 15, 18, 45ff.; and by E. Kitzinger, *The Mosaics of Monreale* (Palermo, 1960), pp. 63-68 and in 'The Role of Miniature Painting', pp. 99-142, esp. p. 119, n. 37. D. Levi, *Antioch Mosaic Pavements*, 2 vols. (Princeton, 1947), 1: 8-9, assumes that modelbooks were used by generations of mosaicists.

useful.[113] Because technical aids have survived from the Middle Ages, their existence in Antiquity becomes even more plausible.[114]

Other possible avenues for the exchange of formal and thematic conventions should also be considered. The history of Roman art is, after all, punctuated by eclecticism and fashionable revivals. Masters who wanted to preserve the traditional repertories of pictorial resources and who wanted their ateliers to produce homogeneous works must have trained their workshop artists to repeat standard motifs as part of their training. Traveling artists would have also spread this knowledge over a wide geographic area.

It is reasonable to assume that a sizeable compendium of pictorial conventions was part of each artist's basic vocabulary and always ready to be applied through a professionally active memory.[115] New images and repopularized older formulas could have readily been assimilated into that memory matrix just as new words and phrases enter common speech. Furthermore, if, as is very likely, manuscript workshops as well as fresco and mosaic ateliers clustered together in one quarter of the city in such major art centers as Rome, a common language of forms would have easily circulated amongst their artists.

113. A reasonable suggestion made by Kitzinger, 'The Role of Miniature Painting', p. 109.

114. See Scheller, *Survey of Model Books*, passim, for a catalog of such materials and a discussion of their use.

115. We are cautioned not to make artists too dependent on technical aids in a very interesting discussion of workshop practices by D.C. Winfield, 'Byzantine Wall Painting Methods', *DOP* 22 (1968): 93-96.

CHAPTER FOUR

Origin of the Pictorial Cycle

Because the Quedlinburg Itala is the oldest extant illustration of any biblical manuscript, and it contains a rare set of detailed instructions to the artists, a study of the origin of its narrative cycle and its relationship to the parental text takes on special importance. The instructions enable us to inquire into workshop practices in the development of this cycle in a manner rarely afforded in the history of art.

COMPARISON WITH OTHER KINGS CYCLES

Among the Old Testament kings, David and Solomon possessed heroic stature for ancient Jews and Christians.[1] Therefore we should expect to find a narrative cycle based on all or part of the four books of Kings among the earliest examples of Old Testament illustrations. Regrettably, the first attempts to represent a series of major events in their lives have been lost. As it so happens, the oldest preserved evidence of a Kings' cycle occurs in the third-century Dura Europos Synagogue frescoes, which depict various episodes relating the story of a considerable array of characters from each of the four Books of Kings.[2] It is reasonable to suppose that these sundry episodes derive from larger and more cohesive cycles.

Fairly extensive Kings cycles were available in Italy by the second half of the fourth century. The Death of Absalom in the Via Latina catacombs in Rome and the Dead Man and the Ass (1 Kings 13:24) on the ivory Lipsanothek of Brescia are minor episodes that are rarely represented. Therefore it is likely that they were extracted from more extensive illustrations of Kings.[3] David's stature in Jewish and Christian messianic thought inspired heroic cycles such as those carved on the wooden doors at S. Ambrogio in Milan and on the Heraclean silver plates from Cyprus, which reflect Theodosianic antecedents. David bowing in penance before Nathan on a late fourth-century relief in Budapest testifies to the existence in this period of the Davidic cycles that later appear in Byzantine psalters.[4] Unfortunately the episodes preserved in these works do not appear in the surviving Itala miniatures.

At least two events represented in our miniatures seem to have been depicted on the walls of contemporary churches. The twenty-first quatrain in Prudentius's *Dittochaeon* celebrates the building of the temple in Jerusalem, and Solomon's dedication of the temple is mentioned in the titulus for Pammachius's church.[5] Both texts were written shortly before the illustration of our manuscript, but whether their pictures resembled those painted on f. 4 must remain a matter of speculation.

Although the Itala's remaining miniatures cannot be compared with other works surviving from the Early Christian period, a few of the pictures are strikingly similar to the same scenes

1. For David's role in early Jewish and Christian thought and art see the sources discussed by J. Danielou, 'David', *RAC*, 3: 594-602; and H. Leclerq, 'David', *DACL*, 4, pt. 1, pp. 295-303. For Solomon cf. H. Leclerq, 'Solomon', *DACL*, 15, pt. 1, pp. 588-602; and C.C. McCown, *The Testament of Solomon* (Leipzig, 1922).

2. Kraeling, *Synagogue*, pp. 393-94 identified twenty-eight scenes from the four Books of Kings in the Dura Europos Synagogue frescoes.

3. Their iconography is discussed by Kötzsche-Breitenbruch, *Via Latina*, pp. 93-95; and Delbrück, *Lipsanothek*, pp. 18-19.

4. For bibliographic references and illustrations of these works of art see my Bibliography for Works of Art Most Often Cited.

5. These examples were noted by Boeckler, p. 150. Cf. Prudentius, *Dittochaeon*, Migne, *PL*, 60: 100; translated by Davis-Weyer, *Early Medieval Art*, p. 29. Also see Pammachius' titulus quoted by Wilpert, *Mosaiken und Malereien*, 2: 646.

6. The chase scene occurs in New York, Pierpont Morgan Lib. M 638, f. 25r. Cf. Cockerell and Plummer, *Miniatures*, fig. 157. Its similarity to our picture 6 is also discussed by Stahl, *Iconographic Sources*, pp. 126-27. Also see the copy of the Bible Moralisée in Oxford, Bodleian Library, Bodl. 270b, f. 134 in A. de Laborde, *La Bible Moralisée* (Paris, 1911), pl. 134. Stahl, pp. 126-27, adds the chase scene in the Pamplona Bible to this group, but all of the movements and gestures in the Itala and Morgan pictures are missing in the Pamplona miniature, Amiens, ms. lat. 108, f. 8v. Cf. F. Bucher, *The Pamplona Bibles*, 2 vols. (New Haven, 1970), pl. 202.

that occur in Medieval manuscripts which incorporate pictorial cycles reputedly dating back to this early period.

The composition of the chase scene in picture 6 also appears on f. 25r in the thirteenth-century Old Testament miniatures in New York, Pierpont Morgan Library M. 638, and in copies of the Bible Moralisée.[6] Saul pursues Samuel and rends his garment, the prophet turns around, raises his hand in a speaking gesture, and runs away in precisely the same manner in all of these codices (fig. 52). Even so, it is doubtful that the Itala's picture is related to these later examples because their other illustrations are totally different from the representations of the same episodes in the Itala; as is indicated by a comparison of miniatures 3, 4, 6, 7, 8, 11, and 12 with very different representations of the same episodes in the Morgan manuscript (ff. 22v, 25r, 37v and 38r)[7] (fig. 51). No doubt, the resemblances between their chase and fighting compositions occurred because the artist who developed the early archetype of the Morgan miniatures and the artist who originated picture 6 independently selected similar topoi from the popular repertory of antique conventions discussed in the preceding chapter.[8]

These issues arise again in a comparison of the burial of Abner (12) with representations of this scene in an eleventh/twelfth-century Byzantine book of Kings in Vatican City, Bibl. Vat., Vat. gr. 333, f. 43v[9] (fig. 50). In both pictures King David follows the four pallbearers who carry Abner's corpse on a bier in accordance with a description of this episode in the text. Far more important, however, are the number of differences between their compositions. The Itala represents two scenes: in the first, David and the men who follow him in the funeral cortege make hand gestures of sorrow; and in the second, David, accompanied by armed guards, converses with a group of his followers who ask him to cease fasting. In the Vatican miniature, on the contrary, David alone follows the bier, and he is not making a mournful gesture. The group of men at the right appear to be vigorously disputing whether David was implicated in Abner's assassination. Clearly the differences far outweight the similarities between the representations of the burial story in these two manuscripts. Therefore it is reasonable to conclude that their similarities are based solely on a passage in the text that is central to the story and on reference to a common pictorial convention widespread in Antique and Byzantine art (fig. 16).

The appearance of Abner before Ishboseth in Vatican f. 42v and in Itala picture 9 are so similar in all their major compositional details that they might be considered descendents of an earlier illustration[10] (fig. 49). Since both manuscripts represent all other episodes in the story of Abner and David in a completely different manner, it is more likely that these two miniatures are not related to each other. Instead they must derive from an omnipresent topos for court scenes which abounds in Ancient and Byzantine art (figs. 18, 28). A comparison of Itala pictures 9 through 12 with the miniatures in Vat. gr. 333 further substantiates that these cycles are unrelated.[11] Moreover, the depictions of Saul's accession to power and subsequent fall from grace in Itala pictures 1 through 8 bear no relation to the representations of those stories in the Vatican Kings.[12]

No other extant cycle of Old Testament Kings can be convincingly related to the Quedlinburg Itala's program. It seems that later generations were not attracted by the antique Roman triumphal imagery which pervades the Itala's illustrations.

THE USE OF IMPERIAL IMAGERY

Triumphal imagery is integral to the very structure of the Itala's illustrations, as the analysis of their pictorial sources so vividly demonstrated in the last chapter. Every element in the composition of picture 5, the submission of Agag in miniature 7 and the ultimate sources of pictures 4, 10 and 12 in Adlocutio scenes can be traced to military models. The methods used to kill Agag (8) and Abner (11) disagree with descriptions in the text but follow popular Roman formulas for paired fighting soldiers.

The extent to which the Quedlinburg Itala relies on military topoi and triumphal imagery sets it apart from other Christian, Medieval and Byzantine Kings cycles. To be sure, its reliance on such formulas was partly motivated by the character of the text, which repeatedly focuses on kings at war, as is the case on f. 2. Nevertheless, the use of military imagery is, on the

7. See the illustrations in Cockerell and Plummer, *Miniatures*, pp. 113, 123, 173, 175. In our discussion of these issues in January 1971 and in his 1974 dissertation H. Stahl, *Iconographic Sources*, pp. 126-27, agreed with my conclusion that the chase scene in the Itala is not related to the pictorial family from which M 638 derived its scene. He also thinks that its archetype used the same common Antique chase convention, and concludes, p. 122, that, given the fragmentary nature of the evidence, the Morgan cycle cannot be compared to any particular Early Christian cycle. Noting other instances when the Morgan miniatures contain formal elements found in Late Antique art led him to suggest that its artists might have referred to a Carolingian manuscript which used comparable Antique formulas.

8. Stahl, *Iconographic Sources*, p. 127, n. 236, has also recognized the similarity of their pictorial conventions, but he too does not consider this evidence of a familial relationship.

9. Vat. gr. 333 has been published by Lassus, *Livre des rois*, p. 70, fig. 81.

10. Illustrated in Lassus, *Livre des rois*, fig. 80, p. 69.

11. The death of Abner in Itala picture 11 is not related to Vat. gr. 333, f. 43. Cf. Lassus, *Livre des rois*, fig. 81. The Vatican ms. does not illustrate the episodes depicted in Itala miniatures 13 and 14. Weitzmann has suggested that the archetype for Vat. gr. 333 was devised in the Early Christian period, and that the Vatican manuscript only contains an abridged copy of the lost pictorial model. Cf. Weitzmann, 'Prolegomena', 106 and 'Cyclic Illustration', p. 74.

12. Vat. gr. 333 does not illustrate the episodes found in Itala miniatures 1-4. Instead the Vatican Kings illustrates scenes from chapters 9 and 11 and very different episodes from chapter 10 on ff. 13-15. Cf. Lassus, *Livre des rois*, figs. 21-25. Although gr. 333, ff. 21-22 illustrate the same episodes found in Itala miniatures 5 and 8, their compositions are totally unrelated. Cf. Lassus, *Livre des rois*, figs. 37-39. The scenes in Itala miniatures 6 and 7 are not illustrated in the Vatican manuscript.

13. Degering, p. 80.

whole, far more extensive than the text would warrant and it often contravenes its meaning. Curiously, there is rarely any indication in the instructions that such models should be used, not even in picture 5 where Degering reconstructed the instructions to read 'de curru' so that they would correlate with the picture.[13] Actually that portion is destroyed, and the remaining space appears too small to accomodate those words. Consequently, it is doubtful that a chariot was ever stipulated in the instructions.

All the kings consistently wear full-dress cuirass armor and paludamentum even though military costume is inappropriate to the meaning of most scenes. This peculiarity is clearly evident in pictures 1 to 3, where, according to 1 Sam. 10, Saul is a young farmer returning to his father's home after he has been secretly anointed by Samuel. He should be wearing the type of short tunic worn by the pilgrim in picture 2, but the artist ceremoniously dressed him in imperial armor. The text to miniature 12 relates that David's men came to the king as he sat dressed in mourning clothes and urged him to cease fasting over the death of Abner; yet, David, in full armor and accompanied by armed bodyguards, addresses his followers in a scene modeled on an Adlocutio. The cuirass is just as inappropriate when Solomon dedicates the temple, and this criticism holds true for the kings in pictures 9 through 13; they should wear court costume.[14]

This consistent use of full-dress armor for all kings repeatedly violates established Roman custom. If, as it seems reasonable to suggest, the Itala workshop had been commissioned to produce deluxe manuscripts for aristocratic patrons on other occasions, its artists should have been aware of the importance which a highly class conscious Late Roman society placed on legally established rules for wearing official dress.[15] Here the Itala is an anomaly, as a survey of the art of the period indicates. Biblical, historical and mythological kings and heroes were generally depicted in a manner appropriate to the context of each scene. In Late Roman art they typically wear a short tunic in their youth, the court costume of an emperor when they are kings, with full-dress armor usually reserved for military scenes. As a matter of course, the heroic David cycles on the S. Ambrogio doors and on the Heraclean silver plates conformed to this general rule.

Other departures from the meaning of the text and instructions occurred when the Itala artists patterned their scenes after official protocol. The biblical passage related to picture 1 implies that the two men who greet Saul are probably his father's farm hands or ordinary Israelite neighbors. In either case, the suitable dress for the men designated by the instructions as 'duo viri' would have been an exomis or simple short tunic. Instead the artist represented them as fully-armed soldiers. It is obvious that they perform an official function by the crosses emblazoned on their shields and by the air of authoritative dignity with which they address Saul, who is dressed as an emperor. We should note how the soldiers' manner contrasts with the lively speaking attitudes of the pilgrims in the next picture. In picture 1 the artist ignored the unceremonious activity required by the directions which request that the two men jump over ditches and speak to Saul. Instead he modeled the scene on a military episode that occurs in official art; our picture resembles the scenes on the Columns of Trajan and Marcus Aurelius in which soldiers report to the emperors[16] (figs. 30, 33).

Similar deviations from the intention of the text occur in picture 3 where Saul's attendant carries the fourth instrument although the text implies that it should have been given to a fourth prophet. (Degering reconstructed the instructions to give the instrument to the boy, but that portion is totally destroyed.)[17] Evidently the artist deemed it more important to adhere to Roman protocol, which required that kings must be accompanied by an escort; this served as a hard and fast rule for the painters of all fourteen miniatures. Here the artist was also guided by his preference for paratactic compositions; by omitting the fourth prophet he avoided crowding his picture with another figure. At least he granted some recognition of the intention of the instructions when he separated the boy attendant from the group of prophesiers by a larger space, a cluster of rocks and the label 'puer Saul'.

To a considerable extent a fascination with imperial imagery, especially its triumphal aspects, was in vogue during the period in which our manuscript was produced. We can find imperial ceremonies and insignia, expressions of triumph and borrowed military formulas in numerous Christian, pagan and secular works of art produced from the middle of the fourth century to the early sixth century. The impact of these ideas in manuscript illustration is evident in the Calendar of 354, Vatican Vergil, Notitia Dignitatum and Ilias Ambrosiana. Imperial imagery was considered appropriate for representing Old Testament kings and leaders in the S. Maria Maggiore nave mosaics, the S. Ambrogio doors and on the lost Theodosianic archetype of

14. Examples of appropriate models of court costume are found on the Missorium and Obelisk base of Theodosius, illustrated in Volbach, *Art*, pls. 53-55. In the late fourth and fifth centuries the men of the imperial family wear a long 'tunica manicata' belted with the 'cingulum', a paludamentum clasped by a gem encircled fibula from which three pendelia are suspended, large embroidered patches on the shoulder of the tunic, tablion on the front and back of the paludamentum, jeweled 'campagi' (shoes), and a gemmed diadem. Imperial costume is discussed by Delbrück, *Kaiserporträts*, passim, and in *Consulardiptychen*, passim; and by Alföldi, 'Insignien', passim. This costume is also worn by the prince on the arch mosaics at S. Maria Maggiore; see Cecchelli, *Mosaici*, pl. 53; Karpp, *S. Maria Maggiore*, fig. 21.

15. These rules are discussed by Alföldi, 'Insignien', 1ff., esp. 51, 68ff.; Delbrück, 'Kaiserornat', pp. 1-21; and Delbrück, *Kaiserporträts*, passim. For a comprehensive bibliography of studies published between 1955-75 on the subject of imperial ceremony and insignia see P. Herz, 'Bibliographie zum römischen Kaiserkult (1955-75)', *ANRW*, II, vol. 16, pt. 2, pp. 874ff.

16. Illustrated in Lehmann-Hartleben, *Trajanssäule*, pl. 51.

17. Degering, pp. 67-68.

the silver David plates discovered in Cyprus. Even Prudentius and John Chrysostom dress Old Testament kings in Roman regalia.[18]

Furthermore, Christ's kingship and his triumph over death were also proclaimed through the adoption of imperial imagery. Examples of this phenomenon in the art and literature of the period are too well known and numerous to mention, and they have already been studied in considerable detail. Here we may simply recall the Junius Bassus sarcophagus of 359, the acclamation of Christ fresco in the catacomb of SS. Pietro and Marcellino and the childhood of Christ cycle at S. Maria Maggiore.[19]

Because themes of imperial triumph played such a vital role in late Roman official politics, and the concept of Christian triumph and world rule were undergoing major developments in contemporary art and literature, we may well ask whether the Quedlinburg Itala's excessive dependence on imperial imagery carried symbolic meaning. In light of this question we should keep in mind that in late Antiquity victory was ideologically seen as a manifestation of the divine bestowal of office and of continued divine favor, first for pagan and then for Christian emperors.[20] By the late third century, many aspects of civilian life were militarized, and many official ceremonies became treated as triumphs.[21] Imperial victory was Christianized in the next century by making a few small changes in established formulas. The addition of a labarum was usually sufficient to indicate that victory was now bestowed on the emperor by the Christian God.[22]

The artistic and literary evidence of the period suggests three possible themes which the Itala cycle may have intended to invoke. Old Testament kings were considered as instruments and types of salvation, as precursors of Roman Christian emperors, and as prophecies of the kingship of Christ.

A significant segment of early Judeo-Christian thought presented David and Solomon in the role of victors over evil forces and as representative types of salvation.[23] These concepts were integral to the Jewish and Christian Solomon amulets, to the David and Goliath images in baptisteries, on catacomb frescoes and sarcophagi, as well as to the heroic David cycle placed under the sign of the cross on the S. Ambrogio doors.[24] The salvation of God's people (now signifying Christians) may have also been implied in the Joshua cycle at S. Maria Maggiore where Joshua may be seen as a foretype of Christ[25] (figs. 16, 20). In most of these works, Roman military imagery clarified the concept of triumph over death and evil. It was not, however, the use of military imagery alone, but the magical, sepulchral or typological context of the aforementioned works which determined their message of Christian salvation.

In the fourth century, Christian emperors were first likened to Moses, David and Solomon, just as pagan emperors had been compared to the ancient heroes, Achilles and Hercules.[26] These

18. See Prudentius, *Dittochaeon*, quatrain 20 translated by Davis-Weyer, *Early Medieval Art*, p. 28; and John Chrysostom, *On S. Phocas Martyr*, Migne, *PG*, 50: 701 f.

19. Various aspects of the development of these concepts in art and literature have been studied by V. Buchheit, 'Christliche Romideologie im Laurentius-Hymnus des Prudentius', *Polychronion, Festschrift Franz Dölger zum 75. Geburtstag* (Heidelberg, 1966), pp. 121-44; J. Kollwitz, 'Das Bild von Christus dem König in Kunst und Liturgie der christlichen Frühzeit', *Theologie und Glaube*, 1 (1947): 95-117; E. Peterson, 'Christus als Imperator', *Theologische Traktate* (Munich, 1951): 149-64; H. P. L'Orange, *Studies in the Iconography of Cosmic Kingship in the Ancient World* (Oslo, 1953), passim; P. Beskow, *Rex Gloriae, The Kingship of Christ in the Early Church*, trans. by E. J. Sharpe (Stockholm, 1962); and W. Hilgers, 'Triumphsymbolik in der altchristlichen Literatur', *Bonner Festgabe Johannes Straub* (Bonn, 1977), pp. 297-306.

20. Consult the following bibliography for a discussion of Roman concepts of divine election of the emperor and for several theories on divinely bestowed victory expressed by pagan and Christian writers: F. Dölger, 'Zur antiken und frühchristlichen Auffassung der Herrschergewalt von Gottes Gnaden', *Antike und Christentum*, 3 (1932): 117-127; Treitinger, *Reichsidee*; J. Straub, *Vom Herrscherideal in der Spätantike* (Stuttgart, 1939); W. Ensslin, *Gottkaiser und Kaiser von Gottes Gnaden* (Munich, 1943); Dvornik, *Early Christian Political Philosophy*.

21. For studies of the militarization of the imperial government see: A. H. M. Jones, 'The Roman Civil Service', *Journal of Roman Studies*, 39 (1949): 38-55; and J. Vogt, *The Decline of Rome. The Metamorphosis of Ancient Civilization*, trans. J. Sondheimer (London, 1967), pp. 96 ff. For influences of this militarization on art cf. H. P. L'Orange, *Art Forms and Civic Life in the Late Roman Empire* (Stockholm, 1958), passim. For sources and descriptions of fourth- and fifth-century triumphs see Alföldi, 'Mon. Zeremoniell', pp. 111-18; Treitinger, *Reichsidee*, pp. 67-71; and C. Barini, *Triumphalia* (Turin, 1952). For representations in art see Kollwitz, *Oström. Plastik*, pp. 63 ff. and 145-62. The entry of Constantine II into Rome is described by Ammianus Marcellinus 16.10 and discussed by Stern, *Calendrier de 354*, pp. 162 ff. The last Roman triumph was celebrated by Honorius after the victory over the Goths in 404 A.D. The clearly pagan associations and character of the triumphal ceremony led to its abandonment by Christians during the fourth century and its replacement by the Adventus. See the discussion by M. J. Deer, 'Der Ursprung der Kaiserkrone', *Schweizer Beiträge zur allgemeinen Geschichte*, 8 (1950): 51-86; S. MacCormack, 'Change and Continuity in Late Antiquity. The Ceremony of Adventus', *Historia. Zeitschrift für Alte Geschichte*, 21 (1972): 721-52.

22. The early fifth-century Column of Arcadius in Constantinople, like that of his father, Theodosius I, self-consciously evoked the second-century Columns of Trajan and Marcus Aurelius in Rome. The cross and labarum on the base of the Arcadius Column clarify that victory is bestowed by the Christian God. The drawings made in 1574 prior to the destruction of the Column were published by Freshfield, 'Notes', pp. 87-104. The official use of the labarum by Christian emperors is mentioned by Eusebius of Caesarea, Gregory of Nazianzus, John Chrysostom and Sozomenos, among others. For full citations of their comments and discussions of Christian symbols on Roman coinage see: A. Alföldi, 'The Helmet of Constantine with the Christian Monogram', *JRS*, 22 (1932): 9 ff.; Grabar, *L'Empereur*, pp. 158-62; Kollwitz, *Oström. Plastik*, 137-39; F. J. Dölger, 'Das Kreuzszepter Konstantins des Grossen', *Schweizer Münzblätter*, 4 (1954): 81 ff.; P. Bruun, 'The Christian Signs on the Coins of Constantine', *Arctos*, 3 (1962); F. J. Dölger, 'Beiträge zur Geschichte des Kreuzzeichens', *JbAC*, 8-9 (1965-66): 7-52; E. Kantorowicz, 'Constantinus Strator', *Mullus, Festschrift Theodor Klauser, JbAC*, supp. 1 (1964): 181-89; K. Hoffman, 'Die Entstehung des "Kaiserbildes im Kreuz", "Historia Augusta" und Labarum', *Akten VII. Int. Kong. Christl. Archäol., Trier, 1965*, Studi di antichità cristiana, 27 (Vatican City, 1969): 559-64; R. H. Storch, 'The Trophy and the Cross: Pagan and Christian Symbolism in the Fourth and Fifth Centuries', *Byzantion*, 40 (1970): 112 ff.; and Holum, 'Pulcheria'.

23. See the studies cited in n. 1, *supra*.

24. There are several third and fourth-century representations of David and Goliath. See for example, the sarcophagi in Marseille and Reims published by LeBlant, *Sarcophages chrétiens*, pp. 17, 35; and the fresco in the third-century baptistery in Dura Europos, in Kraeling, *Synagogue*, pp. 22, 41. For the S. Ambrogio doors see Goldschmidt, *Kirchentür*, passim. The amulets are discussed by Bonner, *Magical Amulets*, pp. 208-12; and Bagatti, 'Medaglie di Salomone'.

25. For Joshua at S. Maria Maggiore see J. Kollwitz, 'Der Josuazyklus von S. Maria Maggiore', *RQ*, 61 (1966): 105-110; and Brenk, *Mosaiken*, pp. 97 ff., esp. 122 ff.

26. Eusebius compared Constantine to Moses in his account of the Battle at the Milvian Bridge. See Eusebius, *Life of Const.* 1.38, in Migne, *PG*, 20:

Old Testament leaders had been elected by God. The emperor's election by the Christian God was expressed by Constantine's advisor, bishop Eusebius of Caesarea, by other Christian writers and in addresses of the bishops and church synods to emperors during the fourth and fifth centuries.[27] It is, nonetheless, difficult to substantiate a correlation because the concept of a Davidic Roman empire is not expounded in the imperial ideology of the fourth and early fifth centuries. The absence of this reference may be due to the extensive loss of antique documents, literature and art, but it is most likely an eloquent silence.[28] It is also possible that the patron of the Quedlinburg Itala may well have been one of the numerous aristocratic critics of imperial power. With these qualifications in mind, we cannot propose with any firm conviction that the Quedlinburg Itala's cycle was conceived as an artistic panegyric implying that Christian emperors were the new David and Solomon.

During the early fifth century, several church leaders taught that Christianity is 'verus Israel', the Old Testament is divine scripture promising the First and Second Coming of Christ, and that the Old Testament kings are forerunners of Christ's Imperium.[29] This conception of Christian history animates the S. Ambrogio doors. The crosses on its upper panels signify that David was anointed by Samuel as God's chosen 'Christ', the ancestor of the true Christ for whom the Old Testament prophecy will be fulfilled when the Christian kingdom is established.[30] The promises made to the Old Testament leaders in the S. Maria Maggiore nave mosaics are fulfilled during the reign of Christ as 'Rex Judaeorum' in typological association with the christological cycle on the triumphal arch.[31]

Even so, after all is said and done, there is no evidence of such typological thinking in the Quedlinburg Itala's surviving illustrations. It is difficult to interpret the gold crosses emblazoned on the shields in picture 1 as an attempt to present Saul as the forerunner of Christ when there is no other evidence which could corroborate this interpretation. The crosses may have only been added as a superficial effort to Christianize the appearance of this cycle.

For many reasons it seems unwarranted to interpret imperial imagery in the Quedlinburg Itala as a vehicle for expounding a religious or political message. The extant miniatures lack the indisputable signs of thoughtful exegesis by which to test such theories. Nor do they reflect the influence of rabbinic or patristic themes, as do so many other Early Christian narrative cycles.[32] The Itala's programmer, to the contrary, was unaware of or insensitive to the importance which church writers gave to the anointing of Old Testament kings.[33] After all, in picture 1 he could have requested the representation of Samuel anointing Saul (1 Sam. 10: 1); instead he asked the artist to illustrate the next verse.

Imperial imagery did not necessarily convey symbolic meaning when used outside its original context. Artists did not use diadem, cuirass and purple paludamentum solely for representing Jewish kings and heroes. These attributes were also worn by their enemies: by King Agag in the Quedlinburg Itala, by Herod at S. Maria Maggiore (if it has been correctly restored) and by Nebuchadnezzar and Pontius Pilate in several fourth-century sarcophagi.[34] If imperial imagery had been considered a vehicle for an ideological message, then the programmer surely would

951-53; discussed by E. Becker, 'Konstantin der Grosse der neue Moses', *Zeitschrift für Kirchengeschichte*, 31 (1910): 161-71. Ambrose exhorted the Roman emperors to follow the example of the Old Testament Kings, especially David. His texts are cited by Dvornik, *Early Christian*, pp. 644-45, 676-82, 736. Also see Athanasius, *Apol. to Constantine, emp.*, 5.20, *PG* 25: 601; Socrates, *Eccles. History*, 7.22, *PG* 67: 788; and Sozomenos, *Eccles. History, Preface*, *PG*, 62: 844-52.

27. See n. 20, *supra*, for discussions of the divine election of the emperor; and the address of Cyril of Constantinople at the calling of the Council of Ephesos in 'Collectio Vaticana, 25', ed. E. Schwartz, *Acta Conciliorum Oecumenicorum*, vol. 1, fasc. 1 (Berlin/Leipzig, 1927-30), p. 115.

28. During a discussion of these issues with Evanghelos Chrysos in November 1976, he suggested that the concept of Davidic kingship was not acceptable imperial ideology in the fourth and early fifth centuries. For the later development of the concept of the Byzantine Emperor as the new David, see Treitinger, *Reichsidee*, pp. 81, 130-35; Dvornik, *Early Christian*, passim; Spain, 'Heraclius and the David Plates'.

29. See Augustine, *de Civ. Dei*, 17. 2-10 *NPNF*, 2: 338-39; and in *de Consensu Evangelistarum*, Migne, *PL*, 34: 1044 and Prudentius, *Dittochaeon*, pict. 20.

30. This concept is discussed by F. Gerke, *Spätantike und frühes Christentum* (Baden-Baden, 1967), pp. 138-39.

31. These ideas are discussed by Brenk, *Mosaiken*, pp. 111, 122ff.; and in a somewhat different approach by S. Spain, 'The Promised Blessing'.

32. There are, for example, Jewish themes on the Lipsanothek of Brescia, discussed by Delbrück, *Lipsanothek*, pp. 91ff.; in the Via Latina catacomb frescoes, they are discussed by Kötzsche-Breitenbruch, *Via Latina*, 104ff. For the influence of Christian exegesis in the Sta. Sabina doors (ca. 420-30) see Grabar, *Christian Iconography*, pp. 142ff.; and at S. Maria Maggiore cf. Brenk, *Mosaiken*, pp. 108ff.; and Spain, 'Promised Blessing', 518ff.

33. The anointing of the Old Testament Kings is discussed by Augustine, *de Civ. Dei* 17, 10. In the *Dittochaeon*, picture 20, Prudentius includes 'oleum et cornu' as King David's attributes and compares him with Christ. Cf. n. 29, *supra*. Models for representing the anointing of Saul would have been available to a workshop in a major art center because the anointing of David by Samuel had already been represented in the Dura Europos Synagogue frescoes and on the S. Ambrogio doors which are discussed by E. Goodenough, *Jewish Symbols in the Greco-Roman Period*, 13 vols. (New York, 1964), 9: 187; 11: fig. 337; Goldschmidt, *Kirchentür*; and H. Buchthal, *Miniatures of the Paris Psalter* (London, 1938), pp. 18-21. Official iconography would not have supplied a model because Christian Roman emperors were not anointed in the fourth and fifth centuries. See 'Onction', *DACL*, 2128-29; and Frank E. Brightman, 'Byzantine Imperial Coronations', *Journal of Theological Studies*, 2 (1901): 378ff. for a discussion of Old Testament, Frankish and Byzantine coronations.

34. Pontius Pilate wears a cuirass on two late fourth-century sarcophagi: on Vatican #151 and on another in San Sabastiano in Rome, illustrated in Deichmann and Bovini, *Repertorium der Sarkophage*, nn. 58, 211. For Nebuchadnezzar see the arcosolium in the catacomb of SS. Marco and Marcellino in Rome in which the artist used the same topos for an emperor that appears in Italia picture 1. A date of ca. 340-350 has been suggested for this fresco by L. de Bruyne, 'Arcosolio'. The representation of Nebuchadnezzar in imperial costume is discussed by C. Carletti, *I tre giovanni ebrei di Babilonia nell'arte cristiana antica* (Brescia, 1975). For Herod at SMM see Brenk, *Mosaiken*, pp. 31-33. De Bruyne, 'Arcosolio', 195ff., suggested that Herod's costume shows his victories are temporary and will be cancelled by the triumphant events above. In sermons of Pope Leo the Great, Herod is a personification of the wicked Roman Empire in contrast to Christ who is the true king. See Leo the Great, *Sermons*, 31.1, 34.2, 36.3, 38.1; and G. A. Wellen, *Theotokos* (Utrecht, 1961), pp. 115-16. While the programmatic complexities in the mosaic cycle might permit us to apply de Bruyne's interpretation to the choice of a cuirass for Herod, it may not be possible to extend that method to the simpler cycle in the Quedlinburg Itala.

have requested this imagery in his instructions, however, he is silent on this matter, even in picture 1, the first miniature in which a king could have appeared.

When viewed within the broader perspective of the history of Old Testament manuscript illustration, it becomes far more likely that the Itala's cycle was conceived as no more than a simple narrative illustration of the biblical text. Moreover, during this early period it was probable that pagans as well as superficially educated Christian converts working side by side in the same workshop could have played a key role in devising the Itala's cycle.[35]

There are two logical and simple explanations for the Quedlinburg Itala workshop's exclusive and often uncritical use of imperial models. Luxury arts of the period frequently borrowed the aura and prestige of official court and military imagery. In our manuscript the slavish repetition of the kings' cuirass costume most likely occurred because the workshop had limited itself, as usual, to repeating only a small number of topoi.

OTHER DEVIATIONS FROM THE TEXT AND INSTRUCTIONS

When in their choice of models the artists proved to be more faithful to Roman pictorial traditions than to the instructions and the Kings text they were conforming to widely accepted working principles. The Vatican Vergil artists, for example, repeatedly included borrowed elements that made little sense in their new Vergilian context. Their sources have been traced back to triumphal, cartographic, bucolic, agricultural and mithraic themes which had been represented in a variety of contexts and media.[36]

We can see this principle at work in picture 6. The instructions define the circumstances under which Samuel's cloak would have been torn by requesting that Saul pursue the running prophet. The artist conflated several moments into one: the prophet flees; Saul tears his cloak; and he turns to Saul to pronounce God's rejection of the king and his house. For the last element the artist may have consulted the text because Samuel's prophecy is not mentioned in the instructions. It is far more likely, however, that the speaking gesture was solely motivated by a popular pictorial source. He faithfully modelled the picture on a conventional chase scheme in which the pursued turns to make a speaking gesture to express rejection of the pursuer.[37] The usual association of this chase formula with bacchic art would not have restricted its suitability in a Christian context because it had long since been widely used in other more neutral scenes. This topos was a logical choice because it contained all the important elements in a ready-made scene that offered the most complete solution to a particular need. It was a fairly common working principle, and, in fact, this precise cliché also proved useful to the Late Antique illustrators of Terence's *Andria* and *Eunuchus*[38] (fig. 48).

The dedication of the temple in picture 14 follows the instructions, but they do not give the artist sufficiently concrete information to guide him in representing the construction of the temple. He chose to depict six workers engaged in various building tasks within a large space defined by a fortified eight-sided city wall. Their lively activity, varied poses and viewpoints contrast remarkably with the monotonous repetition of rigid, flattened standing men in most of the miniatures. For this scene the artist had recourse to the wide range of construction scenes representing the building of ancient cities. Once again he ignored most of the instructions as well as the text because the two men sawing wood with the aid of a tall carpenter's horse are in contravention of 1 Kings 6: 7, which relates that neither hammer, ax or other iron tool was heard in the temple area during construction. The description of the bronze columns and basin which were to have been placed in the courtyard appears to have been ignored.

We find a comparable disregard of the text in Vatican Vergil picture 10 (fig. 21); its text also mentions many buildings under construction which the artist did not represent. Instead his composition is an awkward pastiche of workers, overseers, buildings and machinery that had been selected from a larger repertory of examples which are juxtaposed with frequent compositional incongruities.[39]

An intriguing departure from the instructions occurs in picture 7. They request three scenes: Saul entreating Samuel to pray with him; then Samuel and Saul praying together; and finally, Agag begging Samuel for clemency (1 Sam. 15: 33). The second scene is not in the text. Had the instructions and picture coincided with the text they would only have included the first and third events. In that case both scenes would have been nearly identical, given their common themes of entreaty and the artist's penchant for repeating the same limited number of topoi. The picture might then have resembled the drawing on p. 31.

Perhaps the artist asked the programmer to provide another scene so that his composition would have variety. If, however, the programmer considered scene two a description of verse 31 he certainly read the text carelessly. According to the text Samuel returned and stood behind Saul while the king prayed to the Lord. In the picture Samuel stands in front of the King and they pray together.

At any event, there was only room for two scenes. Had the

35. This general hypothesis is discussed by Weitzmann, 'Book Illustration', p. 125; and Bischoff, 'Scriptoria', pp. 485-86.

36. The Vergil manuscript's sources are discussed in detail by de Wit, pp. 159-74, 205-10, 225-36.

37. The use of this bacchic convention was noted by Boeckler, p. 152; and its correlation with other late Roman works was discussed in the preceding chapter.

38. The lost Late Antique illustrated *Comedies* of Terence are preserved in later copies. The best examples of this chase topos are in Paris, Bibl. nat., lat. 7899 ff. 9v, 18, 26, 40 and 60 illustrated by Jones and Morey, *Manuscripts of Terence*, figs. 42-45, 91, 125, 179, 261, 275.

39. This scene in the Vergil manuscript is discussed by de Wit, pp. 39-43.

artist labeled the first figure Saul, scenes one and two would have been represented in logical order and three would have been omitted. Perhaps that was his original intention, and 'Aga rex' was written in an absentminded moment, thus converting the picture into a reversal of scenes two and three.

It would be incorrect to conclude that the artists consistently deviated from their instructions, when, on the whole, they followed them to a considerable extent in their depiction of episodes, characters and activities. Unless they were told to include specific landscape details, they usually limited themselves to representing figures interacting in simple compositions in which each element was arranged in paratactic alignment from left to right in the order in which it was cited in the instructions. When each picture is compared to its related biblical verses and the precepts it becomes clear that in every case the illustrators either adhered to the instructions or deviated from them by following Roman pictorial conventions. At all events, they appear to have consistently ignored the text.

WORKSHOP PRACTICES: ORIGIN OF THE ILLUSTRATIONS

The instructions to the artists, which are the only examples surviving from that period, and the unusual preliminary sketches on f. 3 provide an extraordinary opportunity to analyze workshop practices. Several of the programmer's contributions to the cycle of illustrations have already been discussed in the first three chapters. On further analysis it will become more evident that he was not an artist, and that his principal focus was on the text. In consultation with the master artist he determined the relationship of the pictures to the text, the choice of stories and activities and the narrative unity of the illustrations. Through careful sifting of the evidence we will distinguish other important contributions made by the programmer and artists to the development of this cycle.

Paleographic and orthographic evidence indicates that the hand which wrote the instructions on f. 3 did not write them on ff. 1, 2 and 4. The sketches and cursive titles which substitute for full instructions on f. 3 should be attributed to the master artist who presumably would not have needed a detailed written guide. After consulting with the programmer about the subject matter of the folios which he intended to paint, he executed quick sketches to serve as memory prompters and wrote cursive titles citing the rank of the principal figures as a reminder to select costumes appropriate to their status.

The sketches resemble shorthand notes more than drawings and generally consist of a circle for each head and a few quickly drawn lines to indicate the placement of a specific number of people in each composition and their principal gesture or posture. The sketches are exceptional in their brevity and stand in marked contrast to a tradition of rather detailed preliminary drawings that have been found on rare occasion beneath manuscript illuminations, frescoes and mosaics.[40] As a rule, Antique and Medieval underdrawings include an entire outline for the figure, the shape and movement of arms and legs, fully delineated facial features, and the careful arrangement of drapery folds, as well as important accessories and attributes. They are true preparatory drawings and are far more elaborate than the few lines found under each picture on f. 3, which act only as mnemonic notations.

The existence of the instructions and sketches prompted Boeckler to suggest that the miniatures were first invented to illustrate this manuscript.[41] Although his theory has been accepted by several scholars,[42] others, most notably Byvanck and Weitzmann, have contended that the instructions and sketches only served to aid the artist in transposing illustrations found in an earlier manuscript of Kings to a new format in the Quedlinburg Itala.[43]

Until now no one has tested either theory by thoroughly analyzing the manuscript. Before presenting my own conclusions I will examine the evidence which supports Boeckler's theory and which argues against it, as well as the material which can be variously interpreted in favor of both opinions.

It has been demonstrated that the Itala artists consistently limited themselves to repeating a remarkably small number of pictorial conventions throughout the manuscript. Therefore we might expect that a group of artists given to such dependence on mechanical aids would have willingly copied a pre-existing cycle had one been made available to their workshop.

The instructions provide strong evidence which suggests that they were written to guide the artists in creating a new Kings cycle. In the first place they were written in far more detail than would have been necessary had they merely been meant to assist the artists in transposing a pre-existing program to a new format. They tell the artists which major and minor biblical characters to include, in what order to arrange them, and what

40. Underdrawings have been found in the Milan Iliad, cf. Bianchi Bandinelli, *Miniatures of the Iliad*, pp. 92-94; and in the Ashburnham Pentateuch, see the facsimile of Gebhardt, *Miniatures*, pp. 19-20; and comments of D. H. Wright in *Art Bull.*, 43 (1961): 251. Drawings in Byzantine manuscripts are discussed by T. Velmans, 'Le dessin à Byzance', *Monuments Piot*, 59 (1974): 138-70. John Chrysostom spoke of underdrawings made by panel painters; see the passages translated by C. Mango, *The Art of the Byzantine Empire*, 312-1453 (Englewood Cliffs, N.J., 1972), pp. 47-48. See Pliny's comments in *Nat. Hist.*, book 35, 36: 68 and 40: 145. Preparatory drawings have also been found under the following mosaics: the arch at S. Maria Maggiore in Rome; the apse of the Capella San Aquilino at San Lorenzo Maggiore, Milan; the dome of S. George, Salonica; and under the apse mosaics of S. Apollinare in Classe.

41. Boeckler, pp. 143-54.

42. Boeckler's theory was accepted by A. Goldschmidt, 'Bildende Kunst, die Quedlinburger Italafragmente', *Deutsche Literaturzeitung*, 26 (1932): 1224; A. Bömer, 'Die neue Prachtausgabe der Quedlinburger Italafragmente', *Zentralblatt für Bibliothekswesen*, 51 (1934): 345-56; Nordenfalk, *Painting*, p. 91; and by D. H. Wright in a review of this book, *Art Bull.*, 43 (1961): 251.

43. See Byvanck, 'Santa Maria Maggiore', p. 18; and K. Weitzmann, *Roll and Codex*, pp. 100, 248; he still maintained this opinion in 'Book Illustration', pp. 104-105. Several other scholars agree with them: Cechelli, *Mosaici*, p. 89; H. Gerstinger, 'Buchmalerei', *RAC*, 2: 749; and Morey, *Early Christian Art*, pp. 154-55.

actions they should perform, and even stipulate important landscape features and objects.

In picture 2, for example, the directions indicate that Saul and his attendant should stand near an oak tree, and they also name the offering that each pilgrim should carry. Had the artist been copying an earlier illustration of this scene, those details would have been apparent in the hypothetical prototype; in which case the instructions need only have read, 'Make three pilgrims greeting Saul'. Instead each offering, the attendant and the tree were specified to assist the artist in composing a new picture. This principle can be demonstrated for every miniature.

The elaborate directions under picture 14 would have been superfluous had a painted model been available. They meticulously describe every aspect of Solomon's posture and gestures as well as every part of the temple decorations, including how the brazen sea should rest on the hind quarters of twelve oxen gazing at the four cardinal points of the heavens. It is significant that the artist ignored most of these elaborate instructions. If they had described an actual picture he would have copied it quite easily. Instead the precepts must have been based on the text.

The repeated deviations of the pictures from the instructions indicate that the programmer was unaware of the pictorial conventions which the artists would actually use. Time and again his instructions fail to mention several of the most essential aspects of the illustrations, particularly their reliance on imperial and military conventions. His first opportunity to stipulate their use occurred in picture 1, but such advice is notably absent. If official imagery had been present in a hypothetical prototype the programmer surely would have mentioned those details; after all, he was, in point of fact, demonstrably precise in requiring so many other motifs. The most striking iconographic characteristics of this cycle would have concerned him because he played a principal role in its formation.

His silence stands in notable contrast to the evidence on f. 3. When the master artist wrote the cursive titles accompanying his sketches, he stressed each person's rank to remind himself when carrying out their task he deviated from the written precepts on ff. 1, 2 and 4, however, ignore imperial imagery. Instead they closely comply with the text because the programmer's training, role and purpose inclined him to focus on its contents.[44]

Evidently, the artists' frequent departures from the instructions and their stress on the official mode reflect the master artist's own contributions. The opportunity to participate in creating a new cycle would have provided him with this latitude. In directing the other artists to use particular pictorial formulas when carrying out their task he deviated from the written precepts because his training and approach to conceptualizing ideas led him to focus on the Roman pictorial repertories which were central to his professional practices.

Additional evidence of the master artist's freedom to make his own contributions to the cycle appear on f. 3, where, as I have already demonstrated, he referred to the same vocabulary of pictorial conventions which he assigned to the other artists. Although on ff. 1, 2 and 4 the artists frequently deviated from the instructions, on f. 3 the master's quick sketches and his illustrations closely correlate with each other. The one exception supports the theory of originality. In the preliminary drawing of Abner's assassination (11) he falls on his back (see drawing *a* on p. 34), but in the painted version, which is clearest on the bookcover impression, his torso remains upright as he falls to his knees (see drawing *b*). We may assume that the artist would have felt free to select whatever conventional pose suited him and then to change his mind.

On the other hand, some of the foregoing characteristics may be interpreted as evidence that the instructions describe existing illustrations which our artists copied. It is also possible that the programmer may have written detailed instructions because he wanted the artists to repeat the contents of a pictorial cycle which he had seen but which would not be available to the artists while they were illustrating their manuscript. Yet, even if the instructions faithfully described another cycle, the Quedlinburg Itala illustrations deviate from them so often that, as pictorial art, the miniatures would still constitute a new set of illustrations.

There is another very rare example of instructions which could cast doubt on Boeckler's theory of originality. In the Barbarus Scaligeri, Paris, Bibl. Nat., lat. 4884, a Latin translation of the 'Alexandrian World Chronicle', the Sacrifice of Isaac and the Exodus from Egypt were never painted.[45] In the blank spaces left for the miniatures, notes were written to indicate the identity and placement in the compositions of every important person, object and landscape element. Because the iconography and placement of these instructions correspond with similar scenes found in the 'Christian Topography' of Cosmas Indicopleustes and in Byzantine Octateuchs, we may conclude that the instructions in this seventh-century chronicle rely on actual illustrations in a Greek manuscript.[46]

Our knowledge of the underdrawings and notations in yet another seventh-century Latin manuscript, the Ashburnham Pentateuch, is limited to the fragmentary clues visible where the paint is thin or it has flaked off the parchment. In several instances the painters deviated from their precepts. Unlike the

44. Delbrück, *Lipsanothek*, pp. 87-88, thought that the scribe also deviated from the text when he wrote the instructions, but the changes which he discussed are only based on Degering's reconstruction of missing portions of the precepts. Delbrück was not certain whether the Itala cycle was original or copied from a prototype.

45. See the discussion of Wolska-Conus, *Cosmas*, 1: 146-47, 152-54, 156; and Bauer and Strzygowski, *Alexandrinische Weltchronik*, pp. 132, 136.

46. The opinion of Wolska-Conus, *Cosmas*, pp. 146-47, 152-56; and Mouriki-Charalambous, *Octateuch*, pp. 181-83.

Itala, which has a homogeneous iconographic character, the Ashburnham Pentateuch has an extraordinarily complex heritage which reassembles several identifiably established scenes.[47]

In contrast with these foregoing manuscripts it has not been possible to associate the Itala's cycle with any other extant Kings illustrations. It may very well be that we will never know whether other examples of the Itala's iconography were never made or have simply not survived. Be that as it may, we cannot fashion universally applicable rules concerning the use of instructions and sketches based on the limited evidence surviving in the Barbarus Scaligeri and Ashburnham Pentateuch.

Kurt Weitzmann noticed that each scene in the Itala would have fit comfortably into the spaces provided by a two column text.[48] His observation relates to his theory that the earliest manuscript illustrations were developed for insertion within the column format of papyrus rolls.[49] Within his theoretical scheme, the scenes in the hypothetical archetype of the Quedlinburg Itala would have been executed as simple line drawings without frames or backgrounds. He also observed that the landscapes are unrelated to the activities in the foreground, and concluded that the landscape elements and frames could have been added when the individual scenes were copied and grouped on one page.[50]

The contents of pictures 7 and 8 may also lead us to question their originality. The confusion in picture 7 may have been due to careless copying if the artist was trying to transfer three pre-existing pictures to the smaller space provided by the Itala's framework. According to other versions of the text related to picture 8, Samuel hewed Agag to pieces with a sword; yet, both the instructions and illustrations in our manuscript give him a spear.[51] Since the Quedlinburg Itala's text contains a number of anomalies, and that portion of the text is lost, we will never know whether it mentioned a spear. It is just as possible that the spear derives from the programmer's careless reading of the text as from a mistake in an earlier illustration. Consequently the spear in picture 8 cannot be claimed as solid evidence in support of either theory.

In the course of writing the precepts, the programmer apparently remained open to changing his mind since he erased and then rewrote them for miniatures 2, 4, 5, 6 and 14.[52] Perhaps he was selecting a limited number of scenes from a larger cycle and decided that other miniatures would make better contributions to the narrative program. An older manuscript using the popular column picture format could have offered him many more pictures from which he could have made his selection than our manuscript's scheme allows.[53]

As we have already noted, the Roman imperial imagery, which plays an integral role in the Itala's structure, also sets it apart from other Kings cycles. It is highly unlikely that those characteristics would have been present in any Kings manuscript illustrated prior to the second quarter of the fourth century. Therefore, as a matter of course, we cannot rule out the possibility that our manuscript copied a recently invented cycle.

It is also possible that the hypothetical model manuscript lacked imperial imagery; in which case the Quedlinburg Itala's artists might have agreed to modernize their model to conform to current interest in the official mode.[54] They may have been accustomed to working with it in the course of illustrating other deluxe manuscripts, and the supervising artist could have directed them to use his selections from a repertory of official conventions. This theory would, at the very least, signify that the workshop made significant changes and contributions to the cycle.

In the final analysis the weight and quality of the evidence supports Boeckler's theory that the programmer wrote the instructions to guide the artists in developing a new series of illustrations. First of all, the instructions were written in far more detail than was necessary if they had been meant to guide the artists in transferring an existing cycle to a new format. It is even more important to recognize that the repeated deviations of the pictures from the instructions demonstrate that the programmer was unaware of the pictorial conventions which the artists would use. This is a particularly critical factor when we consider the stress on imperial imagery. Although it was used persistently and it functioned as a substantive aspect of the iconography, the pro-

47. See the Ashburnham Pentateuch, Paris, Bibl. nat., n. acq. lat. 2334 in the facsimile of Gebhardt, *Miniatures*. Scenes in this manuscript have been compared to Jewish and Christian art from late Antiquity to the end of the Middle Ages by J. Gutmann, 'The Jewish Origin of the Ashburnham Pentateuch Miniatures', *Jewish Quarterly Review*, 44 (1953): 55ff.; and by Hempel, 'Anfänge AT-illus.', 124-29. Wright, *Art Bull.*, 43 (1961): 251, believes that the drawings in the Paris codex helped the artist to make numerous modifications in adapting an established iconography to a complicated new format, but that the scribe wrote the Itala's instructions to guide the artist who was expected to invent a cycle out of stock figures and episodes.

48. Weitzmann, 'Book Illustration', p. 104.

49. A theory developed in Weitzmann's *Roll and Codex* and his other publications.

50. Weitzmann, 'Book Illustration', p. 104.

51. Delbrück, *Lipsanothek*, pp. 87-88, suggested that such deviations on the part of the scribe and artist signify careless reading on their part. He thought that the text and instructions for picture 8 agree, which they do not, and he proposed that the artist's deviation could be attributed to his use of a common pictorial motif.

52. Degering, p. 87, noted that the first set of instructions had been erased. He suggested that the artist asked for a second set which would be easier to illustrate; yet we know that the artist often felt free to deviate from those precepts.

53. Several other fifth and sixth-century manuscripts were illustrated with hundreds of miniatures. De Wit, pp. 195-205, estimated that the Vatican Vergil had approximately 250 illustrations and 400 folios. According to Bianchi Bandinelli, *Miniatures of the Iliad*, pp. 157-62, the Ilias Ambrosiana had between 180 and 200 miniatures or one scene for every 50 to 75 verses. The Cotton Genesis and Vienna Genesis also had hundreds of miniatures as did the prototype of the Vatican Kings, Vat. gr. 333; cf. note 11 *supra*. Several of their pictures were created with conflations from larger cycles according to Weitzmann, *Roll and Codex*, pp. 24ff., 179ff., 190ff.

54. For the range of possibilities in other manuscript copies from conservative and faithful reproduction to extensive change see, for example, the later copies of the Calendar of 354 in Stern, *Calendrier de 354*, passim, and copies of the Utrecht Psalter studied in the bibliography compiled by S. Dufrenne, *Les Illustrations du Psautier d'Utrecht, sources et apports Carolingiens* (Paris, 1978), pp. 13-19.

grammer never mentioned it, even though he was excessively specific in all other details. Whereas his role and training focused his attention on the text, the master artist had freedom to invent illustrations using his own choice of pictorial conventions. This theory is verified by the close correlation of his mnemonic sketches and titles with his final illustrations on f. 3.

Whether viewed from the internal evidence or seen within a broader historical context the arguments favoring the invention of this cycle are very persuasive. The Quedlinburg Itala was illustrated in a cultural climate which encouraged expansion beyond the limited themes of earlier Christian imagery. After the Peace of the Church and the adoption of Christianity as a state religion, a large number of aristocratic converts accustomed to highly evolved pictorial art began to patronize the development of more complex and extensive religious art. Certain principal themes, such as the Childhood and Passion of Christ and the heroic story of David, were depicted in more than one cycle. By the same token, the existence of other pictorial cycles based on the four books of Kings would not, and in fact did not, discourage the creation of new series of illustrations for this popular text. Recent studies of the S. Maria Maggiore mosaics and the Vatican Vergil miniatures indicate that, to a considerable extent, their cycles were also ad hoc inventions.[55] Moreover, Gregory of Tours relates that a fifth-century bishop's wife composed the program which decorated the walls of her husband's church by selecting episodes from a text.[56]

Surely fifth-century Rome, which witnessed the extensive decoration of its basilicas with Old and New Testament themes, would have provided a hospitable milieu for the development of a new Kings cycle, particularly during a period when richly illustrated codices played a significant role in the production of luxury arts. In the following chapter we will establish the period and provenance of our manuscript.

55. Brenk, *Mosaiken*, pp. 178-80, proposes that much of the mosaic cycle is an ad hoc invention; an opinion shared by Kitzinger, 'Role of Miniature Painting', pp. 122ff. De Wit's theory, pp. 16, 169-74, 205f., that the Vatican Vergil artists created a pastiche of non-Vergilian elements is supported by Buchthal's review of his book in *Art Bull.*, 45 (1963): 372-75.

56. This passage in Gregory of Tours's *History of the Franks* is translated in Davis-Weyer, *Early Medieval Painting*, pp. 58-59.

CHAPTER FIVE

Date and Provenance

There is general agreement that the Quedlinburg Itala was made in Italy, and most likely in Rome, however, a variety of dates ranging from the 350's to the early fifth century have been suggested for this manuscript.[1] Because it lacks concrete internal evidence which would indicate its date, the issue has always revolved around its kinship with the S. Maria Maggiore nave mosaics. When Boeckler placed the Itala between 350 and 380, he based his decision as much on Degering's attribution of the text script to Furius Dionisius Filocalus as on the current, although, even then, controversial assignment of the nave mosaics to the patronage of Pope Liberius (352-66).[2] With the rejection of Degering's attribution and the widely accepted redating of the nave mosaics to the papacy of Sixtus III (432-440), it has become necessary to reconsider the date of the Quedlinburg Itala.[3]

Any decision is inevitably linked with the origin of the Vatican Vergil. Both manuscripts may have been produced in the same workshop, or, at the very least, they were products of the same generation and art center. By comparing the style of the Vergil manuscript to the nave mosaics and to a number of late fourth/fifth century ivories and sarcophagi, de Wit concluded that it was written and illustrated in Rome during the 420's.[4] Although his conclusions have been widely accepted, they should be viewed with some caution. He assigned to that decade several portraits and ivories, which are central to his argument even though the evidence does not always permit him to arrive at those dates.[5]

Several attempts have been made to establish a relative chronology for the manuscripts and mosaics based on their relationship to classical traditions, but for many reasons these efforts have only led to equivocal conclusions.[6] In most cases they have rested on comparisons made with the work of the least classicizing artists.[7] This issue has been further complicated by the considerable stylistic variations among mosaicists and the succession of restorations which have altered the original appearance of many panels.[8]

Byvanck and Bianchi Bandinelli shared the opinion that the Itala was made in the 350's, several generations earlier than the Vergil.[9] As they saw it, the Itala was fresher in its iconographic schemes, more naturalistic and less rigid in its figure style, less schematic in its treatment of space, and, on the whole, much closer in style, spirit, and therefore in time to earlier classical painting traditions.[10] Quite the contrary is true. The first and third group of Vergil miniatures (1-9, 26-50) are far more classical in their figure style and spatial compositions (figs.

1. The following dates have been suggested; ca. 350's by Byvanck, 'Antike Buchmalerei, I', 243-51, and Bianchi Bandinelli, *Miniatures of the Iliad*, p. 141; ca. 370's by Boeckler, pp. 181-93, 200; ca. 400 by de Wit, pp. 156-57 and Nordenfalk, *Painting*, p. 93; early fifth century by Bischoff, see note 17 in Chapter One; and the first half of the fifth century by Lowe, see note 24 in Chapter One.

2. See Boeckler, pp. 181-93.

3. For a review of the literature discussing the date of S. Maria Maggiore's mosaics see, Brenk, *Mosaiken*, pp. 1ff.

4. See de Wit's reasons on pp. 151-55.

5. I question several of his observations. The head of Aeneas in min. 24 is a conventional type, not a portrait as he suggested, pp. 84, 151ff. A spear held in the left hand which is covered by a cloak already occurs in the fourth century, whereas he said, p. 154, that it first occurs in the next century. I do not think that the evidence permits us to place all of his comparative ivories precisely in the mid-420's as he has suggested, pp. 153-55; cf. the diptychs of the Lampadarii in Liverpool and of the patrician in Novara in Delbrück, *Consulardiptychen*, nn. 56 and 64.

6. Byvanck, 'Antike Buchmalerei, I', 243-51, and Bianchi Bandinelli, *Miniatures of the Iliad*, p. 141, proposed to arrange the three cycles as Quedlinburg Itala (ca. 350's), Vergil (ca. 420's), Mosaics (ca. 430's); de Wit, pp. 156-57, and Nordenfalk, *Painting*, p. 93, kept them in the same order, but placed the Itala close to ca. 400. Boeckler, pp. 181-93, suggested a contrary order: mosaics (ca. 360's), Quedlinburg Itala (ca. 370's), and Vergil (ca. 390's). Brenk places both manuscripts ca. 400 and the mosaics in the 430's.

7. For example, see the suggestions of Byvanck, *loc. cit.*, pp. 243-51; and Bianchi Bandinelli, *loc. cit.*, p. 141.

8. See the suggestions in n. 6, *supra*. Restorations of the mosaics are described by Brenk, *Mosaiken*, pp. 5, 9ff., 53ff.

9. Cf. n. 7, *supra*.

10. Cf. n. 7, *supra*.

27-29).[11] Both scholars made the mistake of only comparing the Itala with the miniatures painted by the second Vergil artist (10-25), whose work is decidedly anticlassical[12] (figs. 21-26). Since two such antithetical styles can coexist in the same manuscript, basing a comparative chronology on degrees of classicism becomes highly unreliable, particularly when we have conclusively established that all of the artists were using the same modes and formal motifs.

The failure of their method is confirmed by its contradictory conclusions. At one time or another scholars have recommended placing each work in almost every conceivable chronological relationship with the other two.[13] This is largely because each of their artists steered his own wavering course between varying degrees of classicism and Late Antique schematism, flatness and linearity. These fluctuations so thoroughly characterize Late Antique art that attempts to establish a relative chronology based on degrees of classicism are usually untenable.[14] Even in the most philhellenic art of the fourth and fifth centuries the influence of these traditions varies considerably depending on the artist's training, skill and personal style, the traditions of his workshop and his selection of modes and models.

By placing both manuscripts prior to 390, as has been suggested for each of them, they become separated from the mosaics by at least forty years.[15] That distance would imply that the mosaics were deliberately retrospective or that they repeated a style that had remained influential for many decades. The solution to this puzzle is problematic because so many major pieces are missing. There are, nonetheless, many reasons to believe that both manuscripts were produced within the same generation and city as the mosaics.

Several methods may be brought to bear on this question, and all possible evidence which is relevant to this issue will be collected, culled and examined. The style of the miniatures, the official insignia and iconography as well as the paleography, Old Latin text and codicology each offer significant clues. Even works of art in other media can be called into service in an attempt to reconstruct the Quedlinburg Itala's artistic milieu.

By seeking the closest parallels to this manuscript's figure and drapery style we can acquire insight into its date. The proportions of its figures presuppose the reintroduction during the last thirty years of the fourth century of taller and more slender bodies with longer torsos and legs and smaller heads than had previously occurred in that century. These longer proportions continued to be used by artists working in eastern and western centers during the first half of the fifth century. Examples occur in every medium: in the mosaics in S. Giovanni in Fonte, Naples; S. Lorenzo Maggiore, Milan; Galla Placidia and the Orthodox Baptistery in Ravenna; S. Pudenziana and S. Maria Maggiore, Rome; on the Gorgonius sarcophagus and its relatives; on the reliefs of the Theodosianic obelisk base and the 'Stilicho' diptych in Monza (figs. 16, 20, 39, 40, 44, 46).

It is important to recognize that the Itala's figures stand in marked contrast to the figural style favored by classicizing Roman artists during the third quarter of the fourth century. That style, as represented by the Junius Bassus and Two Brothers sarcophagi and the Calendar of 354, featured stunted torsos above very long legs, large hulking shoulders, fleshy protuberances for muscles, large hands and enormous heads (figs. 47, 58). Curiously, both Byvanck and Bianchi Bandinelli have mistakenly compared the Itala to these examples of the 'bello stile'.[16] It is significant that Boeckler avoided comparing the Itala to the art of that generation even though he had first placed our manuscript within that period and he had recognized its classicizing tendency.

Several distinctive poses and gestures find their closest parallels in the art of the late fourth/fifth century. As de Wit has noted, in the Itala and Vergil figures place their weight on their front leg and allow the rear leg to drag behind as the upper body arches slightly backward[17] (fig. 21, 22). This pose does not appear prior to the last third of the fourth century; it was used for Saul and Samuel (2, 4, 7), and in several fifth-century mosaics such as the apostles in the Naples and Ravenna baptisteries and for Joshua and others at S. Maria Maggiore (fig. 20). These figures have in common a remarkably light footed, springy stance (which tends to look like a walking movement) as well as strongly rhythmic, undulating curves moving down the back silhouette[18] (figs. 18, 20). The gesturing arm is usually lengthened and thrust forward at the midsection, and the right hand is greatly enlarged when making an oratorical gesture.

The multiplicity of fine, curving drapery folds flowing across the gracefully moving figure of Samuel (4, 7) in response to his movements indicate that the particular model came from the elegant, softly curving and refined style of the last third of the fourth century, which is so well represented by the statuette of Aelia Flacilla in Paris, the seated Christ in Rome and the reliefs on Theodosius' obelisk base and the Monza diptych[19] (figs. 40, 44). Surely, the immediate forerunner of Samuel would not have been found prior to 370 when negative fold lines and broken drapery sections with irregular outlines prevailed (fig. 58). Samuel's clothing does not, however, represent the most typical style in this manuscript.

11. This was also recognized by Wright, *Art Bull.* (1961): 249; see de Wit, pp. 178ff., for a description of the style of the Vergil miniatures.

12. Cf. n. 7, *supra*.

13. Cf. n. 6, *supra*.

14. Boeckler, p. 165, also advised that this method is unreliable. For an interesting general discussion of these issues see Brendel, *Prolegomena*, passim.

15. See n. 6, *supra*, especially the dates suggested by Byvanck and Bianchi Bandinelli, which would place our manuscript 80 years earlier than the mosaics.

16. Note the comparisons made by Byvanck, *loc. cit.*; Bianchi Bandinelli, *loc. cit.*; and Stern, *Calendrier de 354*, p. 343, n. 1.

17. De Wit, pp. 151-57.

18. This type of figure has also been discussed by Brenk, *Mosaiken*, pp. 141-42, 178, figs. 38.1-38.4.

19. The appearance of this drapery style in Lateran sarcophagus 174 may, to some extent, be due to recarving by a restorer.

All of the other drapery is flat, stiff, angular and simplified to just a few major folds which coincide with the stiff, rectilinear bodies. This reflects important changes from the soft, smooth transitions and fluid gentle curves of the first phase of Theodosianic art to the stiff angularity and harder, sharper, linear effects that became progressively dominant beginning with the turn of the fifth century. Analogous transformations occur in eastern and western artistic centers in a variety of media.[20] In Rome, as well as in other Italian cities, the curvilinear style begins to be supplanted by the hard, angular linearity seen in many S. Maria Maggiore mosaic panels and in the ivory diptych of a patrician in Novara (ca. second quarter 5th cent.) (fig. 20, 43).

The small, smoothly curving oval faces with pointed chins used for all of the Itala figures contrast sharply with the bulbous and square-jawed heads that dominated throughout much of the fourth century (compare figs. 53, 54, 56, 58). Here as well, the shape of the heads in the Itala presupposes the development of the long, smooth, oval faces first used in eastern and western centers in the late fourth century; they appear, for example, on the Missorium of Theodosius, Arcadius's portrait and the Monza diptych[21] (figs. 39, 44).

In our manuscript most of the men wear their hair cut short, with a fringe across the forehead and a wisp curving forward at the sidelocks. This style, so commonly seen in Roman portraits since Augustus, reappeared generation after generation, but even modest variations in its overall silhouette correlate with the other stylistic changes which have been described. The hairline begins just above the ears, curves far out at the temples and then continues smoothly to the top of the head where it ends in a shallow, depressed arc. The forehead is high and wide below the fairly straight fringe of hair (figs. 53, 54, 56). Close comparisons to the shape of this hairdo can be found in so many works of art produced in a variety of media during the first half of the fifth century, that we can recognize it as a popular contemporary convention. It appears, for example, in the diptych of Probianus, somewhat later in the diptychs of Consul Felix (428 A.D.) and the patrician in Novara, in the first and third group of miniatures in the Vatican Vergil, in several S. Maria Maggiore panels (see Jacob meeting Esau), and on a portrait from Ephesos now in Munich[22] (figs. 28, 43, 55, 57).

Several insignia of official status confirm the range of dates suggested by the figural style. Abner (9, 11) wears the cruciform gold fibula with an exaggerated long staff which was reserved for high ranking dignitaries from the fourth through sixth centuries. Extant examples have been dated as early as the reign of Constantine.[23] The oldest artistic representations of this fibula with its elongated staff reaching almost up to the wearer's ear first begin to appear in official art in the late fourth century. Excellent comparisons can be made with the fibulas on the Missorium and obelisk base of Theodosius, and on the fifth-century diptychs of Probianus and the patricians in Novara and Monza (figs. 39, 40, 43, 44). The embroidered shoulder patch and the large square tablion sewn across the breast of the chlamys worn by a courtier in picture 14 also appear as official insignia on the same ivories.[24] To the best of my knowledge, the tablion does not occur in this position prior to the fifth century.[25]

The first extant example in official art comparable to the large gold crosses emblazoned on the soldier's shields in picture 1 was once found on the early fifth-century base of Arcadius's column in Constantinople, provided the drawings published by Freshfield can be trusted. There is no solid historical evidence of crosses placed on shields or used as military standards in the fourth century, and prior to 420 the cross rarely appeared on coins.[26] Here the Itala artist followed recently established imperial models.

Byvanck argued that the plain band diadem in the Itala provided incontrovertible proof that the manuscript cannot be dated later than the 350's, when, in his opinion, the flat band was replaced by the jeweled diadem.[27] Actually, this change had already occurred late in Constantine's reign.[28] A survey of imperial portraits and coins indicates that representations of Roman emperors and caesars wearing the band diadem are very rare.[29] This simple fillet had been worn, however, by Hellenistic kings and ancient heroes. It is important to recognize that it continued to be depicted on several other late fourth and fifth-

20. These stylistic changes have been discussed by Kollwitz, *Oström. Plastik*, passim; E. Kitzinger, 'A Marble Relief of the Theodosian Period', *DOP*, 14 (1960): 20-26; G. Matthiae, *La pittura romana del medioevo* (Rome, 1965), 1: 50, in a comparison of the S. Pudenziana and S. Maria Maggiore mosaics; by H. P. L'Orange, *Studien zur Geschichte des spätantiken Porträts* (Leipzig, 1933), pp. 78-80; and L'Orange, 'Der subtile Stil'.

21. This type of head has been discussed by L'Orange, 'Subtile Stil', 68-75.

22. I do not accept Byvanck's attempt, *loc. cit.*, p. 246, to limit a comparison of the kings' heads to portraits of Constans I and Constantine II. The kings' hairdo is so generalized and badly damaged in every example in the Itala that it can only be compared in the most general way to hairstyles worn by Roman emperors between ca. 325 and the early fifth century.

23. See the examples published by Heurgon, 'Tresor de Ténès', 45-51; and Noll, 'Kaiserfibel von 316', 221-44. The fibula as an insignia of rank is also discussed by A. Riegl, *Die spätrömische Kunst-Industrie nach den Funden in Österreich-Ungarn* (Vienna, 1901), pp. 267-68.

24. Late Roman clothing and insignia of rank are discussed by Alföldi, 'Insignien', passim; and Delbrück, *Consulardiptychen*, pp. 244-47.

25. This opinion is also shared by Rinaldi, 'Costume romano', 224.

26. For a discussion of Christian symbols on Roman coins see n. 22 in chapter 4. See the 'Long-Cross Solidi' on coins minted in Constantinople between 420-22. The labarum appears on several 4th cent. coins; and the cross occasionally replaced Victory on the imperial globus represented on the coins of Valentinian II (383-88). A fuller discussion of these issues is presented by Holum, 'Pulcheria', 153ff.

27. Byvanck, 'Antike Buchmalerei, I', p. 250.

28. The change in the emperor's diadem is discussed by Delbrück, *Kaiserporträts*, pp. 56-65, and in 'Kaiserornat', 1ff.; Alföldi, 'Insignien', 263-68; and M. R. Alföldi, *Die Constantinische Goldprägung* (Bonn, 1963), pp. 135-44, where she challenges some of Delbrück's ideas on the development of the diadem.

29. For examples of the flat band diadem worn by Constantine the Great, Crispus and Delmatius on coin portraits see Delbrück, *Kaiserporträts*, p. 58, pl. 2, n. 21; p. 78, pl. 5, n. 7; and p. 82, pl. 8. The plain band diadem is also worn by Nebuchadnezzar on the lid of the S. Ambrogio sarcophagus illustrated in Grabar, *Christian Iconography*, fig. 24; by Joshua in the mosaics; and by Aeneas in the Vergil miniatures.

century works of art including the S. Maria Maggiore mosaics and the Vergil miniatures (figs. 16, 21, 22).

The old-fashioned round fibula worn by the Itala kings does not provide a reliable gauge for dating our manuscript even though this simple design was replaced during Constantine's reign by a more elaborate imperial fibula with three pendelia. Nevertheless, the simpler form continued to be represented long afterward in unofficial art by those who failed to modernize their sources.[30]

Because outdated motifs typically lived on in art for many generations after they were no longer used in daily life, their appearance here can only indicate the origin and age of some of the Itala's models. They correlate with several other antiquarian forms and ceremonies which have already been identified in our miniatures as well as in other works of art in this period.

An Old Testament Kings cycle based on traditional triumphal iconography would have been unthinkable before the establishment of Christianity as a state religion, and such imagery does not appear to have affected Old Testament programs until the last decades of the fourth century. Imperial imagery formed an integral part of the Itala's cycle, and it proved to be a major influence on the S. Maria Maggiore mosaic program, thus serving to set both of them apart from earlier and later representations of the same themes.[31] As the last two chapters have demonstrated, during this period official art also provided an important source of motifs for many other ateliers producing luxury arts.

The paleography has corroborated the art historical evidence. The best comparisons with the style of the script in the text, instructions and labels can be made with manuscripts produced in Italy between the mid-fourth and fifth centuries. An even narrower range of dates has been provided by the letter forms in the artists' labels, which, up to this time, have not been found in a datable manuscript prior to the 440's, however, this evidence must be used with circumspection. Although the letters in question tend to be associated with manuscripts written in the latter half of that century, considerable latitude should be used in paleographical dating during this period.

The production of a Vetus Latina version of the four books of Kings is compatible with a fifth-century date because these early Latin texts continued to be copied throughout the century despite the availability of Jerome's new translation.[32] Even Jerome's caustic criticism of large and lavishly decorated Christian codices did not halt the production of the type of deluxe manuscript exemplified by the Quedlinburg Itala.[33]

When all of the evidence is assembled a clearer picture of the date of this codex emerges. Our manuscript was written and illustrated by a Roman workshop no earlier than the first third of the fifth century, and very likely during the 420's or 430's. A date earlier than ca. 400 is unacceptable, and the later range of dates seem probable for a number of reasons. This conclusion is based on: the paleography of the gold labels, the presence of crosses on the shields in picture 1, the tablion on the courtier's mantle (14), the angularity of the figure and drapery style, the shape of the hairdoes, and the illustrations' close relationship, on so many artistic levels, with the S. Maria Maggiore mosaics.

THE MILIEU

An investigation of the pictorial sources of our manuscript indicated that numerous comparisons with its forms and motifs can be found in works of art produced in Italy and in other late Roman artistic and political centers in the eastern empire. Repeatedly, however, the closest correlations were found in Italian art, especially in works made in the city of Rome. The same conclusions have been drawn by scholars studying the sources of the Vergil and mosaics.[34] The striking similarities between these three cycles in so many details have made it evident that the manuscripts were also made in Rome, and that they were all products of the same generation.

These three workshops merged classicizing quotations with Roman imperial conventions. Although many of their antiquarian motifs had been developed originally in the first and second centuries, they were repeated as standard formal elements during the intervening centuries and hence were still available to illustrate Christian, pagan and secular art. Furthermore, studies of the Vergil miniatures and mosaics have indicated that, to a considerable extent, they were also invented by their artists, who were expected to devise new pictures from stock formulas on the basis of verbal rather than written instructions.[35] Apparently, fifth-century Rome could still provide its artists with a repertory

30. Round gem encircled fibulae are worn by Constantine the Great and his descendants with and without three pendants. For the fibula without pendelia see Delbrück, *Kaiserporträts*, pls. 1.6, 3.33, 4.47, 7.4 and 9.1. Magnentius was the last emperor to wear his fibula either with or without pendants; cf. Ibid., pl. 12.4, 12.5. The prince/king on the arch mosaic at S. Maria Maggiore (fig. 46) wears a fibula with two pendelia. The artist must have forgotten to include the third one, unless this section of the mosaic was incorrectly restored. For a discussion of the imperial fibula see Alföldi, 'Insignien', 183. According to Constantine Porphyrogenitus, *De cerimoniis*, 1. 43-45, the investiture ceremony of a new Augustus included pinning on his special fibula. This scene is represented on a sardonyx in the Leningrad Hermitage Museum which has been dated to 423 A.D. by Delbrück, *Kaiserporträts*, fig. 73, pp. 211-14.

31. For a discussion of this observation in relation to triumphal imagery used at S. Maria Maggiore see the variety of viewpoints expressed by Brenk, *Mosaiken*, esp. pp. 178-81; Spain, 'Promised Blessing', 518ff.; and Kitzinger, 'Role of Miniature Painting', pp. 130ff.

32. These issues have been discussed in chapter 1, cf. nn. 13-14 for a bibliography.

33. Jerome's comment and examples of deluxe fifth-century codices are noted in chap. 3, n. 24.

34. See the comments by de Wit, pp. 205-210; and further comments on this observation offered by Buchthal in *Art Bull.* (1963): 372-75; and in 'Note on the Vatican Vergil', 167-71. The sources of the Vergil miniatures have been closely linked with the art of metropolitan Rome by T. B. Stevenson, *The Miniatures of the Vatican Vergil* (Ph.D. diss.: New York Univ., 1970), esp. pp. 123-28. The sources used by the S. Maria Maggiore artists have been methodically researched by Brenk, *Mosaiken*; see his conclusions, on pp. 178-81, concerning the invention of much of the cycle. His opinion is shared by Kitzinger, 'Role of Miniature Painting', pp. 126ff.; and *Byzantine Art in the Making*, pp. 66-75.

35. See the comments of de Wit, Buchthal, Stevenson, Brenk and Kitzinger in n. 34.

of models and an artistic milieu which encouraged the development of new pictorial cycles.

Within a few years after the sack of the city in 410, a series of popes began to decorate their basilicas with extensive Old and New Testament programs. Rome was not the only important center of artistic activity. For generations emperors and empresses, bishops and aristocrats had been building and decorating churches, baptisteries and monumental tombs in many Italian cities. Sarcophagi, silver, and ivories also attest to the high level and quality of artistic production in Rome, Milan and Ravenna.

The Quedlinburg Itala scarcely qualifies as the 'Bible of the Poor' which served as Paulinus of Nola's justification of religious art.[36] On the contrary, the richness of this codex indicates that it was made either for the personal library of a wealthy patron or as a gift. Considering the lavish donations to churches of wall paintings and of gold, silver and ivory appointments recorded in the literature of this period, a church library might have been the intended recipient of the Quedlinburg Itala.[37]

The persistent echo of late fourth and fifth-century formal and iconographic motifs in Medieval manuscripts indicates that the Quedlinburg Itala is the rare survivor of an active period of manuscript illumination. As Weitzmann and Nordenfalk have so amply demonstrated, the change from roll to codex stimulated the development of ideas for decorating this new format.[38] We must also recognize that the Itala artists devised new illustrations for the popular Kings text during a period of iconographic invention. The miniatures were created in a transitional period; whereas their style and imagery are profoundly rooted in the traditions of ancient Roman art, our codex also belonged to a new age when manuscript illumination was rapidly becoming a major artistic form. It would maintain that status for more than a millennium.

36. Paulinus of Nola, *Carmina* 27: 512-95 translated in Davis-Weyer, *Early Medieval Art*, pp. 18-19.

37. Lavish donations to churches in the fourth and fifth centuries are cited by L. Duchesne, ed., *Le Liber Pontificalis*, 2nd ed., 3 vols. (Paris, 1886), 1: 170-268; and in Davis-Weyer, *Early Medieval Art*, pp. 11, 13, 18-40, 57-59.

38. See the discussion of Weitzmann, 'Book Illustration', pp. 96-125; and C. Nordenfalk, 'The Beginning of Book Decoration', *Beiträge für G. Swarzenski* (1951), pp. 1-20.

Bibliographic Abbreviations of frequently cited Sources

PERIODICALS AND DICTIONARIES

AJA	*American Journal of Archaeology.*
ANRW	*Aufstieg und Niedergang der römischen Welt.*
Archäol. Anz.	*Archäologischer Anzeiger.*
Art Bull.	*Art Bulletin.*
Atti d. Pont. Acc. Rom. d. Arch., Memorie	*Atti della Pontificia Accademia Romana di Archeologia, Memorie.*
Atti d. Pont. Acc. Rom. d. Arch., Rendiconti	*Atti della Pontificia Accademia Romana di Archeologia, Rendiconti.*
Cah. Arch.	*Cahiers Archéologiques.*
Corsi di cultura	*Corso di cultura sull'arte Ravennate e bizantina.*
CRAI	*Académie des Inscriptions et Belles Lettres, Comptes Rendus.*
DACL	Cabrol F. and H. Leclerq, *Dictionnaire d'archéologie chrétienne et de liturgie*, 15 vols. in 30 (Paris, 1924-53).
DOP	*Dumbarton Oaks Papers.*
JbAC	*Jahrbuch für Antike und Christentum.*
JDAI	*Jahrbuch des deutschen archäologischen Instituts.*
JRS	*Journal of Roman Studies.*
Mem. Amer. Acad. Rome	*Memoirs of the American Academy in Rome.*
Met. Mus. J.	*Metropolitan Museum Journal.*
Mon. Piot	*Monuments et mémoires publiées par l'Academie des Inscriptions et Belles-Lettres. Fondation Eugène Piot.*
RAC	*Reallexikon für Antike und Christentum.*
RINASA	*Rivista dell'Instituto Nazionale d'Archeologia e Storia dell'Arte.*
Riv. Archeol. Crist.	*Rivista di archeologia cristiana.*
Röm. Mitt.	*Mitteilungen des deutschen archäologischen Instituts, Röm. Abteilung.*
RQ	*Römische Quartalschrift.*

ARTICLES AND BOOKS

Alföldi, 'Mon. Zeremoniell'
A. Alföldi, 'Die Ausgestaltung des monarchischen Zeremoniells am römischen Kaiserhofe', *Röm. Mitt.* 44 (1934): 103 ff.; republished in *Die monarchische Repräsentation im römischen Kaiserreiche*, Darmstadt, 1970.

Alföldi, 'Insignien'
A. Alföldi, 'Insignien und Tracht der römischen Kaiser', *Röm. Mitt.* 50 (1935): 1-171; republished in *Die monarchische Repräsentation im römischen Kaiserreiche*, Darmstadt, 1970.

Bagatti, 'Medaglie di Salomone'
B. Bagatti, 'Altre Medaglie di Salomone Cavaliere e loro origine', *Riv. Archeol. Crist.* 47 (1971): 331-42.

Bauer and Strzygowski, *Alexandrinische Weltchronik*
A. Bauer and J. Strzygowski, *Eine Alexandrinische Weltchronik*, Denkschriften d. Akad. d. Wiss., Wien, Phil.-Hist. Kl., vol. 51, pt. 2, Vienna, 1905.

Becatti, *Colonna*
G. Becatti, *La colonna coclide istoriata*, Rome, 1960.

Berger, *Notitia Dignitatum*
P. Berger, *The Notitia Dignitatum*, Ph.D. diss., New York Univ., 1974.

Bianchi Bandinelli, *Miniatures of the Iliad*
R. Bianchi Bandinelli, *Hellenistic Byzantine Miniatures of the Iliad (Ilias Ambrosiana)*, Olten, 1955.

Bischoff, 'Scriptoria'
B. Bischoff, 'Scriptoria e manoscritti mediatori di civiltà dal sesto secolo alla riforma di Carlo Magno', *Centri e vie di irradiazione della civiltà nell'alto medioevo*, Settimane di studi sull'alto medioevo, vol. 11, Spoleto, 1964; republished in *Mittelalterliche Studien*, vol. 2, Stuttgart, 1967.

Boeckler
Cf. Degering and Boeckler.

Bonner, *Magical Amulets*
C. Bonner, *Studies in Magical Amulets Chiefly Graeco-Egyptian*, Ann Arbor, Mich., 1950.

Brendel, *Prolegomena*
O. Brendel, *Prolegomena to a Book on Roman Art*, Mem. Amer. Acad. Rome, vol. 21, Rome, 1953.

Brenk, *Mosaiken*
B. Brenk, *Die frühchristlichen Mosaiken in S. Maria Maggiore zu Rom*, Wiesbaden, 1975.

Brilliant, *Septimius Severus*
R. Brilliant, *The Arch of Septimius Severus in the Roman Forum*, Mem. Amer. Acad. Rome, vol. 29, Rome, 1967.

Brilliant, *Gesture and Rank*
R. Brilliant, *Gesture and Rank in Roman Art, The Use of Gestures to Denote Status in Roman Sculpture and Coinage*, New Haven, 1963.

Bruns, *Obelisk*
G. Bruns, *Der Obelisk und seine Basis auf dem Hippodrom zu Konstantinopel*, Istanbuler Forschungen, vol. 7, Istanbul, 1953.

de Bruyne, 'Arcosolio'
L. de Bruyne, 'Arcosolio con pitture recentamente ritrovato nel cimitero dei SS. Marco e Marcellino', *Riv. Archeol. Crist.* 26 (1950): 195-216.

Buchthal, *Art Bull.* (1963)
H. Buchthal, Review of de Wit, 'Die Miniaturen des Vergilius Vaticanus', *Art Bull.* 45 (1963): 372-75.

Buchthal, 'Note on the Vatican Vergil'
H. Buchthal, 'A Note on the Miniatures of the Vatican Vergil Manuscript', *Mélanges Eugène Tisserant*, vol. 6, Studi e Testi, 236, Vatican City, 1964, 167-71.

Byvanck, '*Sta Maria Maggiore*'
A. W. Byvanck, 'Das Problem der Mosaiken von Santa Maria Maggiore', *Festschrift Hans R. Hahnloser*, Stuttgart, 1961, pp. 18ff.

Byvanck, 'Antike Buchmalerei, I'
A. W. Byvanck, 'Antike Buchmalerei: I. Die Datierung der Berliner Itala', *Mnemosyne*, ser. 3, vol. 6 (1938): 241-51.

Cameron, *Claudian*
A. Cameron, *Claudian: Poetry and Propaganda at the Court of Honorius*, Oxford, 1970.

Carder, *Land Surveying Ms.*
J. N. Carder, *Art Historical Problems of a Roman Land Surveying Manuscript: The Codex Arcerianus A. Wolfenbüttel*, New York, 1978.

Cecchelli, *Mosaici*
C. Cecchelli, *I mosaici della basilica di Santa Maria Maggiore*, Rome, 1956.

Cockerell and Plummer, *Miniatures*
S. C. Cockerell and J. Plummer, *Old Testament Miniatures*, New York, 1969.

Davis-Weyer, *Early Medieval Art*
C. Davis-Weyer, *Early Medieval Art, 300-1150*, Sources and Documents in the History of Art Series, ed. H. W. Janson, Englewood Cliffs, N.J., 1971.

Dawson, *Landscape Painting*
C. M. Dawson, *Romano-Campanian Mythological Landscape Painting*, Yale Classical Studies, vol. 9, New Haven, 1944.

Degering/Boeckler
H. Degering and A. Boeckler, *Die Quedlinburger Italafragmente*, 2 vols., Berlin, 1932 (facsimile).

Deichmann and Bovini, *Repertorium der Sarkophage*
F. W. Deichmann and G. Bovini, *Repertorium der christlich-antiken Sarkophage*, vol. 1, Rom und Ostia, 2 vols., Wiesbaden, 1967.

Deichmann, *Ravenna*
F. W. Deichmann, *Ravenna, Hauptstadt des spätantiken Abendlandes*, vol. 1, *Geschichte und Monumente*, Wiesbaden, 1969; vol. 2, *Kommentar*, Wiesbaden, 1974; vol. 3, *Frühchristliche Bauten und Mosaiken von Ravenna*, 2nd ed., Wiesbaden, n.d.

Delbrück, *Consulardiptychen*
R. Delbrück, *Die Consulardiptychen und verwandte Denkmäler*, 2 vols., Berlin, 1926-29.

Delbrück, 'Kaiserornat'
R. Delbrück, 'Der spätantike Kaiserornat', *Antike* 8 (1932): 1-21.

Delbrück, *Kaiserporträts*
R. Delbrück, *Spätantike Kaiserporträts*, Berlin, 1933.

Delbrück, *Lipsanothek*
R. Delbrück, *Probleme der Lipsanothek in Brescia*, Bonn, 1952.

Dorigo, *Late Roman Painting*
W. Dorigo, *Late Roman Painting*, New York, 1971.

Düning
A. Düning, 'Ein neues Fragment des Quedlinburger Itala-Codex', *Quedlinburger Gymnasialprogramm* 1888: 1-24.

Dvornik, *Early Christian*
F. Dvornik, *Early Christian and Byzantine Political Philosophy, Origins and Background*, 2 vols., Dumbarton Oaks Studies, vol. 9, Washington, D.C., 1966.

Ehrensperger-Katz, 'Villes fortifiées'
I. Ehrensperger-Katz, 'Les représentations de villes fortifiées dans l'art paléochrétien et leurs dérivées byzantines', *Cah. Arch.* 19 (1969): 1-27.

Ferrua, *Via Latina*
A. Ferrua, *Le pitture della nuova catacomba di Via Latina*, Vatican City, 1960.

Freshfield, 'Notes'
E. H. Freshfield, 'Notes on a Vellum Album Containing Some Original Sketches of Public Buildings and Monuments Drawn by a German Artist Who Visited Constantinople in 1574', *Archaeologia* 72 (1922): 87-104.

Gaehde, 'Carolingian Bible of San Paolo'
J. E. Gaehde, 'Carolingian Interpretations of an Early Christian Picture Cycle to the Octateuch in the Bible of San Paolo f.l.m. in Rome', *Frühmittelalterliche Studien* 8 (1974): 351-84.

Gebhardt, *Miniatures*
O. von Gebhardt, *The Miniatures of the Ashburnham Pentateuch*, London, 1883 (facsimile).

Gerstinger, *Wiener Dioscurides*
H. Gerstinger, *Der Wiener Dioscurides*, Graz, 1965 (facsimile).

Goldschmidt, *Kirchentür*
A. Goldschmidt, *Die Kirchentür des heiligen Ambrosius in Mailand*, Straßburg, 1903.

Goodenough, *Dura Synagogue*
E. R. Goodenough, *Symbolism in the Dura Synagogue*, Jewish Symbols in the Greco-Roman Period, vols. 9-11, New York, 1964.

Grabar, *L'Empereur*
A. Grabar, *L'Empereur dans l'art byzantin: recherches sur l'art officiel de l'empire d'orient*, Paris, 1936.

Grabar, *Christian Art*
A. Grabar, *The Beginnings of Christian Art*, London, 1967.

Grabar, *Christian Iconography*
A. Grabar, *Christian Iconography, A Study of Its Origins*, Bollingen Series, vol. 35, New York, 1968.

Gutmann, *Dura Europos Synagogue*
J. Gutmann, *The Dura Europos Synagogue: A Re-Evaluation (1932-72)*, Missoula, Mont., 1973.

Hamberg, *Studies*
P. Hamberg, *Studies in Roman Imperial Art*, Copenhagen, 1945.

Heurgon, 'Tresor de Ténès'
Heurgon, Jacques, 'Le Tresor de Ténès', *Bulletin de la Société nationale des antiquitaires de France* (1957): 45-51.

Hempel, 'Anfänge AT-Illus.'
H. L. Hempel, 'Zum Problem der Anfänge der AT-Illustration', *Zeitschrift für die Alttestament. Wiss.* 69 (1957): 104-31.

Holum, 'Pulcheria'
Holum, Kenneth G., 'Pulcheria's Crusade A.D. 421-22 and the Ideology of Imperial Victory', *Greek, Roman and Byzantine Studies* 18 (1977): 153-72.

Jones and Morey, *Manuscripts of Terence*
L. W. Jones and C. R. Morey, *The Miniatures of the Manuscripts of Terence*, Princeton, 1930-31.

Kalavrezou-Maxeiner, 'Imperial Chamber'
I. Kalavrezou-Maxeiner, 'The Imperial Chamber at Luxor', *DOP* 29 (1975): 225-51.

Karpp, *S. Maria Maggiore*
H. Karpp, *Die frühchristlichen und mittelalterlichen Mosaiken in Santa Maria Maggiore zu Rom*, Baden-Baden, 1966 (a photographic study).

Kessler, *Bibles from Tours*
H.L. Kessler, *The Illustrated Bibles from Tours*, Studies in Manuscript Illumination, vol. 7, Princeton, 1977.

Kitzinger, 'Role of Miniature Painting'
E. Kitzinger, 'The Role of Miniature Painting in Mural Decoration', *The Place of Book Illumination in Byzantine Art*, Princeton, 1975, pp. 99-142.

Kitzinger, *Byzantine Art in the Making*
E. Kitzinger, *Byzantine Art in the Making*, Cambridge, Mass., 1977.

Koehler, *Schule von Tours*
W. Koehler, *Die Karolingischen Miniaturen*, vol. 1, *Die Schule von Tours*, 2 vols. and plates, Berlin 1930-1933.

Koeppel, 'Profectio und Adventus'
G. Koeppel, 'Profectio und Adventus', *Bonner Jahrbücher*, 169 (1969): 130-195.

Kötzsche-Breitenbruch, *Via Latina*
L. Kötzsche-Breitenbruch, *Die neue Katakombe an der Via Latina in Rom*, *JbAC*, suppl. 4, Munster-Westphalia, 1976.

Kollwitz, *Oström. Plastik*
J. Kollwitz, *Oströmische Plastik der Theodosianischen Zeit*, Berlin, 1941.

Kraeling, *Synagogue*
C.H. Kraeling, *The Synagogue*, *The Excavations at Dura Europos, Final Report*, vol. 8, pt. 1, New Haven, 1956.

Lassus, *Livre des rois*
J. Lassus, *L'Illustration byzantine du livre des rois*, *Vat. gr. 333*, 2nd ed., Paris, 1973.

Laubscher, *Galeriusbogen*
H.P. Laubscher, *Der Reliefschmuck des Galeriusbogens in Thessaloniki*, Berlin, 1975.

LeBlant, *Sarcophages chrétiens*
E. LeBlant, *Les sarcophages chrétiens de la Gaule*, Paris, 1886.

Lehmann-Hartleben, *Trajanssäule*
K. Lehmann-Hartleben, *Die Trajanssäule. Ein römisches Kunstwerk zu Beginn der Spätantike*, 2 vols., Berlin and Leipzig, 1926.

L'Orange and von Gerkan, *Konstantinsbogen*
H.P. L'Orange and A. von Gerkan, *Der spätantike Bildschmuck des Konstantinsbogens*, 2 vols., Berlin, 1939.

L'Orange, 'Subtile Stil'
H.P. L'Orange, 'Der subtile Stil. Eine Kunstströmung aus der Zeit um 400 nach Christus', *Antike Kunst* 4 (1961): 68-75.

Lowe, 'Some Facts'
E.A. Lowe, 'Some Facts about Our Oldest Latin Manuscripts', *The Classical Quarterly* 19 (1925): 197-208, reprinted in Lowe, *Palaeographical Papers* 1: 187-202.

Lowe, 'More Facts'
E.A. Lowe, 'More Facts about Our Oldest Latin Manuscripts', *The Classical Quarterly* 22 (1928): 43-62, reprinted in Lowe, *Palaeographical Papers*, 1: 251-74.

Lowe, *CLA*
E.A. Lowe, *Codices Latini Antiquiores*, 11 vols., Oxford, 1934-72.

Magi, *Calendario dipinto*
F. Magi, *Il calendario dipinto sotto S. Maria Maggiore*, Atti d. Pont. Acc. Rom. d. Arch., Memorie, vol. 11, Vatican City, 1972.

Morey, *Early Christian Art*
C.R. Morey, *Early Christian Art*, Princeton, 1942.

Mouriki-Charalambous, *Octateuch*
D. Mouriki-Charalambous, *The Octateuch Miniatures of the Byzantine Manuscripts of Cosmas Indicopleustes*, Ph.D. diss., Princeton Univ., 1970.

von Mülverstedt
G.A. von Mülverstedt, 'Das Itala-Fragment', *Zeitschrift des Harz-Vereins für Geschichte und Altertumskunde*, 7 (1876): 251-63.

Noll, 'Kaiserfibel von 316'
R. Noll, 'Eine goldene Kaiserfibel aus Niederemmel vom Jahre 316', *Bonner Jahrbücher* 174 (1974): 221-44.

Nordenfalk, *Painting*
C. Nordenfalk and A. Grabar, *Early Medieval Painting*, New York, 1957.

Nordenfalk, *Zierbuchstaben*
C. Nordenfalk, *Die spätantiken Zierbuchstaben*, Stockholm, 1970.

Petersen et al., *Markus-Säule*
E. Petersen, A. von Domaszewski and G. Calderini, *Die Markus-Säule auf Piazza Colonna in Rom*, 2 vols., Munich, 1896.

Pliny, *Nat. Hist.*
Pliny, *Natural History*, Loeb Classical Library.

Rinaldi, 'Costume Romano'
L. Rinaldi, 'Il costume romano', *RINASA*, 13-14 (1964-65): 230ff.

Rostovtzeff, 'Architekturlandschaft'
M. Rostovtzeff, 'Die hellenistische-römische Architekturlandschaft', *Röm. Mitt.* 26 (1911): 1-186.

Ryberg, *Rites*
I.S. Ryberg, *Rites of the State Religion in Roman Art*, Mem. Amer. Acad. Rome, vol. 22, Rome, 1955.

Ryberg, *Panel Reliefs*
I.S. Ryberg, *Panel Reliefs of Marcus Aurelius*, New York, 1967.

Scheller, *Survey of Model Books*
R.W. Scheller, *A Survey of Medieval Model Books*, Haarlem, 1963.

Schönebeck, *Mailänder Sark.*
H.U. von Schönebeck, *Der Mailänder Sarkophag und seine Nachfolge*, Studi di antichità cristiane, vol. 10, Vatican City, 1935.

Schultze, *Quedlinburger Itala*
V. Schultze, *Die Quedlinburger Itala-Miniaturen der königlichen Bibliothek in Berlin, Fragmente der ältesten christlichen Buchmalerei*, Munich, 1898.

Schum
W. Schum, 'Das Quedlinburger Fragment einer illustrierten Itala', *Theologische Studien und Kritiken* 49 (1876): 121-34.

Seeck, *Notitia Dignitatum*
O. Seeck, *Notitia Dignitatum*, Berlin, 1876.

Spain, 'Heraclius and the David Plates'
S. Spain, 'Heraclius, Byzantine Imperial Ideology, and the David Plates', *Speculum* 52 (1977): 217-37.

Spain, 'Promised Blessing'
S. Spain, 'The Promised Blessing: the Iconography of the Mosaics of S. Maria Maggiore', *Art Bull.* 61 (1979): 518ff.

Stahl, *Iconographic Sources*
H. Stahl, *The Iconographic Sources of the Old Testament Miniatures, Pierpont Morgan Library, M. 638*, Ph.D. diss., New York University, 1974.

Stern, *Calendrier de 354*
H. Stern, *Le calendrier de 354: étude sur son texte et ses illustrations*, Paris, 1953.

Thompson, *Palaeography*
E.M. Thompson, *An Introduction to Greek and Latin Palaeography*, Oxford, 1912.

Treitinger, *Reichsidee*
O. Treitinger, *Die oströmische Kaiser- und Reichsidee nach ihrer Gestaltung im höfischen Zeremoniell*, Jena, 1938.

Volbach, *Elfenbeinarbeiten*
W.F. Volbach, *Elfenbeinarbeiten der Spätantike und des frühen Mittelalters. Römisch-germanisches Zentralmuseum*, Mainz, 1952; second edition, 1976.

Volbach, *Art*
W.F. Volbach, F. and M. Hirmer, *Early Christian Art*, Munich, 1958.

Waetzoldt, *Kopien*
S. Waetzoldt, *Die Kopien des 17. Jahrhunderts nach Mosaiken und Wandmalereien in Rom*, Vienna, 1964.

Weitzmann, 'Chronicles'
K. Weitzmann, 'Illustrations for the Chronicles of Sozomenos, Theodoret and Malalas', *Byzantion* 16 (1942-43): 87ff.

Weitzmann, *Joshua Roll*
K. Weitzmann, *The Joshua Roll: A Work of the Macedonian Renaissance*, Studies in Manuscript Illumination, vol. 3, Princeton, 1948.

Weitzmann, *Ancient Book Illum.*
K. Weitzmann, *Ancient Book Illumination*, Martin Classical Lectures, vol. 16, Cambridge, Mass., 1959.

Weitzmann, *Roll and Codex*
K. Weitzmann, *Illustrations in Roll and Codex*, 2nd ed., Princeton, 1970.

Weitzmann, 'Prolegomena'
K. Weitzmann, 'Prolegomena to a Study of the Cyprus Plates', *Met. Mus. J.* 3 (1970): 97-111.

Weitzmann, 'Cyclic Illustration'
K. Weitzmann, 'The Selection of Texts for Cyclic Illustration of Byzantine Manuscripts', *Byzantine Books and Bookmen*, Washington, D.C., 1975, pp. 69-99.

Weitzmann, *Studies*
K. Weitzmann, *Studies in Classical and Byzantine Manuscript Illumination*, ed. Herbert L. Kessler, Chicago, 1971.

Weitzmann, 'Illustration of the Septuagint'
K. Weitzmann, 'The Illustration of the Septuagint', *Studies in Classical and Byzantine Manuscript Illumination*, ed. H. L. Kessler, Chicago, 1971, pp. 45-75.

Weitzmann, 'Jewish Pictorial Sources'
'The Question of the Influence of Jewish Pictorial Sources on Old Testament Illustration', *Studies in Classical and Byzantine Manuscript Illumination*, Chicago, 1971, pp. 76-95.

Weitzmann, 'Book Illustration'
K. Weitzmann, 'Book Illustration of the Fourth Century: Tradition and Innovation', *Studies in Classical and Byzantine Manuscript Illumination*, ed. H. L. Kessler, Chicago, 1971, pp. 96-125.

Weitzmann, ed., *Age of Spirituality*
K. Weitzmann, ed., *Age of Spirituality, Late Antique and Early Christian Art, Third to Seventh Century*, catalogue of the exhibition at the Metropolitan Museum of Art 1977-78, New York, 1979.

Wilpert, *Mosaiken und Malereien*
J. Wilpert, *Die römischen Mosaiken und Malereien der kirchlichen Bauten vom IV. bis XIII. Jahrhundert*, 4 vols., Freiburg i.Br., 1924.

de Wit
J. de Wit, *Die Miniaturen des Vergilius Vaticanus*, Amsterdam, 1959.

Wolska-Conus, *Cosmas*
W. Wolska-Conus, *Cosmas Indicopleustes, Iconographie Chrétienne*, Sources Chrétiennes, vol. 141, Paris, 1968.

Wright, *Art Bull.* (1961).
D.H. Wright, Review of Grabar and Nordenfalk's 'Early Medieval Painting', *Art Bull.* 43 (1961): 245-55.

Bibliography for Works of Art most often cited

CHRISTIAN RELIEF SCULPTURE

Doors, S. Ambrogio, Milan, David cycle, fragments in the church museum, wood, ca. end of 4th cent.
Goldschmidt, *Kirchentür*; Volbach, *Art*, pl. 102.

Doors, S. Sabina, Rome, Old and New Testament scenes, cypress wood, ca. 422-440.
Kantorowicz, E. H., 'The "King's Advent" and the Enigmatic Panels in the Doors of Santa Sabina', *Art Bull.* 26 (1944): 207-313; Volbach, *Art*, pls. 103-105; Weitzmann, ed., *Age of Spirituality*, no. 438, pp. 486-88.

Relief fragment, Penitence of David, Budapest, Museum of Fine Arts, marble, from Asia Minor, ca. late 4th cent.
E. Eszlary, 'On the Development of Early Christian Iconography. A Fourth Century Fragment from Asia Minor in the Budapest Museum of Fine Arts', *Acta Historicae Artium Academiae Scientarum Hungaricae* 8 (1962): 215-40; Z. Kadar, 'Un rilievo frammentario del Museo di Budapest', *Riv. Archeol. Crist.* 38 (1962): 149-50.

Sarcophagi, details: David and Goliath, Marseille and Reims, marble 4th cen.
LeBlant, *Sarcophages chrétiens*, pp. 17, 35.

Sarcophagus of Gorgonius, Ancona, marble, Rome, late 4th cent.
Schönbeck, *Mailänder Sark.*, pp. 108, 115; M. Ioli, *Il sarcofago paleocristiano di Catervio nel duomo di Tolentino*, Studi di antichità cristiane, vol. 9, Bologna, 1971.

Sarcophagus of Junius Bassus, Vatican City, Grottoes under S. Peters, marble, Rome, 359 A.D.
F. Gerke, *Der Sarkophag des Junius Bassus*, Berlin, 1936; Deichmann and Bovini, *Repertorium der Sarkophage*, vol. 1, no. 680; Weitzmann, ed., *Age of Spirituality*, no. 386, pp. 427-29. — Fig. 58.

Sarcophagus, Lateran 174, Vatican City, Grottoes under S. Peters, marble, prob. Rome, ca. 3rd quarter 4th cent.
Volbach, *Art*, pls. 44-45.

Sarcophagus, S. Ambrogio, Milan, marble, Rome, end of 4th cen.
Schönebeck, *Mailänder Sark.*, passim; Volbach, *Art*, pl. 46-47.

Sarcophagus of the Two Brothers, Vatican City, Museo Pio Cristiano, marble, Rome, ca. mid 4th cent.
Deichmann and Bovini, *Repertorium der Sarkophage*, vol. 1, no. 45, pp. 43ff., pl. 15.

Sarcophagi, detail: Pontius Pilate, Vatican, Museo Pio Cristiano, no. 151, and San Sebastiano, marble, Rome, 4th cent.
Deichmann and Bovini, *Repertorium der Sarkophage*, vol. 1, no. 58, p. 211.

FRESCOES

Dura Europos, Synagogue, frescoes: Old Testament Scenes, ca. 245-46.
Kraeling, *Synagogue*; Goodenough, *Dura Synagogue*.

Herculaneum, fresco: Dirce, 1st cent.
(Lost, known through a drawing published by Dawson, *Landscape Painting*, p. 95, pl. 12, no. 32.) — Fig. 14.

Pompeii, House of Sacerdos Amandus, fresco: Fall of Icarus, 1st cent.
Dawson, *Landscape Painting*, pl. 14, pp. 99, 121, 140ff. — Fig. 11.

Tomb fresco of Q. Fabius and M. Fannius, Rome, Conservators' Museum, from the Esquiline, Republican, 1st cent. B.C.
M. Swindler, *Ancient Painting*, New Haven, 1929, fig. 568.

Labors of the Months frescoes, in a public building under S. Maria Maggiore, Rome, 1st half 3rd cent.
Magi, *Calendario dipinto*, p. 48, suggests a date between 300-350, cf. his reconstruction drawings, pls. 43ff. A date in the second quarter of the third century is more likely; cf. Inabelle Levin, 'A Reconsideration of the Date of the Esquiline Calendar and of its Political Festivals', *AJA* 86 (1972): 429-35, and H. Mielsch's review of Magi's book in *Gnomon* 48 (1976): 500-502.

Hypogaeum of the Aurelii, Rome, fresco: Sermon in a city, 1st half of 3rd cent.
C. Cecchelli, *Monumenti cristiano-eretici di Roma*, Rome, 1944; F. Wirth, *Römische Wandmalerei vom Untergang Pompeiis bis ans Ende des dritten Jahrhunderts*, Berlin, 1934, pl. 48. — Fig. 10.

Luxor, temple of Ammon, imperial frescoes, Tetrarchic.
Kalavrezou-Maxeiner, 'Imperial Chamber', 225-51.

Catacomb of S.S. Marco and Marcellino, Rome, fresco: Nebuchadnezzar, arcosolium, 4th cent.
de Bruyne, 'Arcosolio', 195-216.

Via Latina catacomb, Rome, frescoes, 4th cent.
Ferrua, *Via Latina*; Kötzsche-Breitenbruch, *Via Latina*. — Fig. 12.

Diana Chapel under Via Livenza 4a, Rome, frescoes: Diana the Huntress, 4th cent.
L. Usai, *Dialoghi di Archeologia*, (1972). — Fig. 8.

Hypogeum of Trebius Justus, Rome, frescoes, late 4th cent.
C. Casalone, 'Note sulle pitture del Ipogeo di Trebio Giusto a Roma', *Cah. Arch.*, 12 (1962): 53-64.

Catacomb of SS. Pietro and Marcellino, Rome, Acclamation of Christ, vault fresco, early 5th cent.
Dorigo, *Late Roman Painting*, fig. 179.

S. Paolo f.l.m., Rome, nave frescoes: Old and New Testament scenes, ca. mid 5th cent., destroyed by fire in 1823. See the water color drawings of 1634 in Vatican City, Bibl. Vat., Barb. lat. 4406, and of ca. 1790 in Vatican City, Bibl. Vat., Vat. lat. 9843.
Waetzoldt, *Kopien*, pp. 22, 55ff., figs. 318ff., 408; J. White, 'Cavallini and the Lost Frescoes of S. Paolo', *J. Warburg and Courtauld Institutes*, 19 (1956): 84-95.

ILLUSTRATED MANUSCRIPTS

Alexandrian World Chronicle, Barbarus Scaligeri, Paris, Bibl. nat., Lat. 4884, 7th cent.
Wolska-Conus, *Cosmas*, 1: 146-47, 152-56; Mouriki-Charalambous, *Octateuch*, pp. 181-83.

Alexandrian World Chronicle, Moscow Pushkin Museum, copy of post 392 original.
Bauer and Strzygowski, *Alexandrinische Weltchronik*, 144ff.

Ashburnham Pentateuch, Paris, Bibl. nat., n. acq. lat. 2334, Spain or N. Africa, ca. early 7th cent.
Gebhardt, *Miniatures* (facsimile); B. Narkiss, 'Towards a Further Study of the Ashburnham Pentateuch', *Cah. Archéol.* 19 (1969): 45-59.

Bible Moralisée, Oxford, Bodleian Lib., Bodl. 270b, cf. fol. 134, French, 13th cent.
A. Laborde, *La Bible Moralisée illustrée conservée à Oxford, Paris, et Londres*, vol. I, Paris, 1911, pl. 134.

Bible of S. Paolo f.l.m., Rome, Carolingian, ca. 870.
Gaehde, 'Carolingian Bible of San Paolo', 351-84.

Book of Kings, Vatican City, Bibl. Vat., Vat. gr. 333, Byzantine, 11th/12th cent.
Lassus, *Livre des rois.*—Figs. 49, 50.

Calendar of 354, Vatican City, Bibl. Vat., cod. Barb. lat. 2154, copy made for Peiresc in Paris, originally written in Rome by Furius Dionysius Filocalus in 354.
Stern, *Calendrier de 354.*—Fig. 47.

Comedies of Terence, Vatican City, Bibl. Vat., Vat. lat. 3868; and Paris, Bibl. nat., lat. 7899, Carolingian copies of the lost Late Antique illustrated ms. based on Medieval intermediaries.
Jones and Morey, *Manuscripts of Terence.*—Fig. 48.

Corpus Agrimensorum Romanorum, Codex Arcerianus, Wolfenbüttel, Herzog-August-Bibl., cod. Guelf. 36.23, Italy(?) ca. 500 A.D., and Vatican City, Bibl. Vat., Pal. lat. 1564 (Carolingian), 9th cent., copies of the lost antique original ms. of the 5th cent.
C. Thulin, *Die Handschriften des Corpus Agrimensorum Romanorum*, Abh. Preuss. Akad. d. Wiss., Phil.-Hist. Kl., Anhang II, Berlin, 1911; Carder, *Land Surveying Ms.*; H. Butzmann, *Corpus Agrimensorum Romanorum, Codex Arcerianus A der Herzog-August-Bibliothek zu Wolfenbüttel (Cod. Guelf. 36.23 A)*, Leiden, 1970 (facsimile).

Cotton Genesis, London, Brit. Lib., cod. Cotton Otho B. VI, (Byzantine), poss. Alexandria, 5/6 cent.
K. Weitzmann, 'Observations on the Cotton Genesis Fragments', *Late Classical and Medieval Studies in Honor of Albert Mathias Friend Jr.*, ed. K. Weitzmann, Princeton, 1944, pp. 112-31; J.J. Tikkanen, 'Die Genesismosaiken von S. Marco in Venedig und ihr Verhältnis zu den Miniaturen der Cottonbibel', *Acta Societatis Scientiarum Fennicae* 17 (1889): 99ff.

Dioscurides, Vienna, Nat. Bibl., cod. med. gr. 1, Byzantine, Constantinople, ca. 512.
Gerstinger, *Wiener Dioscurides* (facsimile).

Homilies of Gregory of Nazianzus, Paris, Bibl. nat., gr. 510, cf. fol. 374, Julian the Apostate cycle, Byzantine, Constantinople, 9th cent.
Weitzmann, 'Chronicles', 87ff.

Ilias Ambrosiana, Milan, Bibl. Ambrosiana, cod. F. 205 Inf., poss. Constantinople, 5th/6th cent.
Bianchi Bandinelli, *Miniatures of the Iliad*; A. Calderini, A. M. Ceriani, A. Mai, *Ilias Ambrosiana*, Fontes Ambrosiani, vol. 28, Bern and Olten, 1943 (facsimile).

Joshua Roll, Vatican City, Bibl. Vat., Pal. gr. 431, Byzantine, Constantinople, 10th cent.
Weitzmann, *Joshua Roll*.

Moutiers-Grandval Bible, London, Brit. Lib., add. ms. 10546, Tours, Carolingian, 9th cent.
J. Duft et al., *Die Bibel von Moutiers-Grandval*, Bern, 1971; Kessler, *Bibles from Tours*.

Notitia Dignitatum, Munich, Staatsbibl., c.l.m. 10291, ff. 178r-222r. Renaissance copy of a lost ms. of ca. 425 A.D.
Seeck, *Notitia Dignitatum*; Berger, *Notitia Dignitatum*.

Old Testament Miniatures, New York, Pierpont Morgan Lib., M 638, Paris, mid-13th cent. (other leaves are in Paris and Aachen); cf. Kings Cycle on ff. 18-46.
Cockerell and Plummer, *Miniatures*; Stahl, *Iconographic Sources.*—Figs. 51, 52.

S. Augustine Gospels, Cambridge, CCC, ms. 286, Italian, late 6th cent.; cf. fol. 125R.
F. Wormald, *The Miniatures in the Gospels of St. Augustine, Corpus Christi College MS. 286*, Cambridge, 1954.

Tabula Peutingeriana, Vienna, Nat. Bibl., cod. 324, 13th cent., based on a lost 4th cent. prototype.
J. Hermann, *Die Frühmittelalterlichen Hss. des Abendlandes*, Die illuminierten Hss. und Inkunabeln der Nationalbibliothek in Wien, vol. I, Leipzig, 1923.

Vergilius Romanus, Vatican City, Bibl. Vat., Vat. lat. 3867, Italy(?), late 5th cent.
Picturae Ornamenta ... codicis Vaticani Latini 3867 qui codex Vergilii Romanus audit. Codices e Vaticanis selecti II, Rome, 1902 (facsimile).

Vergilius Vaticanus, Vatican City, Bibl. Vat., Vat. lat. 3225, prob. from Rome, ca. 420.
de Wit, *Miniaturen Vergilius Vat.*—Figs. 21-29.

Vienna Genesis, Vienna, Nat. Bibl., cod. theol. gr. 31, Byzantine, Constantinople or Syria(?), 6th cent.
W. von Hartel and F. Wickhoff, *Die Wiener Genesis*, Vienna, 1895 (facsimile); H. Gerstinger, *Die Wiener Genesis*, 2 vols., Vienna, 1931 (facsimile).

Vivian Bible (First Bible of Charles the Bald), Paris, Bibl. nat., lat. 1, Tours, Carolingian, mid 9th cent.
Koehler, *Die Schule von Tours*; Kessler, *Bibles from Tours*.

BIBLIOGRAPHY FOR WORKS OF ART

IVORIES

Diptych, Asklepios and Hygieia, Liverpool, Merseyside County Museums, M. 10044, ivory, Rome, early 5th cent.
Delbrück, *Consulardiptychen*, 1: 215ff., 2: pl. 55; Volbach, *Elfenbeinarbeiten*, 1976, no. 57, pl. 15; Weitzmann, ed., *Age of Spirituality*, no. 133, pp. 155-58.

Diptych of Consul Asturius, Darmstadt, Museum, ivory, Rome, ca. 449(?).
Volbach, *Elfenbeinarbeiten*, 1976, no. 3, pl. 2; Delbrück, *Consulardiptychen*, 1: 95ff., 2: pl. 4.

Diptych: christological scenes, Milan, Cathedral Treasury, ivory, N. Italy(?), 2nd half of 5th cent.
Volbach, *Elfenbeinarbeiten*, 1976, no. 119, pl. 37; Volbach, *Art*, pls. 100-101.

Diptych of Constantinus III(?), Halberstadt, Cathedral Treasury, ivory, Rome, ca. 417(?).
Delbrück, *Consulardiptychen*, 1: 87ff., 2: pl. 2; Volbach, *Elfenbeinarbeiten*, 1976, no. 35, pl. 8.—Fig. 42.

Consular diptych, Bourges, Museum, ivory, from Rome, ca. 435(?).
Volbach, *Elfenbeinarbeiten*, 1976, no. 36; Delbrück, *Consulardiptychen*, 1: 157ff., 2: pl. 37.

Diptych of Consul Felix, Paris, Bibl. nat., Cabinet des médailles, 41, ivory, from Rome, ca. 428, engraving of lost verso published by Mabillon; cf. Delbrück.
Delbrück, *Consulardiptychen*, 1: 93ff., 2: pl. 3; Volbach, *Elfenbeinarbeiten*, 1976, no. 2, pl. 1; Weitzmann, ed., *Age of Spirituality*, no. 45, p. 46.—Fig. 82.

Diptych of a patrician, Novara Cathedral, Museo del Duomo, ivory, N. Italy, ca. 425.
Delbrück, *Consulardiptychen*, 1: 248ff., 2: pl. 64; Volbach, *Elfenbeinarbeiten*, 1976, no. 64, pl. 20; Weitzmann, ed., *Age of Spirituality*, no. 54, pp. 56-58.—Fig. 43.

Diptych of Consul Probianus, Berlin, Staatsbibl. Preuss. Kulturbesitz, Ms. theol. lat. fol. 323, ivory, Rome, ca. 400.
Volbach, *Elfenbeinarbeiten*, 1976, no. 62, pl. 18; Delbrück, *Consulardiptychen*, 1: 250ff., 2: pl. 65; Weitzmann, ed., *Age of Spirituality*, no. 53, pp. 55-56.

Diptych of Probus with portraits of Emperor Honorius, Aosta, Cathedral Treasury, ivory, Rome(?), ca. 406.
Delbrück, *Consulardiptychen*, 1: 84ff.; 2: pl. 1; Volbach, *Elfenbeinarbeiten*, 1976, no. 1, pl. 1.

Diptych of 'Stilicho' (ca. 360-408), Monza, Cathedral Treasury, ivory, Italy, early 5th cent.
Delbrück, *Consulardiptychen*, 1: 242ff., 2: pl. 63; Volbach, *Elfenbeinarbeiten*, 1976, no. 63, pl. 19.—Fig. 44.

Diptych of the Symmachi and Nicomachi, Paris, Musée de Cluny, CL 17048; and London, Victoria and Albert Museum, 212-1865, ivory from Rome, ca. 388-401.
Volbach, *Elfenbeinarbeiten*, 1976, no. 55, pl. 29; Delbrück, *Consulardiptychen*, 1: 209ff., 2: pl. 54.

Lipsanothek, Brescia, Museo del' Età Cristiano, ivory casket, N. Italy, last third of the 4th cent.
Delbrück, *Lipsanothek*. His date, ca. 312-15, is unacceptable; J. Kollwitz, *Die Lipsanothek von Brescia* (Berlin, 1933) suggests last third of the fourth century; Volbach, *Art*, pls. 88-89; Volbach, *Elfenbeinarbeiten*, 1976, no. 107, pl. 31.

Pyxis: Christ teaching etc., Berlin, Staatliche Museen Preussischer Kulturbesitz, Frühchristliche-Byzantinische Sammlung, ivory, N. Italy, ca. 400.
Volbach, *Art*, pl. 95; Volbach, *Elfenbeinarbeiten*, 1976, no. 161, pl. 53.

METALWORK

Amulets: Solomon on horseback, Jewish and Christian, Syro-Palestinian.
Bonner, *Magical Amulets*, pp. 208-12; Bagatti, 'Medaglie di Salomone', 331-42.

David plates, New York, Metropolitan Mus. of Art, silver, prob. from Constantinople, found in Cyprus, ca. 629-30.
Weitzmann, 'Prolegomena', 97-111; Spain, 'Heraclius and the David Plates', 217-37.

Missorium of Theodosius I, Madrid, Real Academia de la Historia, silver, eastern empire, 388.
Delbrück, *Kaiserporträts*, p. 200, pls. 94-98; Weitzmann, ed., *Age of Spirituality*, no. 64, pp. 74-76.—Fig. 39.

Reliquary casket, Milan, S. Nazaro Maggiore, silver, N. Italy(?), ca. late 4th cent.(?).
Volbach, *Art*, pls. 113-15. Its authenticity is questioned by C. R. Morey, 'Silver Casket of San Nazaro in Milan', *AJA*, 23 (1919): 101-25.

MOSAICS

S. Apollinare in Classe, apse mosaic and underdrawing, mid-6th cent.
M. Mazzotti, 'Sinopie Classensi', *Felix Ravenna*, 103-104 (1972): 211-22; G. Bovini, 'Les "sinopie" ... Saint Apollinaires-in-Classe', *CRAI* (1974): 97-110; Deichmann, *Ravenna*, 1: 257ff.; 3: 383-413.

Capella S. Aquilino, San Lorenzo Maggiore, Milan, apse mosaics, 4th/5th cent.
A. Calderini, G. Chierici and C. Cecchelli, *La Basilica di San Lorenzo Maggiore in Milano* (Milan, 1951), pp. 217-22.

S. Giovanni in Fonte, Naples, mosaics, early 5th cent.
J. L. Maier, *Le baptistère de Naples et ses mosaïques* (Freiburg, 1964).

Mausoleum of Galla Placidia, Ravenna, mosaics, ca. 424-50.
Deichmann, *Ravenna*, 1: 158ff.; 2, 1: 61ff.; 3: pls. 1-31.

Orthodox Baptistery, Ravenna, mosaics, mid-5th cent.
S. K. Kostof, *The Orthodox Baptistery of Ravenna* (New Haven, 1965).

S. Costanza, Rome, apse mosaics, 2nd half 4th cent.
H. Stern, 'Les Mosaïques de l'église de Ste.-Constance à Rome', *DOP*, 12 (1958): 157-218.

S. Maria Maggiore, Rome, arch and nave mosaics, ca. 432-440.
Brenk, *Mosaiken*; Karpp, *S. Maria Maggiore* (photographic study); Cecchelli, *Mosaici*.—Figs. 16-20, 45, 46.

S. Pudenziana, Rome, apse mosaic, early 5th cent.
Wilpert, *Mosaiken und Malereien*, pls. 42-46; G. Matthiae, *Mosaici medioevali delle chiese di Roma* (Rome, 1967), pp. 55ff., pls. 12ff., figs. 36ff.

S. George, Salonica, dome mosaics and underdrawings, ca. mid 5th cent.
H. Torp, *Mosaikkene i St. Georg-Rotunden i Thessaloniki* (Oslo, 1963) suggests a date of ca. 380-90 for the mosaics. E. Kleinbauer, 'The Iconography and the Date of the Mosaics of the Rotunda of Haghios Georgios, Thessaloniki', *Viator*, 3 (1972), 27-108; he wants to date them ca. mid to third quarter of the 5th cent., p. 68. Cf. p. 29 for underdrawings.

OFFICIAL RELIEF SCULPTURE

Column of Theodosius, Istanbul, marble, destroyed, fragments remain, Constantinople, ca. 380's.
Kollwitz, *Oström. Plastik*, pp. 3ff., pls. 1ff.; Becatti, *Colonna*.

Column of Marcus Aurelius, Rome, late 2nd cent.
Petersen et al., *Markus-Säule*; Becatti, *Colonna*.—Figs. 33-35, 45.

Column of Trajan, Rome, early 2nd cent.
Lehmann-Hartleben, *Trajanssäule*; Becatti, *Colonna*.—Figs. 30-32.

Arch of Constantine, Rome, ca. 315-17.
L'Orange and von Gerkan, *Konstantinsbogen*; R. Bianchi Bandinelli, *Rome, the Late Empire*, New York, 1971, pp. 73-80.

Arch of Galerius, Salonica, 3rd/4th cent.
Laubscher, *Galeriusbogen*; Grabar, *Christian Art*, fig. 153.—Fig. 37.

Arch of Septimius Severus, Lepcis Magna, early 3rd cent.
R. Bartoccini, 'L'Arco quadrifonte dei Severi a Lepcis', *Africa Italiana*, 4 (1931): 101ff.; Brilliant, *Gesture and Rank*, fig. 4.40.

Arch of Septimius Severus, Rome, early 3rd cent.
Brilliant, *Septimius Severus*.—Fig. 13.

Obelisk base of Theodosius I, Istanbul, hippodrome, marble, Constantinople, ca. 392.
Bruns, *Obelisk*; Volbach, *Art*, pls. 54-55.—Fig. 40.

Triumph of Marcus Aurelius, Rome, Conservators' Museum, marble panel, from Rome, late 2nd cent.
Ryberg, *Panel Reliefs*, pp. 15ff., pl. 9a.—Fig. 36.

Column of Arcadius, Constantinople, marble, early 5th cent., destroyed, fragments, see drawings of 1574, Cambridge, Trinity College, Ms. 0.17.2, paper.
Freshfield, 'Notes', 87-104; Becatti, *Colonna*, pp. 151-288, pls. 56, 61, 63, 72-76; Kollwitz, *Oström. Plastik*, pp. 17ff., pls. 3-9.

PORTRAITS AND STATUES

Statuette of Christ, Rome, Museo Naz. Romano, marble, prob. Constantinople, ca. 370-80.
B. Brenk, 'Ein Scheinsarkophag im Metropolitan Museum in New York', *Kolloquium über spätantike und frühmittelalterliche Skulptur*, II (Mainz, 1970), pp. 54-57; Weitzmann, ed., *Age of Spirituality*, no. 469, pp. 524-25.

Portrait statuette of Aelia Flacilla, Paris, Bibl. nat., Cabinet des médailles, 13, marble, found in Cyprus, from Constantinople, ca. 380-90.
Delbrück, *Kaiserporträts*, pp. 163-65, pl. 62; Weitzmann, ed., *Age of Spirituality*, no. 20, pp. 26-27, pl. 1.

Portrait of Arcadius, Istanbul, Archeological Museum, marble, Constantinople, found near the Forum Tauri, ca. 395-400.
N. Firatli, *AJA*, 55 (1951): 67-71.

Portrait, Munich, Glyptothek, marble, from Ephesos, 1st half of 5th cent.
L'Orange, 'Subtile Stil', p. 73, pl. 28, 3-4.—Fig. 55.

Colossal imperial statue, Barletta, outside the Church of S. Sepolcro, bronze, from Constantinople, ca. mid 5th cent.
Delbrück, *Kaiserporträts*, pp. 219-26; H.-G. Severin, *Zur Porträtplastik des 5. Jahrhunderts nach Chr.*, Miscellanea Byzantina Monacensia, 13, Munich, 1972, no. 21, pp. 106-15; Weitzmann, ed., *Age of Spirituality*, no. 23, 29-30.

NOTE ON THE REPRODUCTION OF THE MANUSCRIPT

These color illustrations were produced in response to requests of numerous scholars who have urged me to make the Quedlinburg Itala more widely known. The photographic study will act as a companion to the facsimiles of other Late Antique and Christian manuscripts which continue to be published.

While studying these color plates readers should be aware that, due to technical limitations, the illustrations have a slightly yellowish cast, and they do not convey the rosiness of pinks and reds, especially of the pink strips in the skies. Moreover, the fine gold lines, which were generously spun over nearly all solid forms in the original illustrations, could not be reproduced.

NOTE ON THE TRANSCRIPTION

The transcription is based on Degering's transcription, supplemented by my own inspection. (For the right margin of f. 4v, cf. the offset on f. 3v.) The following conventions are used:

- ligatures are resolved;
- ( ) includes letters not written in full but implied by the use of an abbreviation;
- the strokes over the *nomina sacra* (cf. p. 17) are retained;
- where the original has *scriptio continua*, spaces have been introduced between words; where the original has spaces between words (which function as punctuation, cf. p. 17), a comma has been introduced; where the original has punctuation by an interpunctum, a point is printed;
- [ ] indicates text believed to have been present originally, but now lost through physical damage;
- .... indicates letters which, though not completely lost, are not identifiable with certainty;
- ⟦ ⟧ indicates letters which were erased, but for which a reconstruction was proposed by Degering;
- ` ´ indicates letters added as an afterthought.

SOURCES OF THE ILLUSTRATION

With particular gratitude we mention two photo sources:

Prof. Karpp for the S. Maria Maggiore mosaics (figs. 16-20, 45-46);

the Deutsche Archäologische Institut, Rome, for figs. 7 (DAI 72.642), 9 (59.1973), 10 (56.1540), 11 (66.1798), 13 (33.49), 30-32 (31.319, 311, 329), 33 (55.835), 38 (65.140), 40 (38.600), 41 (67.1754).

Photographs of Vatican manuscripts (Vatican Vergil, figs. 21-29, 53-54, 56, and figs. 47, 49-50) are from Vatican, Bibl. Apost. Vaticana, Archivio fotografico; those of the New York manuscript (figs. 51, 52) from New York, Pierpont Morgan Library.

Other sources are mentioned in the captions ('Delbrück' refers to his *Consulardiptychen*).

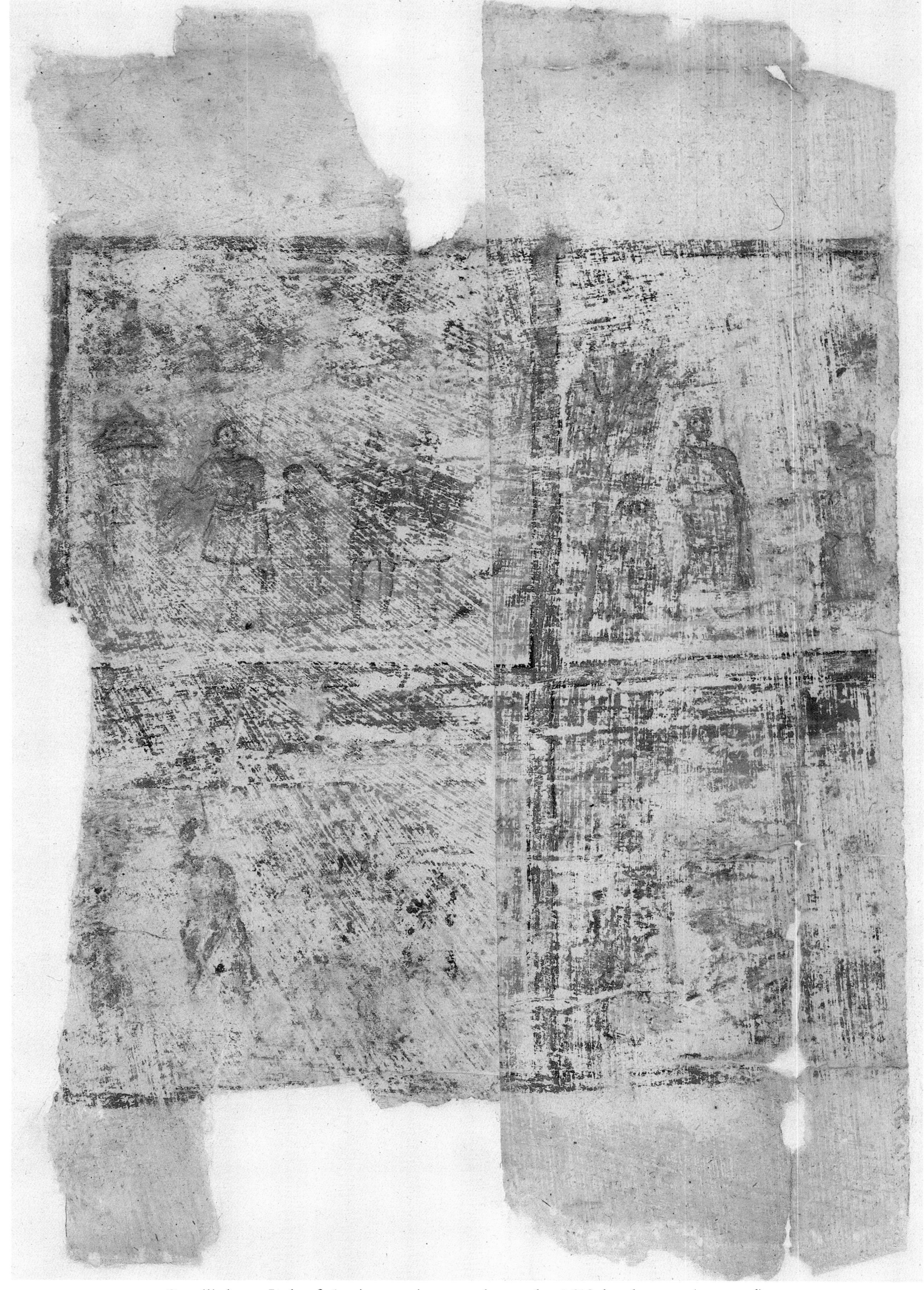

Quedlinburg Itala, f. 1r, impressions made on the 1618 bookcover (reversed).

Quedlinburg Itala, f. 1r = Pictures 1-4.

Quedlinburg Itala, f. 1v.

et erat]ụir ex filiis benia
min et]nomen ei erat
cis fili a]bieḷ f̣ili sararae
fili bac]hir f̣ili aret fili
uiri ie]mnaei ⟦aret fili⟧
uir pot]ens . et huic fi
lius er]ạt , et nomen ei
erat sa]ul ṣtatura bo
nata ui]r bonus , non
erat ui]r nemo melior
super]ḥunc in filiis is
trahel] , neque longior
super u]meros eius . su
per tot]am terram
et perier]unt asinae pa
tris sau]lis cis , et dixit
cis ad s]ạul fịḷium suum .
tolle (unum)] e pueriṣ et sur
gite et i]te , eṭ quaẹṛịtẹ
asinas] , ṭṛạṇṣịẹṛunt
per mo]nteṃ ẹpḥṛạịṃ
et tra]nsieṛunṭ pẹṛ
terra]m selc̣ḥa , et ṇọṇ
inuen]eruṇṭ , et ṭṛạṇ
sieru]nt per terram
easace]n , et ṇọṇ ịṇụẹ

nerunt , et transierunt
per terram lamin, et
non inuenerunt , et
intrauerunt in sipha(m) .
et saul dixit puero suo
qui cum eo erat , ueni
reuertamur , ne rele
uatus pater meus , neg
legat de asinis , et solli
citus sit pro nobis . et di
xit ei puer . ecce homo
d̅e̅i̅ . in hac est ciuitate .
et homo praeclarus .
et quidquid locutus fue
rit continget . et nunc
eamus . ut indicet no
bis uiam nostram , in
qua profecti sumus .
et dixit saul puero suo .
ecce ibimus , et quid offe
remus ei , quoniam pa
nes defecerunt nobis .
ut offeramus homini
d̅e̅i̅ . quod sụf̣f̣ịciaṭ no
bis . et respoṇḍịṭ pụẹṛ
ṣạụli et dixịṭ , ẹc̣c̣ẹ ịṇụẹ(ṇ)

Quedlinburg Itala, f. 1v: 1 Samuel 9:1-8.

2r

Pict.
5-8

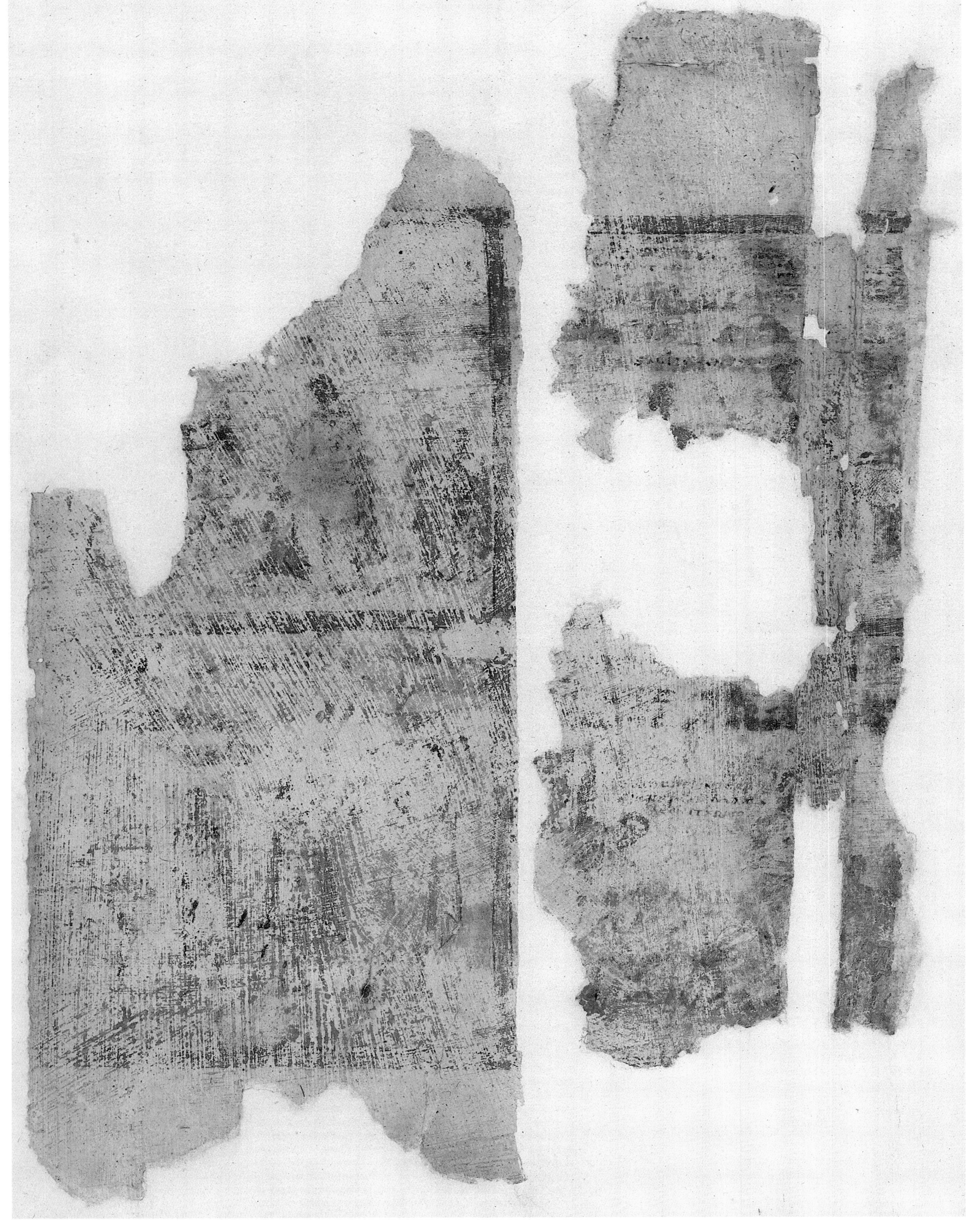

Quedlinburg Itala, f. 2r, impressions made on the 1618 bookcover (reversed).

Quedlinburg Itala, f. 2r = Pictures 5-8.

2v

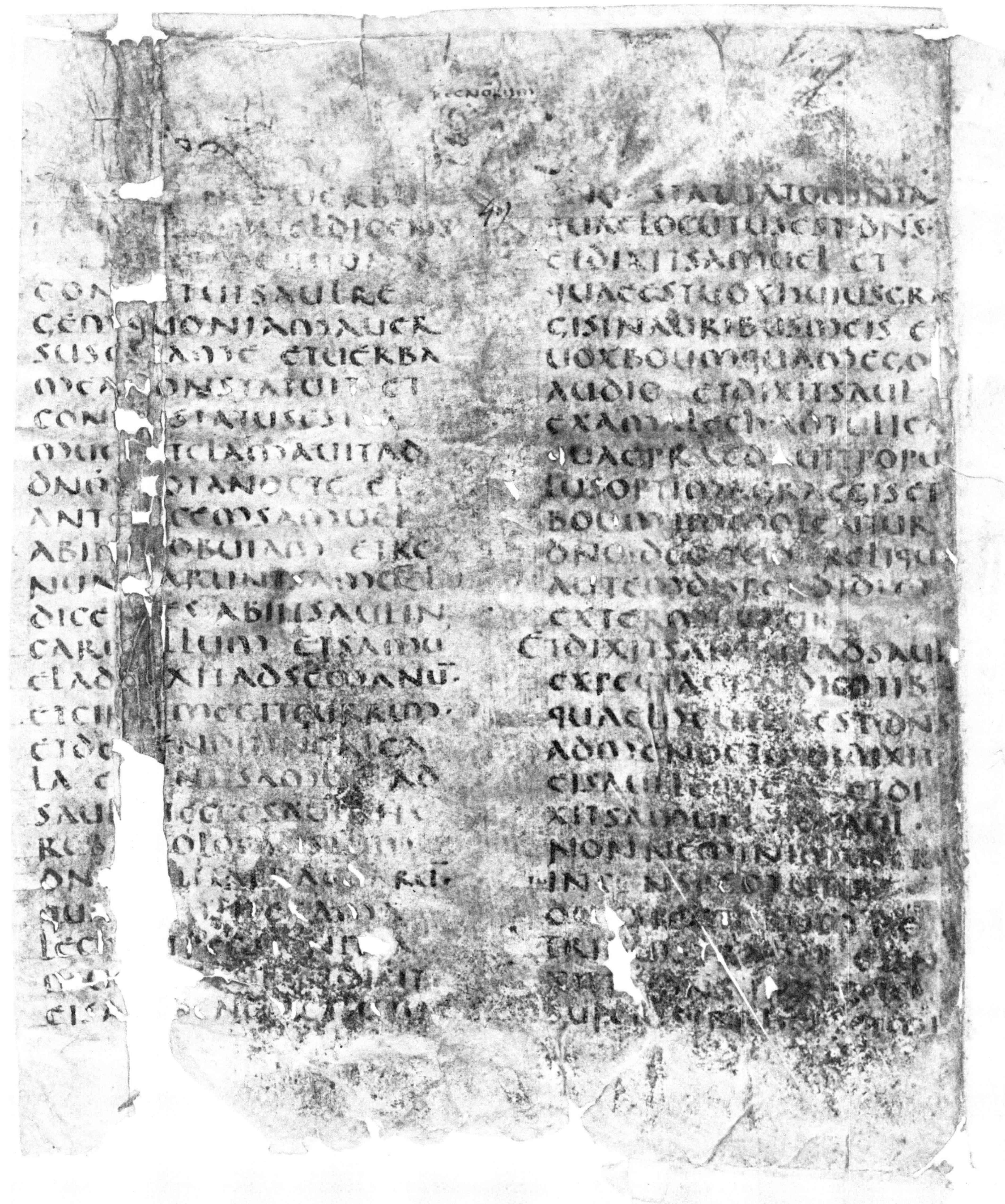

Quedlinburg Itala, f. 2v.

ẹṭ f̣ạc̣ṭ[u]m est uerbu(m)
d(omi)ni̇ . ạḍ ṣạṃuel dicens
p̣ạenitẹṭ me , quoniạ(ṃ)
con[st]itui saul re
gem , quoniam auer
sus es[t] a me , et uerba
mea non statuit , et
con[tri]status est ṣa
mue[l , e]t clamauit ad
d(omi)n(u)m . [t]ota nocte , et
ante [lu]cem samuel
abiiṭ iṇ obuiam , et re
nun[ti]arunt samuel
dicenṭes , abiit saul in
carmellum , et samu
el adduxit ad se manu(m) .
et circ̣ụmegit currum .
et de[sc]endit in galga
la , e[t ue]nit samuel ad
saul[, e]t ecce saul offe
reb[at h]olocaustum
d(omi)n[o . in]itia praedaru(m) .
qua[e adt]ulit ex ama
lech[, e]t perueṇit [s]a
mu[el ad sa]ụḷ . et dixit
ei sa[ul .]benedịctụṣ ṭụ

d(omi)no . statuat omnia
quae locutus est . d(omi)n(u)s .
et dixit samuel , et
quae est uox huius grae
gis in auribus meis , eṭ
uox boum quam ego
audio , et dixit saul .
ex amalech . adtuli ea
quae praedạuit popu
lus optima graegis et
boum immolentur
d(omi)no . deo . tuo . reliqua
autem disperdidi et
exterminaui .
et dixit samụẹl ad saul
expecta et indico tibị
quae locutus est . d(omi)n(u)s .
ad me nocte . et dixit
ei saul loquere , et di
xit samuel ad ṣaul .
nonne minimus eras
`tu´ in conspectu tuọ .
du[x] spectorum , de
tri[b]u istrahel , et un
xit t[e] . d(omi)n(u)s . iṇ regẹṃ
super istraḥẹḷ . et mi

Quedlinburg Itala, f. 2v: 1 Samuel 15:10-17.

transierunt iordane(m)
et abierunt totam prae
tenturam , et uenerunt
in castra madiam , et
ioab reuersus est de
post abenner , et con
graegarunt totum
populum , et uisi sunt
a pueris dauid decem
et nouem pueris , et asa
el , et pueri dauid percus
serunt de filiis benia
minin . ccclx . uiros ab
illo . et sustulerunt a
saelem , et sepelierunt
illum in monimento
patris illius in bethle(m)
et abierunt tota nocte
ioab et uiri illius , et lu
xit illis in chebron . et
facta est pugna magna
inter domum saul , et

inter domum[dauid
et dauid ibat e[t uires
cebat , et dom[us saul ibat
et infirmaba[tur . et na
ti sunt dauid f̣[ilii in
chebron , et e[rat pri
migenitus il[lius am
mon ex achiṇ[aam is
trahẹ[li]tide [et secun
dus il[liu]s da[luia ex
abigạẹa de[carmel
lo , [et te]ṛṭiu[s abessa
lon filius m[aachath
filiae thlom[ai regis
gezir . et qu[artus or
nias filius a[ggith , et
quinṭus sap[hathia
filiụs abit[alis , et
ṣextus ieth[eraam
e[x] agla uxor[e dauid
ist[i nati] sun[t dauid
in ch[ebro]n . [

Quedlinburg Itala, f. 3r: 2 Samuel 2:29-3:5.

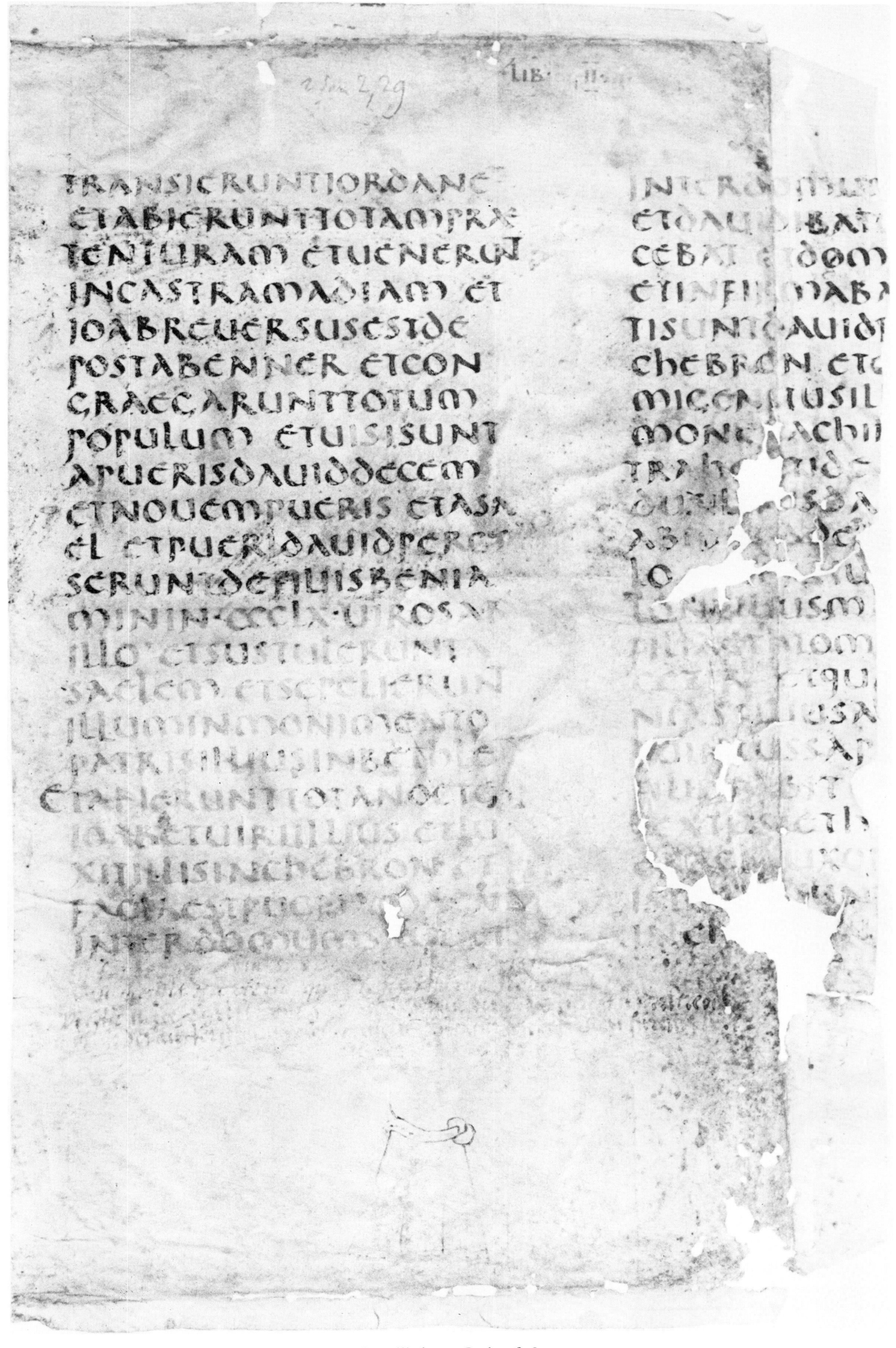

Quedlinburg Itala, f. 3r.

Quedlinburg Itala, f. 3v = Pictures 9-12.

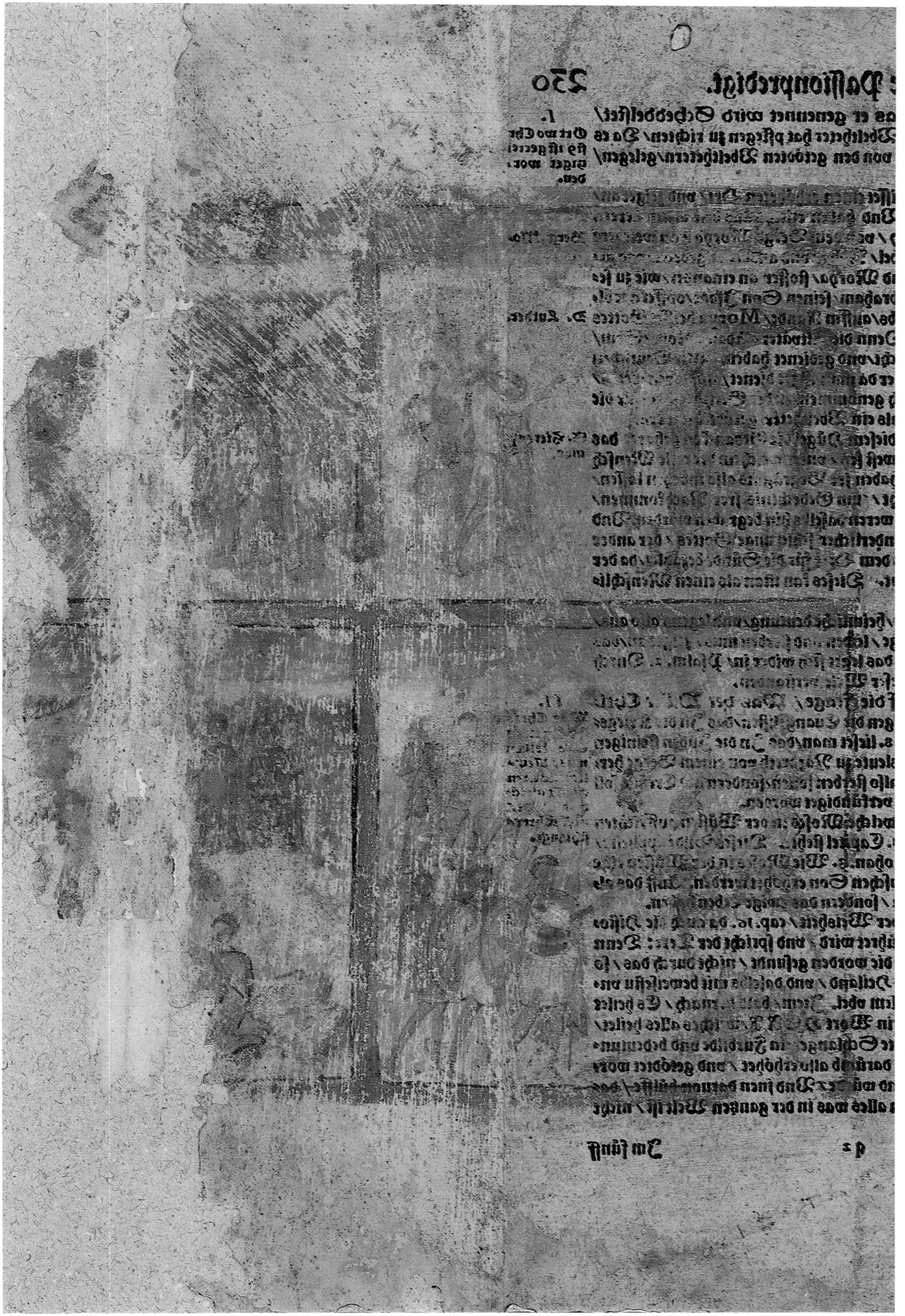

Quedlinburg Itala, f. 3v, impressions made on the 1618 bookcover (reversed).

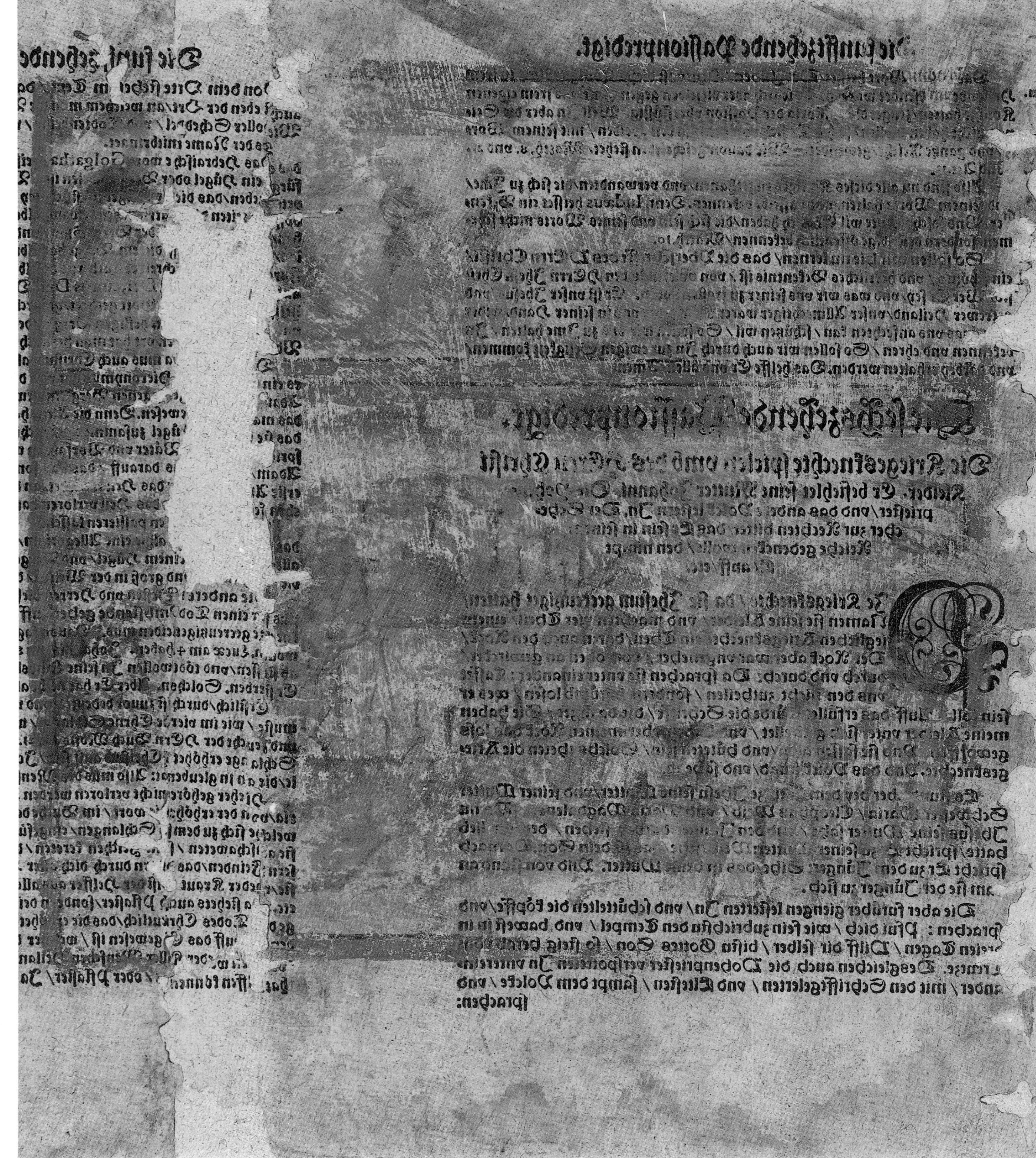

Quedlinburg Itala, f. 4r, impressions made on the 1618 bookcover (reversed).

Quedlinburg Itala, f. 4r = Pictures 13-14.

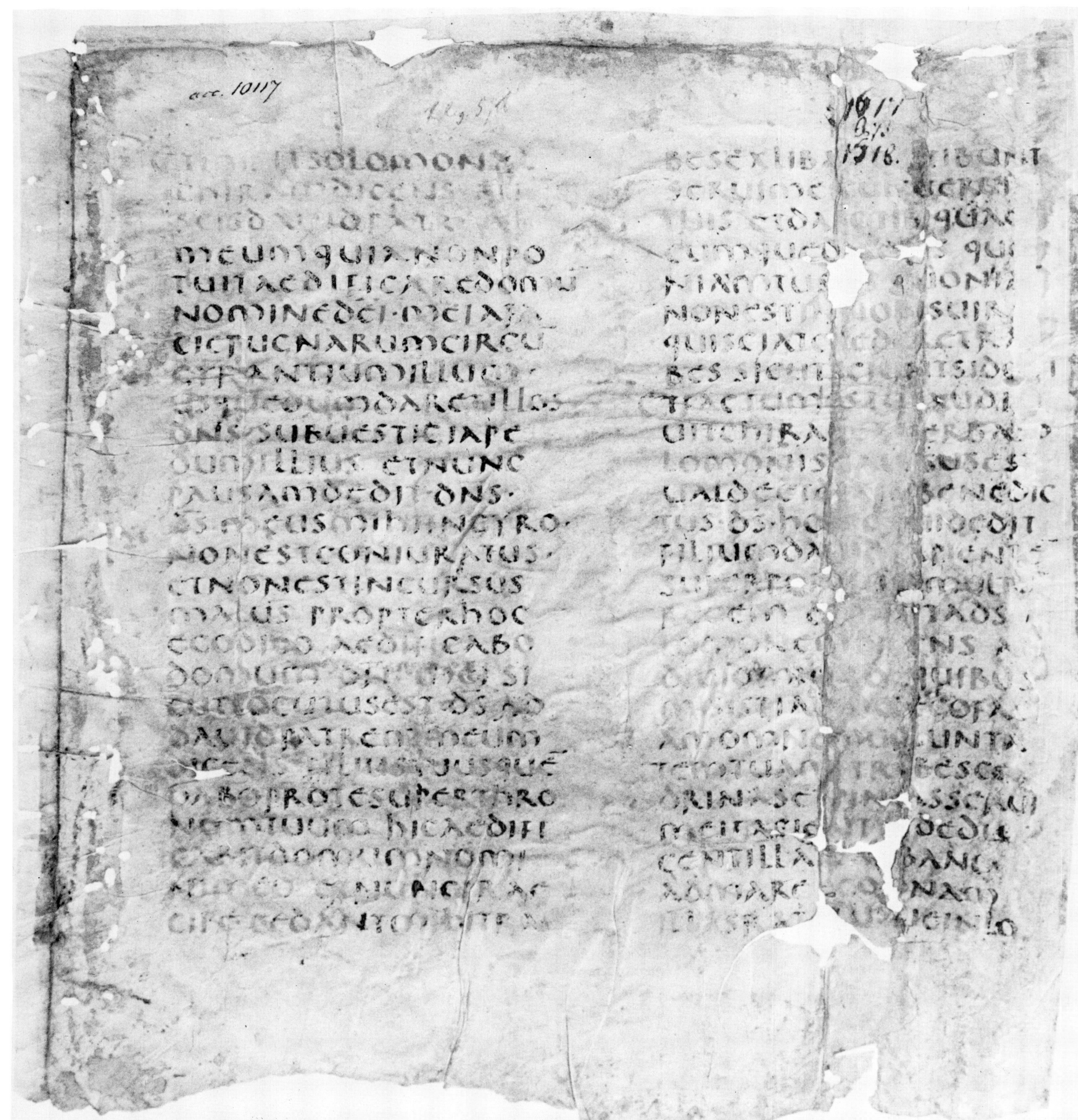

Quedlinburg Itala, f. 4v.

et miṣit solomon ad
chiram dicens . tu
scis dauid patrem
meum quia non po
tuit aedificare domu(m)
nomine d̄ēī . mei a fa
cie pugnarum circu(m)
gyrantium illum .
usque dum daret illos
d̄(omi)n̄(u)s̄ . sub uestigia pe
dum illius , et nunc
pausam dedit . d̄(omi)n̄(u)s̄ .
d̄(eu)s̄ . meus mihi in gyro .
non est coniuratus .
et non est incursus
malus , propter hoc
ego dico . aedificabo
domum . d̄(omi)n̄ī . mei si
cut locutus est . d̄(eu)s̄ . ad
dauid patrem meum
dicens . filius tuus que(m)
dabo pro te super thro
num tuum , hic aedifi
cabit domum nomi
ni meo . nunc p̣rae
cipe . cedant mihi tra
bes ex libaṇo , ẹt ibunt
serui meị cum ṣeruis
tuis , et dabo tibi quae
cumque dịx̣eṛịs , quo
niam tu s[ci]s , quonia(m)
non est in nobis uir
qui sciat caedere tra
bes , sicut sciunt sidoni
et factum est uṭ audi
uit chira ṛex uerba ṣo
lomonis g̣auịsus esṭ
ualde et dixiṭ . benedic
tus . d̄(eu)s̄ . hoḍịe qui dedit
filium dauid sapiente(m)
super popụḷụṃ multu(m)
regem , eṭ ṃịṣịt ad so
lomonem diċẹns , au
diui omṇịạ dẹ quibus
misisti aḍ ṃẹ . ego facị
am omnem uolunta
tem tuam . trabes ce
drinas et pinẹas serui
mei facient [et] dedu
cent illaṣ [ex li]bano
ad mare , ẹgo pọnam
illas rat[es] usq̣ue in lo

Quedlinburg Itala, f. 4v: 1 Kings 5:2-9.

cum quemcụmque di
xeris mihi , et exponam
illa sibi , et ṭụ tolles .
sed et tu facieṣ uolun
tatem meam , ut des pa
nes domui ṃẹae , et da
bat chira ṣọlomọni
trabes cedṛinas et
omnem ụọlụntaṭem
eius faciebaṭ , et solo
mon dedit regi chirae
xx . choroṣ ṭriṭici mạ
chit domui eius . eṭ . xx .
beth olei : secundụm
hoc dabat solomon re
gi chirae in annum .
et . d(omi)n(u)s . dedit sapienti
am solomoni sicut lō
cutus est ei , et erat pax
inter chiram et solo
monem , et posuerunt
ambo testamentum
inter se , et abduxiṭ
rex solomon homine(m)
contributionem ex o(m)
nibus istrahel , et erat

contributio . xxx . uiḷro
rum , et misit illos in
libanum , ut decem mi
lia in mensem opus
facerent et succede
rent . mense erant in
libano . et duobus me(n)
sibus in domibus suis .
et erat adoniram su
per contributos . et
erant solomoni . lxx .
portantes sublatio
nes , et . xc . qui cedeba[nt
in montem lapidem .
praeter principes qui
constituerant supeṛ
opera solomonis tri[a
milia et .dc . magistr[i
qui faciebant opera .
et praepararunt la
pides et trabes tribus
annis
et factum est in quadriḷn
gentesimo et quadra
gesimo anno profec
tionis istrahel ex ae

Quedlinburg Itala, f. 5r: 1 Kings 5:9-6:1.

CUMQUEUENI[illegible]QUEDI
XERISMIHI[illegible]XTOMAM
[illegible]LASIB[illegible]ET[illegible]TOLLES[illegible]
SEDETTUFAC[illegible]SUOLUN
TATEMMEAM UIDESPA
NESDOMUI[illegible]AE ETDA
BATCHIRA[illegible]MONI
TRABESCE[illegible]NAS[illegible]
OMNE[illegible]NTA[illegible]
EIUSFAC[illegible]ETSOLO
MONDED[illegible]CHIRAE
[illegible]HOF[illegible]IA
ENTEDOM[illegible]
BETHOLEI SECUN[illegible]
HOEDABATSO[illegible]
EICHIRAEINANN[illegible]
ET·DNS·DEDITSAPIENTI
AMSOLOMONISICUTLO
CUTUSESTEI ETERATPAX
INTERCHIRAMETSOLO
MONEM ETPOSUERUN
AMBOTESTAMENTUM
INTERSE ETABDUXIT
REXSOLOMON HOMINE
CONTRIBUTIONEMETO
NIBUSISTRAHEL ETERAT

CON[illegible]IBUTIO·XXX·[illegible]
[illegible]UM ETMISITILLOSIN
[illegible]ANUM UNDECEMMI
LIAIN[illegible]SEMOTUS
FACERENT ETSUCCEDE
RENTMENSE ERANTIN
LIBANO ETDUOBUS[illegible]
DIBUSINDOMIBUSSUIS
ETERAT ADONIRAMSU
PERCONTRIBUTOS
ERANTSOLOMONI LXX
PORTANTESSUBLATIO
NES ET·XC·QUICEDERAN
INMONTEMLAPIDEM
PRAETERPRINCIPESQUI
CONSTITUERANTSUPER
OPERASOLOMONISTRIA
MILIA ET·DC·MAGISTRI
QUIFACIEBANTOPERA
ETPRAEPARARUNTLA
PIDESETTRABESTRIBUS
ANNIS
ETFACTUMESTINQUADRI
CENTESIMOETQUADRA
GESIMOANNOPROFEC
[illegible]IONISISTRAHELEXAE

Quedlinburg Itala, f. 5r.

[illegible]PTO IN ANNO QUAR
[illegible] MENSE SECUNDO
REGNANTE REGE SOLO
MONE IN ISTRAHEL·
ET PRAECEPIT REX ET SUS
TULERUNT LAPIDES MA
NOS LAPIDES PRAETIO
SOS ET POSUERUNT IN
FUNDAMENTO DOMUS
ET LAPIDES NON POLITOS
POLIERUNT PUERI SOLO
MONIS ET PUERI CHI
RAE ET MISERUNT IL
LOS IN ANNO QUARTO
QUO FUNDAUIT DOMU
DNI IN MENSE XIIII IN
SECUNDO MENSE IN
UNDECIMO ANNO IN
MENSE BABAL HIC ME
SIS EST OCTAUUS ET CO
SUMMATA EST DOMUS
IN OMNEM RATIONEM
SUAM ET IN OMNEM
CONSTITUTIONEM SUA
ET DOMUM [illegible] AEDI
FICAUIT R[illegible] DNO XL·

CUBITIS LATITUDO EIUS
ET AELAM ANTE FACIEM
TEMPLI XX CUBITIS IN LO
GITUDINE MERAUIN LA
TITUDINE DOMUS ANTE
FACIES DOMUS ET DECE
CUBITIS LATITUDO EIUS
ERAT ET AEDIFICABIT DO
MUM ET CONSUMMA
UIT ILLA ET FECIT IN DO
MO FENESTRAS PROSPI
CIENTES ABSCONSAS·
ET DEDIT IN PARIETEM
DOMUS CYMATIA IN CY
RO TEMPLI ET DABIR LA
TERA SUPTUS QUINQUE
CUBITORUM IN CUBITO
LATITUDO EIUS ET TER
TIUM SEPTEM CUBITIS
LATITUDO EIUS QUONI
AM DIASTEMATA DEDIT
IN DOMO IN CIRCUITU
DOMUS A FORIS UT NO
TANGANTUR PARIETES
DOMUS ET DOMUS AEDI
FICARETUR LAPIDIBUS

Quedlinburg Itala, f. 5v.

g]ypto , in anno quar
t]o mense secundo
regnante rege solo
mone in istrahel .
et praecepit rex et sus
tulerunt lapides mag
nos , lapides praetio
sos , et posuerunt in
fundamento domus .
et lapides non politos
polierunt pueri solo
monis . et pueri chi
rae . et miserunt il
los in anno quarto
quo fundauit domu(m)
d(omi)ni . in mense xiiu in
secundo mense in
undecimo anno in
mense behal , hic me(n)
sis est octauus , et co(n)
summata est domus
in omnem rationem
suam , et in omnem
constitutionem sua(m) .
et domus quam aedi
ficauit r[e]x . d(omi)no . xl .

cubitis latitudo eius
et aelam ante faciem
templi . xx . cubitis in lo(n)
gitudinem erat in la
titudine domus ante
facies domus , et dece(m)
cubitis latitudo eius
erat , et aedificabit do
mum , et consumma
uit illa , et fecit in do
mo fenestras prospi
cientes absconsas .
et dedit in parietem
domus cymatia in gy
ro templi et dabir la
tera suptus quinque
cubitorum in cubito
latitudo eius . et ter
tium septem \`in´ cubitis
latitudo eius , quoni
am diastemata dedit
in domo , in circuitu
domus a foris , ut no(n)
tangantur parietes
domus , et domus aedi
ficaretur lapidibus

Quedlinburg Itala, f. 5v: 1 Kings 6:1-7.

Fig. 7. – Sacral-idyllic landscape, Pompeii.

Fig. 8. – Nymphaeum in Via Livenza, Rome: Diana the Huntress. (Photo: Dorigo.)

Fig. 9. – Sacral-idyllic landscape from Boscotrecase, Naples, Museo Naz. 147.501.

Fig. 10. – Hypogaeum of the Aurelii, Rome: Sermon in the City.

Fig. 11. – Fall of Icarus, House of Sacerdos Amandus, Pompeii.

Fig. 12. – Via Latina Catacomb, Rome: Ascension of Elijah. (Photo: Pont. Comm. Archeol. Sacra, Rome.)

Fig. 13. – Arch of Septimius Severus, Rome, Panel 3: Capture of Babylonia and Seleucia.

Fig. 14. – Punishment of Dirce, drawing from a lost fresco in Herculaneum. (Photo: Dawson.)

Fig. 15. – Coin of Constantine the Great, Trier. (Photo: Cah. Archeol., 19.)

Figs. 16, 17. – S. Maria Maggiore nave mosaics: Joshua; carrying the Ark across the Jordan; Jacob and Laban.

Figs. 18, 19. – S. Maria Maggiore nave mosaics: Hamor and Sichem address Jacob and Dina's brothers; Moses speaks to the Israelites; Fall of the Quails.

Fig. 20. – S. Maria Maggiore nave mosaic: Joshua and the Angel; Return of the Spies.

Fig. 21. – Vatican Vergil (Vatican, Bibl. Apostolica Vaticana, Vat. lat. 3225), f. 13r, picture 10: Aeneas and Achates observe the building of Carthage.

Figs. 22, 23. – Vatican Vergil, ff. 16v, 17r, pictures 11, 12: Dido receives Aeneas; Venus sends Cupid disguised as Ascanius.

Figs. 24, 25. – Vatican Vergil, ff. 22r, 36v, pictures 16, 24: Ascanius' hair flames; Aeneas and Creusa; Dido reproaches Aeneas.

Fig. 26. – Vatican Vergil, f. 24v, picture 18: Aeneas at the tomb of Polydorus.

Figs. 27, 28. – Vatican Vergil, ff. 45v, 63r, pictures 31, 42: Aeneas and the Sybil; Latinus and the Trojans.

Fig. 29. – Vatican Vergil, f. 73v, picture 49: The camp of Ascanius.

Fig. 30. – Column of Trajan, section 51: Trajan receives a delegation.

Figs. 31, 32. – Column of Trajan, sections 44, 60: Trajan receives homage; Building a fortified wall.

Fig. 33. – Column of Marcus Aurelius: Emperor in an encampment.

Figs. 34, 35. – Column of Marcus Aurelius, sections 101, 115: Emperor flanked by his generals; Adlocution. (Photos: Becatti.)

Fig. 36. – Marcus Aurelius panel, Rome: Triumph. (Photo: Ist. Centr., Rome.)

Fig. 37. – Arch of Galerius, Salonica: Galerius makes a sacrifice. (Photo: Grabar.)

Fig. 38. – Severan relief, Palazzo Sacchetti, Rome.

Fig. 39. – Missorium of Theodosius, Madrid. (Photo: Volbach.)

Fig. 40. – Obelisk base of Theodosius, Istanbul.

Fig. 41. – Constantine the Great, Rome, Campidoglio.

Fig. 42. – Diptych of Constantius III, Halberstadt Cathedral Treasury. (Photo: Delbrück.)

Fig. 43. – Diptych of a patrician, Novara. (Photo: Delbrück.)

Fig. 44. – So-called 'Stilicho' diptych. Monza. (Photo: Volbach.)

Fig. 45. – S. Maria Maggiore nave mosaics and Column of Marcus Aurelius, details (from figs. 16, 34).

Fig. 46. – S. Maria Maggiore arch mosaic: Ruler of Aphrodisius.

Fig. 47. – Calendar of 354, October (Vatican, Bibl. Apost. Vaticana, Barb. lat. 2154, f. 21r).

Fig. 48. – Terence, *Eunuchus* (Paris, Bibl. nat., lat. 7899, f. 60). (Photo: Jones and Morey.)

Figs. 49, 50. – Vatican, Bibl. Apost. Vaticana, Vat. gr. 333, ff. 42v, 43v: Abner before Isboseth; Death and Burial of Abner.

Figs. 51, 52. – New York, Pierpont Morgan Library, M.638, ff. 36v, 25r: Abner kills Joab's brother, Saul tears Samuel's cloak.

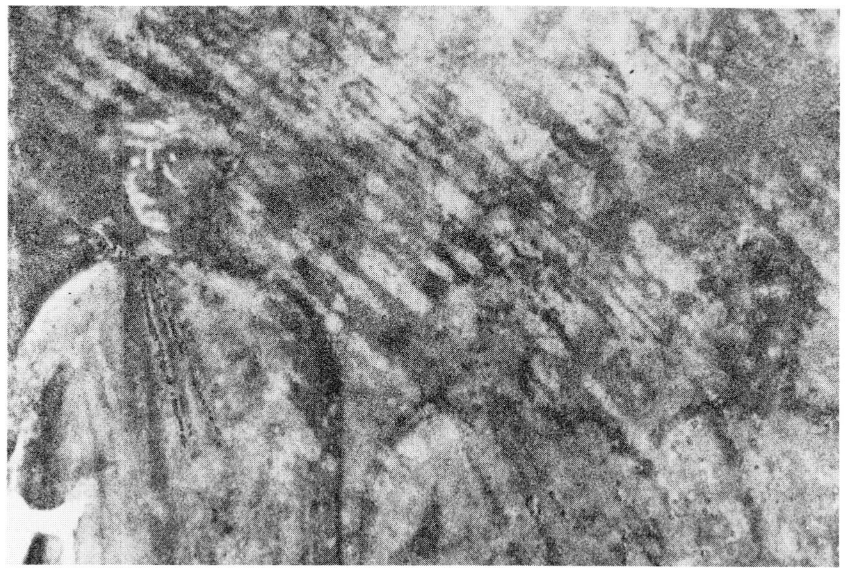

Figs. 53, 54. – Quedlinburg Itala, pictures 4 and 9, details: Samuel's head; Abner and his attendants.

Fig. 55. – Munich Glyptothek, Portrait from Ephesos.
(Photo: Munich, Glyptothek.)

Fig. 56. – Quedlinburg Itala, picture 10, detail: Heads of the Israelites.

Fig. 57. – Diptych of Consul Felix (428), Paris.

Fig. 58. – Junius Bassus sarcophagus (359), Rome: Sacrifice of Isaac. (Photo: Grabar.)